The *Empathy* Factor

Your Competitive Advantage for Personal, Team, and Business Success

MARIE R. MIYASHIRO

PuddleDancer
PRESS

2240 Encinitas Blvd., Ste. D-911, Encinitas, CA 92024
email@PuddleDancer.com · www.PuddleDancer.com

For additional information:
Center for Nonviolent Communication
5600 San Francisco Rd., NE, Suite A, Albuquerque, NM 87109
Ph: 505-244-4041 · Fax: 505-247-0414 · Email: cnvc@cnvc.org · Website: www.cnvc.org

The Empathy Factor
Your Competitive Advantage for Personal, Team, and Business Success
© 2011 PuddleDancer Press
A PuddleDancer Press Book

Good to Great. Copyright © 2001 by Jim Collins. Reprinted with permission from Jim Collins.

PuddleDancer Press, Permissions Dept.
2240 Encinitas Blvd., Ste D-911, Encinitas, CA 92024
Tel: 760-652-5754 Fax: 760-274-6400
www.nonviolentcommunication.com; email@puddledancer.com

Ordering Information
Please contact Independent Publishers Group, Tel: 312-337-0747; Fax: 312-337-5985;
Email: frontdesk@ipgbook.com or visit www.ipgbook.com for other contact
information and details about ordering online

Author: Marie R. Miyashiro
Editor: Peggy Henrikson
Indexer: Phyllis Linn
Cover and Interior Design: Lightbourne, www.lightbourne.com

Manufactured in the United States of America

1st Printing, October 2011

10 9 8 7 6 5 4 3

ISBN: 978-1-892005-25-0

Library of Congress Cataloging-in-Publication Data

Miyashiro, Marie R.
  The empathy factor : your competitive advantage for personal, team, and business success / by
Marie R. Miyashiro.
    p. cm.
  Includes bibliographical references.
  ISBN 978-1-892005-25-0 (pbk. : alk. paper)
1. Social interaction. 2. Communication in organizations. 3. Empathy. I. Title.
HM1111.M593 2011
  650.101'9--dc22
                       2011006889

Praise for *The Empathy Factor*

"Empathy has always been a core part of Marie Miyashiro. Now she has transformed that valued human relations quality and skillfully turned it into a powerful communications force for the business community. *The Empathy Factor* will help thoughtful business people add substance and dimension to relationships within the workforce—colleagues and customers. Breakthrough thinking from cover to cover that will lead to more meaningful discourse and heightened impact."

—JAMES B. HAYES, Former Publisher, FORTUNE Magazine

"*The Empathy Factor* provides great insight into almost diametrically opposed business needs, personal and corporate. Not only does it explain why they exist, but provides sound techniques to achieve synergy between the two—in turn, making the employee and business more productive. This should be required reading for any manager or supervisor."

—BILL MOORE, Senior Vice President, Ipitek Corporation;
Former Vice President and General Manager, Ortel Corporation;
Former Corporate Marketing Manager, Hewlett-Packard

"The concepts in the book are brilliant, and its ultimate premise—that empathy significantly supports workplace productivity and collaboration—is powerful. I love the material presented and, even more, am thrilled to be able to put the concepts into practice every day in the work I do with my clients. Miyashiro shows how today's managers can build organizations using empathy as the core driver of their success. In the end, those who read this will not only learn the power of Connect-Think-Do but will understand the even more powerful Connect-Think-Lead."

—JERRY COLONNA, *Upside* magazine's 100 Most Influential People
of the New Economy, *Forbes ASAP's* Best Venture Capitalists in
the Country, and *Worth's* 25 Most Generous Young Americans

"Marie Miyashiro's comprehensive discussion of empathy in the workplace resonates with integrity. As I read *The Empathy Factor,* the Integrated Clarity model of organizational needs came to life. I saw immediate applications for anyone who works as a consultant to organizations, whether for-profit, nonprofit, or social enterprise. Marie embodies the capacity to relate to ourselves with compassion as we create possibilities for alternate futures to emerge."

—CATHERINE W. BROOKER, M.A., Founder and Principal Consultant, Social Futures Group; Former Senior Organization Development Consultant, Sun Microsystems

"I came away from *The Empathy Factor* with new insights, new skills, and a much stronger appreciation of the crucial importance of 'connecting.' And I agree: the payoffs of putting this value into practice are huge! Now, those payoffs— capacity to innovate, resilience under pressure, and overall organizational effectiveness—are within much easier reach, thanks to the wisdom provided in this wonderful book."

—SAM KANER, Ph.D., Author, Consultant, Expert in Multi-Stakeholder Collaboration; Founder of the San Francisco-based international consulting firm, Community At Work

"Marie makes her point and encourages her reader's belief not only in the 'theory' of empathy but also the 'reality' that one can achieve. Business climates can truly benefit from her expertise and *The Empathy Factor* is a good read! I encourage anyone who wants to open their mind to a better way of communicating to open a copy of this book."

—ROBIN D. LANE, Vice President of the Board of Directors, Arizona Women's Golf Association; Former Major Account Sales Representative, Sun Microsystems

"*The Empathy Factor* is a book that points at new ways to think about the difficult and complex problems facing organizations and the world. As an organizational consultant and coach for twenty years, I personally implemented with great success the methodologies Marie provides in her book. Her unique approach helps my clients increase their capacity to collaborate, resolve entrenched conflicts, and innovate."

—JEAN-PHILIPPE BOUCHARD, MA, PCC, Partner and
Senior Organizational Consultant, Prologue Consultants Inc.;
Certified Nonviolent Communication Trainer

"*The Empathy Factor* offers cutting edge insight on the root causes of the challenges that today's companies and organizations face and how teams can achieve game-changing transformation to achieve ultimate buy-in, accountability, morale, and teamwork. If you're ready for real and sustainable change and what is sure to be the next big thing in the business world—needs-responsive organizations—you will want to read *The Empathy Factor*."

—DIAN KILLIAN, Ph.D., Founder and Director,
The Center for Collaborative Communication;
Coauthor, *Connecting Across Differences*

"Organizations have needs just as people in organizations have needs—an amazingly refreshing perspective! Marie has beautifully illustrated how the power of empathy can humanize the workplace and help transform our world."

—SYLVIA HASKVITZ, M.A., R.D., CNVC Certified Trainer,
Consultant and Author, *Eat by Choice, Not by Habit*

"*The Empathy Factor* is at once accessible and far-reaching in its implications. In page after page filled with real-life examples and tips, Marie Miyashiro makes the case that empathy is entirely learnable, eminently practical, and core and central to an organization's capacity to achieve its mission. Far from a 'soft' distraction, the needs-awareness allows everyone to zoom-in on what matters most, the source of focus and efficiency in achieving business and personal goals. I recommend this book highly for anyone who wants to gain a handle on how to make organizations adapt to the rapidly changing constraints of our times."

—MIKI KASHTAN, Ph.D., Co-Founder, Lead Facilitator
and Trainer, Bay Area Nonviolent Communication

"I LITERALLY stayed in my bedroom one weekend to read the entire book—no outside connection. I only came out of the room to eat. My copy is now full of highlighted, underlined, circled sections with lots and lots of post-it notes. By the way, I'm not at all a reader (ashamed to say), especially books for work. But this book, I was blown away. I HAD to read it all. Basically, I'm saying I'm a huge fan."

—SHOKO MIYAGI, Ph.D., Training Officer, University of
Wisconsin Madison, Facilities Planning and Management

"Fabulous! With this book, Marie has made several very important contributions to the body of work concerning effective leaders. She makes a clear connection between the vitality of organizations and the ability of its leaders to harness the vast potential energy generated by engaging human beings in the landscape of their feelings. Equally important, she has taken the widely heralded virtue of empathy and made it very accessible with numerous pragmatic strategies and tools. A must-read for any emerging leader!"

—ULRICH NETTESHEIM, Managing Partner, Passages Consulting;
Lecturer, Haas School of Business at University
of California Berkeley; Founder, Umanity

CONTENTS

DEDICATION

For my father and mother, Chico and Frances, who met my needs for love and stability from the day I was born.

For my sister, Laura, for providing a perpetual source of support and encouragement, and for my brother-in-law, Bob, a steady voice of wisdom and humor.

For my grandmother, Kame, who showed me how to live in both worlds of truth—of what is seen and what is invisible.

For Stacey, for showing me how to trust and love again.

For Muffin, for showing me how doggies give and receive empathy, too.

For my son, Alex, who taught me about family, love, and fun.

For Marshall, for giving us the gift of Nonviolent or Compassionate Communication.

For my clients, who taught me everything.

ACKNOWLEDGMENTS

I express my gratitude first to my clients who showed the curiosity and courage to embrace what I think of as a powerful way to communicate, lead, and work. We travel this road together, and I feel appreciation for their companionship and expressions of thanks for the value this process added to their professional and personal lives.

I am grateful for the opportunity to study with Marshall Rosenberg, Ph.D. and to be both his student and coauthor of the chapter in *The Change Handbook,* which outlines applying Nonviolent Communication™ (NVC) and its organizational counterpart, Integrated Clarity®, to the workplace. Marshall's teachings remain as the inspiration for my work and my life aspiration to live more compassionately as often as I can remember. This book project evolved through his publisher, PuddleDancer Press, giving me the opportunity to express the meaning I find in my work and the hopes I have of how it can add value to the world of organizations.

I am forever grateful to Neill Gibson, the publisher's representative, who championed this book project with my publisher. Many times during the course of this multi-year project, it was Neill's belief in this work that sustained my own faith in it and generated my energy for it. I thank Meiji Stewart, as publisher, for making the resources available to bring forth another publication about the empathic connection process of NVC and the first book of its kind intended for a mainstream business audience.

I am grateful to Jerry Colonna for his foreword and his encouragement and belief in the role this work can play in the new economy. I hope that his support will encourage many business and organizational leaders, employees, and stakeholders to discover value in these pages.

Sylvia Haskvitz, one of the original trainers certified in the NVC process by the Center for Nonviolent Communication, supported my learning and applying NVC from the first moment she knew of my interest in it. As a friend and colleague, she models the process as a lifelong practice. I have learned about NVC, friendship, compassion, love, and healthy eating from her. All along the way, Sylvia's experiences with organizations and businesses reinforced our joint belief that there was value in the idea of organizational needs as a bridge to meeting more individual needs in the workplace and the marketplace. Sylvia also reviewed the book for consistency with NVC language and principles and made helpful suggestions. She's been a valuable part of my life and firm, Elucity Network, Inc., and this book project began with her suggesting it to PuddleDancer Press.

Tiffany Meyer was instrumental in bringing my work into publication for the first time with the suggestion and proposal writing for a chapter in *The Change Handbook*. She also played a pivotal role in organizing a series of workshops I conducted through the Oregon Network for Compassionate Communication in the formative years of this work. Her hand is also seen in the marketing and support of this book.

This book is a reality because my editor, Peggy Henrikson, held all the pieces together with a balance of joy and rigor that I found uplifting and productive. On a demanding schedule, she kept me and others involved in its publication on track with every detail and proved to be a master of book editing and manuscript development. She was inspired by the concepts in these pages, began practicing it as we worked on chapters together, and always extended to me the openhearted connection of professional collaboration that we showcase in the book. Peggy played the role of editor, researcher, and project manager, sometimes viewing media files of online trainings I conducted as a way to help me begin a first draft of a chapter. She already understood the ways of living and working compassionately. This project simply helped her find a new language and framework for it. I am lucky I found Peggy.

In the early stages of this book project, Jan Henrikson guided me, edited the first chapter I wrote, and conducted interviews with me and transcribed them into documents that were later used as resources. I thank her for the time she spent getting this project started.

Jan Knight of Bancroft Information Services also provided much of the key secondary market research in the form of books, publications, and articles that contributed to the research presented.

I am grateful for the work of Palma Odano, Shannon Bodie, and the rest of the publishing team for their dedication and professionalism to this project.

I am grateful to Peggy Holman, one of the editors of the second edition of *The Change Handbook,* for noting that the Nonviolent Communication and Integrated Clarity combination was a significant contribution to the field of organizational change work. She also gave valuable feedback and encouragement about my earliest writings describing this combined process.

Jan Gordley, Jennifer La Hue-Smith, Cindy Klinge, and the entire team at Gordley Design Group helped produce the illustrations and have been a client partner in applying this work over the years. All of them have inspired me in their own way. The Gordley team also supported the marketing efforts for this book. I am grateful for their partnership and for all the ways we've been able to apply this work to business.

For their courage and enthusiasm in spreading needs-based programs that bring empathy into previously uncharted work arenas, I am grateful to my clients Laurel Parker, AECOM; Bruce Dusenberry, president of Horizon Moving Systems; Anita Seyer at GTE; Maurice Sevigny, former dean of the University of Arizona College of Fine Arts; Ron Jones, former president of the International Council of Fine Arts Deans and president of the Memphis College of Art; Raymond Tymas-Jones, dean of the University of Utah College of Fine Arts; Teresa Welborn, deputy director of the Arizona Department of Transportation Communication and Community Partnerships division; and Brian Arthur, former assistant director for the Applied Behavioral Health Policy group.

Catherine Brooker suggested the initial book outline to make the case for empathy and NVC's role in empathy training. Frank Cole was the first reader and helped confirm the way key concepts are presented. James B. Hayes, Peggy Milford, Bill Moore, Paul Weber, Laura and Bob Jessee, Jan Knight, Joelle Lien, Brent Schneider, Christine Peringer, and the Kindred Spirits business group served as special readers who offered constructive suggestions and encouragement with early drafts or concepts. I thank them for their generosity of time and heart.

Thank you to Jim Collins, William Bridges, Kimball Fisher, Jerry Porras, Marshall Thurber, and Judith Orloff Faulk for their groundbreaking work, which has inspired mine. To others who have contributed to the completion of this work but may not be listed here, I express my gratitude.

To my meditation teacher, G.C., I am grateful beyond measure for teaching me how to connect with the deepest part of me in service of life and others. This well of silence supported the completion of this book and the attainment of a dream.

FOREWORD

by JERRY COLONNA, Co-Founder, Flatiron Partners
and Former Partner, JP Morgan Partners

Over the years, I've been aware of the potential for greater workplace productivity and deeper meaning through work. I began my study of business as a journalist, chronicling the struggles of new and established companies. Later, I helped develop successful new businesses as a venture capitalist, starting two well-regarded firms and ultimately joining JP Morgan Chase's private equity unit, JP Morgan Partners. Often as a result, I served on more than a hundred boards of directors, working with both for-profit companies and nonprofit organizations. I've watched great companies become born and grow into large success stories and large companies falter and miss opportunities. I've watched small nonprofit organizations struggle through the maturation process, some succeeding, many failing. And through it all, every one of them, and every one of the people endeavoring to do the sacred work of creating something of lasting and enduring value, could have benefited from the lessons laid out in *The Empathy Factor: Your Competitive Advantage to Personal, Team, and Business Success.*

More recently, I began providing coaching services for teams and individuals. I've witnessed firsthand the transformative power of empathy, when my clients experience what Miyashiro calls the process of forming "empathic connection." Instead of the two-dimensional think-and-do cultures prevalent in our workplaces, the book advocates for a third dimension, Connect-Think-Do, placing a primacy on engaging with one another in our full humanness before we do the work.

This cutting-edge book highlights a growing body of research that validates the practice of empathy as a key business advantage. Most important, it details a proven and repeatable method for developing and practicing empathy as a workplace skill. The method described, Nonviolent Communication (NVC), represents one of the largest empathy practice communities in the world. To this largely interpersonal model, Miyashiro adds a framework for teams and organizations that she calls Integrated Clarity® because of the way the individual, team, and larger organization can operate more collaboratively as a unified whole.

She writes:

> Our workplaces are two dimensional because the process of empathic connection requires a literacy and comfort with two human qualities that have been systematically devalued and misinterpreted in the world around us. Our organizations are born out of this same consciousness and simply replicate this world condition in our workplaces. These two misunderstood qualities are: 1) our ability to be fluently aware of our feelings without judgment of them and 2) our ability to then connect these feelings to related human needs that are being met or unmet.

Miyashiro makes a compelling case for wider-spread use and awareness of the core NVC techniques—not just in situations where the violence of our interactions is apparent, but also in places where we don't necessarily see the violence being perpetrated.

The Empathy Factor is a call for ending this subtle, persistent, and awful violence to the Self done every day in the name of profits and productivity. But more than a call to action, it offers proof that—ironically—building a more compassionate, empathic workplace is precisely the path to greater productivity and, consequently, profits.

For at its heart, *The Empathy Factor* is a business book in every sense of the phrase. Not only that, it's a joy to read. On first pass, the book may not appear erudite, but it is. The style is very accessible, with callouts and real-world examples. The book builds on Miyashiro's twenty-eight-plus years of consulting, observing, and guiding a variety of for-profit and nonprofit organizations as well as her extensive research and comprehensive analysis.

Santa Clara County Library District

408-293-2326

Checked Out Items 4/14/2018 11:55
XXXXXXXXXX8745

Item Title	Due Date
1. The case for marriage : why married people are happier, healthier, and better off financially 33305016235420	5/5/2018
2. Nonviolent communication : a language of life 33305227853649	5/5/2018
3. The happiness advantage : the seven principles of positive psychology that fuel success and performance at work 33305225671639	5/5/2018
4. The empathy factor : your competitive advantage for personal, team, and business success 33305238953131	5/5/2018

No of Items: 4

Amount Outstanding: $1.50

24/7 Telecirc: 800-471-0991
www.sccl.org
Thank you for visiting our library.

I'm honored to write this foreword. The concepts in the book are brilliant, and its ultimate premise—that empathy significantly supports workplace productivity and collaboration—is powerful. I love the material presented and, even more, am thrilled to be able to put the concepts into practice every day in the work I do with my clients.

Miyashiro shows how today's managers can build organizations using empathy as the core driver of their success. In the end, those who read this will not only learn the power of Connect-Think-Do but will understand the even more powerful Connect-Think-Lead.

Jerry Colonna is the co-founder with Fred Wilson of Flatiron Partners, which became one of the most successful, early-stage investment programs in the country. He also became a partner with JP Morgan Partners, the private-equity arm of JP Morgan Chase, and now serves as a director, trustee, or advisor to a number of for-profit and nonprofit organizations. He was listed in *Upside* magazine's 100 Most Influential People of the New Economy, *Forbes ASAP*'s Best Venture Capitalists in the Country, and *Worth*'s 25 Most Generous Young Americans.

PART I

Understanding Empathy and Needs-Based Awareness

ONE

Introducing the Third Dimension
and Integrated Clarity®

"Greed is out. Empathy is in."

—Frans de Waal, *The Age of Empathy: Nature's
Lessons for a Kinder Society*

As humanity evolves, we are constantly being invited to expand our view of ourselves and the world. This creates enormous changes in our workplaces and the way we relate to one another at work. But sometimes it isn't easy for us to comprehend that next dimension in our evolution.

This book introduces a way to bring empathy into the workplace—to create a new dimension of increased harmony, productivity, and success to both individuals and organizations. As I spoke of this new paradigm in the fall 2004 keynote address for the University of Arizona's College of Fine Arts' opening convocation, I told the following story of Flatland and Spaceland. My talk marked the beginning of a thirteen-month strategic planning and dialogue project I was hired to conduct with the college management and staff. They were about to be introduced to a new dimension—the one you will experience and other managers, employees, and business owners are coming to know, if you put into action what you read in this book.

MOVING FROM FLATLAND TO SPACELAND

The day before the convocation, Dean Maurice Sevigny asked me what I was planning to talk about. He had a regular practice of reading all the latest management and organization development books as a way to support his college in an economy of dwindling funds for the arts. I think he was surprised by my answer.

I asked him if he knew of a book called *Flatland*.[1]

"No, I haven't read that one," he said. "When was it published?"

"Eighteen eighty-four," I replied.

"Eighteen eighty-four!" The dean laughed, but his look begged further clarification so I briefly explained my plan.

The next day, I began my talk with the story of *Flatland,* a short novel written by Englishman Edwin Abbot. It's a story about a two-dimensional world where inhabitants can only perceive length and width. They are called Flatlanders. The main character is a Square, who is married to a Line and has two sons, both Hexagons.

One dark night, the Square is visited by a Sphere, a three-dimensional ball. In Flatland, when a three-dimensional ball-shaped object passes through their world, Flatlanders can't comprehend its depth or fullness.

The Sphere explains that it's from Spaceland, a third dimension, but soon grows frustrated at the Square's ignorance.

"What do you mean you don't understand the third dimension?" he asks. "I'm from space. I can go above and beyond Flatland."

The Square replies: "Well, we can do that, too. We go North and South."

You can see the problem with trying to explain a third dimension in words.

With more confusion and nothing concrete to support the idea of another dimension, the Square becomes increasingly fearful.

Eventually, the only way he can know the third dimension is to physically experience it rather than try to grasp it intellectually. So the Sphere takes him to visit Spaceland. But when he travels into the three-dimensional reality of Spaceland, instead of gaining greater understanding, the Square is more disoriented than ever. He can't reconcile his limited understanding of the world order he's used to with what he's experiencing as a strange new truth.

Happily, in the end, he does excitedly grasp the new world of Spaceland. But sadly, he is unable to convey his new reality to any of the other Flatlanders.

His hope endures, however, that one day the possibilities of Spaceland may "find their way to the minds of humanity in Some Dimension, and may stir up a race of rebels who shall refuse to be confined to limited Dimensionality."

The Square demonstrates many qualities we all possess when confronted with change and something new we don't understand. At first he goes into denial. Then he's confounded. He's curious. Then he gets angry. At one point he becomes fearful. He doesn't want to or thinks he's incapable of seeing things from a new perspective, a new depth. Finally, through actual experience, he accepts and is thrilled with the new dimension.

This book calls for a "new race of rebels" who are willing to explore a way of being that's wider, deeper, and fuller, not to mention more effective, than our current worlds of being and business normally express.

The ideas presented here are what many call innovative and revolutionary—both metaphorically because they represent a new way of doing business, and literally because they can lead to the kind of innovation that creates dramatic positive change.

Workplace Thinking and Doing—A Two-Dimensional Approach in a Three-Dimensional World

I worked in a Flatland of my own the first eight of my twenty-nine years as a communication and organization development consultant. I was a two-dimensional consultant working in the two-dimensional worlds found in the business, nonprofit, and government agencies that were my clients. In these worlds, the two dimensions consisted of *thinking* and *doing*. I found problems and fixed them, only to see the same problems arise again after the fix. Consultants in Flatland are in perpetual demand because they fix the symptoms but not the root causes.

To some degree, we all work in Flatland. In the two-dimensional world of thinking and doing, the organizational dialogue goes something like this: "If we think hard enough about our problems or goals, we will be able to develop a plan to do all the 'right' things to be successful." The traditional work culture places tremendous value on the intellect, on data; on taking action and staying busy to implement "the plan." This culture measures our worth and success in terms of how much thinking and doing we can get done in a day. In fact, workers and managers who can get more than a day's work done are richly rewarded. The value of people in the two-dimensional workplace comes down to getting the job done, irrespective of a person's quality of character or the demonstration of values. Some organizations are even *one* dimensional: "Don't think. Just do what I say." In these types of organizations, performance and profit are valued more highly than people—all types of stakeholders, from employees to the community at large—sometimes even at the expense of the consumer.

This imbalance may be overt but more likely it's subtle, leaving us with a quiet discomfort, difficult to articulate but clearly present. Slogans, well-intentioned morale-boosting activities, and corporate communications that pronounce the opposite can mask our experience. When we do experience that oh-so-rare brush with being regarded in our full humanness—not just our capacity to think and do—we are acutely aware of how much we've been longing for it. When we come across people in an organization who really get who we are as unique people, it reminds us of what is positively possible and mostly absent.

We need only turn to the news headlines of the past few years or our own personal history to find further evidence of less-than-human experiences in the workplace. The global economic crisis we're recovering from has been a crisis of values and morality, not one of the dollar, euro, or yen. In the preface of the World Economic Forum 2010, Klaus Schwab and John J. DeGioia wrote, "The current economic crisis should warn us to fundamentally rethink the development of the moral framework and the regulatory mechanisms that underpin our economy, politics and global interconnectedness."[2] The previous year, in December 2009, the Forum had conducted a unique new opinion poll through Facebook. Respondents—the majority of whom were under thirty years old—were asked how they see the role of values in the economy today. Of the more than one hundred thirty thousand respondents from France, Germany, India, Indonesia, Israel, Mexico, Saudi Arabia, South Africa, Turkey, and the United States, strikingly, more than two-thirds believe the current economic crisis is also a crisis of ethics and values.

Only in a two-dimensional world can so many people be financially and emotionally bankrupted while a select few experience unheard of profit at their expense. This is not a system problem alone. Something is fundamentally out of balance in the way we participate within that system, as well. Sadly, we have become unwitting accomplices to conditions that pull on our purse strings as well as our hearts.

Building on Brilliance

I would have bumped along obliviously like the Square had I not been introduced to the third dimension by those who had already discovered Spaceland where the answers live.

In the 1980s, I studied with teachers such as Marshall Thurber and his colleague Judith Orloff Faulk, and my thinking was remade by their teachings and philosophy. Thurber, in turn, is the only person to have been a protégé of two of the greatest thinkers of our modern times, Dr. W. Edwards Deming, the father of the quality management movement, and R. Buckminster Fuller, inventor, architect, engineer, mathematician, poet, and cosmologist. One of the main tenets I took away from this work included a fundamental understanding that the vast majority of interpersonal conflicts in organizations are systems issues, not people issues. To address people issues before addressing the way the whole system or the team influences these relationships is trying to nurture a seed in sand instead of fertile soil. It's the combination of good soil and sound seed that yields the tree. I know this from my own experiences. If you put people who essentially get along into a system with limited resources, for example, the situation creates unintended competition for these resources—and guess what? The people don't get along, as well. Conversely, if you take people who have little commonality and probably wouldn't get along very well at a dinner party and place them into a thoughtfully structured organizational or team setting, they thrive—both interpersonally and in terms of team productivity. The key, then, is to structure an environment that makes the group's shared goals easy to see by all and supports their common reality.

Effective political campaigns shine as prime examples of this. You walk into the campaign office and immediately and everywhere on the walls you see how the team is stacking up against the goals of the campaign and its competitors. All understand what the "finish line" is and the timeframe around it. Basic resources are available to all without having to jump through hoops to find them or ask for them. And when one team sees that its precinct is not winnable, it rolls its personnel and resources over into an area where its efforts can make a difference instead of protecting its territory. Information and resources are shared widely. For the most part, people are clear about what they are accountable for and what authority they have.

People who work and volunteer for political campaigns can represent unusual cross-sections of the socioeconomic scale because "politics makes strange bedfellows," as the saying goes. Yet people get along because they're all focused on the same mission and shared goals. The system supports this, and in turn, the people feel supported.

The vast majority of interpersonal conflicts in organizations are systems issues, not people issues.

During my decades of experience in business communication, I observed my share of organizational identity crisis, pain, dissatisfaction, misunderstandings, and depressed productivity and morale. After my studies in interpersonal and organizational communication at Northwestern University, I worked for two of the largest communication companies in the world, Time, Inc. and a Hill and Knowlton company. I encountered thousands of people—employees, managers, owners, members, volunteers—in hundreds of organizations. On many occasions, I was the recipient of their frantic questions: "What do we do next?" "What can we do?"

At present, these concerns are growing in number and intensity as the world's rate of change picks up pace exponentially. In the 1960s, Buckminster Fuller estimated that starting approximately five thousand years ago, a new invention or innovation came along about every two hundred years that changed what he called "the critical path of humanity."[3]

The path of humanity and the nature of the world and business are changing exponentially.

By AD 1, this number became every fifty years. By AD 1,000, every thirty years. And by the Renaissance, every three years a new invention came along that changed the nature of the world. By the Industrial Revolution, the timing was reduced to six months. And Fuller estimated that by the 1920s, the interval was three months, ninety days. He called this "accelerating acceleration." According to physicist Peter Russell, that timing is down to days if not hours.[4]

Dealing With the Frantic Pace of Change

So why is it that the rate of successful change in organizations is normally as slow as molasses in January? Of all those that embark on some kind of management strategy to deal with change in their outer or inner environment, I've heard estimates that only 25 to 30 percent make it, and the rest struggle along.

From my observations, the main reason organizations that try to manage change fail is their tendency to treat human systems as though they were mechanical processes. They're asking questions that view their human processes as mechanistic—such as asking in strategic planning sessions, "What do we do next?" From a human perspective, it's more critical to begin with values explorations, especially fixed values such as those that define an organization's or team's identity. In this context, the question isn't, "What do we do next?" The question is, "Who are we as an organization?" An inquiry of being, not doing.

While a values focus isn't new, the approach presented here is, in that organizational or team identity is defined as a "universal need." This need is addressed within the framework of an interpersonal and organizational "needs consciousness" that serves as the foundation for sustainable change and success in the workplace.

Fear of the Future

Along with the frantic uncertainty, fear arises. Do you discern fear in yourself and your colleagues about the future? What happens when people in organizations are motivated by fear? They unintentionally create a cycle of contracting opportunities, resources, and energies. The book *The Luck Factor* by Richard Wiseman, psychology chair at the University of Hertfordshire, England, presents the results of an eight-year study of people who were lucky and those who were unlucky. The researchers found that the lucky ones had certain psychological traits. Primarily, these people did not operate from fear but rather with an expectation of good fortune.[5] That's what thriving organizations do. They operate from a vision of their own greatness in the future. And to do that, they go beyond the traditional paradigm.

The innovations in this model address both interpersonal and organizational needs within the single framework of a "needs consciousness" that serves as the foundation for sustainable change and success in the workplace.

My early teachers, out of the school of Marshall Thurber and Buckminster Fuller, frequently used the phrase "the brightness of the future," which has stayed with me. The organization's job is to focus on the brightness of the future and keep others focused on the brightness—without ignoring the pain.

Catapulted Into Spaceland

I had been working as an organization development consultant for twenty-two years when I met Marshall Rosenberg in 2004, and his teachings would sig-

Thriving organizations focus on a vision of their own greatness in the future.

nificantly alter my life and work. I was not surprised in 2005 to hear this man who had worked to bring peace to such groups as warring street gangs and clashing African tribes say he thought American businesses are some of the most violent places on earth.[6]

As I studied the model of Nonviolent Communication (NVC) that Rosenberg taught, I understood what he meant. I could see the unconscious and unintentional disregard for the feelings and needs of people, both in everyday relationships and in the world of the businesses, nonprofits, universities, and government agencies with which I worked. I observed that the workplace is full of what I call silent pain. I like to tell the groups I work with that I estimate about 30 to 50 percent of what is said in workplace meetings is not what is heard. One woman remarked, "Is that all?" Most others nod silently.

Within months of learning NVC, I witnessed the wonders it worked in meeting the needs of individuals and creating more productive work relationships. I noticed a shift in the way team members listened to one another. They were listening from a deeper, more effective place. *A place of empathy—of being able to see, feel, and experience what the other person was experiencing.* Consider the following situation in which I initiated deeper understanding with a simple question based on my own curiosity.

An estimated 30 to 50 percent of what is said in workplace meetings is not what is heard.

A female employee shared her frustration about others not following a particular work process she was in charge of creating. Her colleagues began offering suggestions to fix the problem, but she was so focused on expressing her pain that she couldn't hear their suggestions. When I finally asked her if any of the suggestions were of value to her, she replied, "What suggestions?" I then asked if she was frustrated because she valued respect and considered following the work process a demonstration of respect.

Her answer was: "Yes . . . yes, that's it. I want respect. I work hard to put these schedules together and want others to respect the process, too." Having experienced being listened to at this new level of her needs, she paused, took a breath, then raised her arms in the air with a big smile and said, "Now I'm ready for some suggestions!"

Her unmet need for respect was acknowledged so she could move from wanting to be understood to being willing to hear strategies and suggestions from others. This simple acknowledgment made the process more effective for all.

NVC focuses on an explicit process for developing and deepening the practice of empathy. This involves connecting with the feelings and needs in ourselves and others in service of promoting greater understanding all around. I'm convinced this idea works on an expanded level for teams and organizations as well as for individuals because of what I've read in the research and seen in my own consulting practice.

From the beginning of my work with organizations, first as a corporate communications specialist and now as an organizational consultant, I was aware that organizations had needs, too—related to the needs of the people in them, but distinct. To be clear, organizations differ from people in that they don't have an inherent right to exist; they exist only to service human needs. However, the degree to which organizational needs themselves are met or unmet can determine whether the organization thrives or even survives.

In one of our discussions, Rosenberg and I talked about bringing NVC into organizations. I was familiar and comfortable with the world of business and organizations, so I set out to combine NVC with a process that would meet the needs of organizations and teams. I wanted to bring the empathy factor into all levels of a business, enhancing every function of its operation and resulting not only in higher morale but greater productivity and profits.

Eureka! Integrated Clarity was born.

My work now includes this new dimension, the power of empathy through Nonviolent Communication (also known as Compassionate Communication), thanks to Marshall Rosenberg, trainers for the Center for Nonviolent Communication such as Sylvia Haskvitz, Miki Kashtan, and others. This model became the centripetal force that pulled all my previous learning about people and organizations into an integrated whole.

Integrated Clarity outlines a practical, doable empathy process for meeting individual as well as organizational needs resulting in higher morale and greater productivity and profits.

Now, when I go into an organization I'm aware of the pain but there's no need to focus on it. The process of Integrated Clarity (IC) enables both healing to happen and the brightness of the future to evolve. Appreciating what is and building on the strengths of individuals and their teams create the foundation for successful change.

It's About Connection

This book is about helping you create more choice, power, and productivity for yourself and the teams and organizations with which you engage. How? By unearthing and energizing that most vital and often overlooked third dimension—the human dimension of connection. A connection based on empathy.

Three distinct levels of empathic connection are constantly at play in our workplaces: connecting to our own internal state, connecting with others—from co-workers to end consumers—and connecting with the whole team or organization. However, in many—if not most—situations, the quality of these connections is not meeting critical human needs such as trust, respect, autonomy, understanding, and meaning. Because people are essential to organizations, when these needs go unmet, productivity, services, and profits also suffer.

Feelings and Needs

Our workplaces are two dimensional because the process of empathic connection requires a literacy and comfort with two human qualities that have been systematically devalued and misinterpreted in the world around us. Our organizations are born out of this

Workplace connections often don't meet critical human needs, and as a result, productivity, services, and profits suffer along with the people.

same consciousness and simply replicate this world condition in our workplaces. These two misunderstood qualities are:

1. our ability to be fluently aware of our feelings without judgment of them and
2. our ability to then connect these feelings to related human needs that are being met or unmet.

Our workplaces add another level of complexity because feelings and needs are submerged in a system-wide context of day-to-day urgencies where a vast number of human interconnections play out at the same time. This systemic condition further obscures our abilities to perceive feelings and needs, which are often not readily discernible even without the complexities of the workplace.

A breakthrough in our understanding of such abilities was accomplished in 1983 by the American developmental psychologist Howard Gardner, who presented his theory of multiple intelligences. This theory proposed that humans have a range of abilities that can't be measured by IQ tests. Of the nine intelligences currently suggested by Gardner, two are Intrapersonal and Interpersonal intelligences, which we will explore in depth in this book in terms of developing empathic connections with ourselves and others.

Building on Gardner's breakthrough, psychologist Daniel Goleman published his bestselling book *Emotional Intelligence* in 1995, and he continues to research and promote the contribution of emotional intelligence to workplace effectiveness. Goleman's views on empathy and leadership are discussed in Chapter Two.

With this and other solid backing, why hasn't workplace

consideration of empathy taken hold more quickly? Our problem seems to derive from our entrenched conditioning in using the emotions of fear, guilt, shame, and anger as workplace motivators instead of proficiency with connecting to our own and others' feelings and needs. In the two-dimensional world, these negative emotions are the motivators for productivity. In the three-dimensional world, they are obstacles.

Defining "feelings" and "needs" is not as simple as we might first think. These concepts have been submerged, misrepresented, and misunderstood in our collective consciousness for thousands of years. Our assumptions and even scientific data about feelings and needs are contradictory. Our language muddies the waters further as, for example, "feelings," "emotions," "needs," "desires," and "wishes" are often used interchangeably but with very different meanings.

A meaningful, effective, and repeatable practice of empathy that can be learned for workplace application depends on understanding feelings and needs. To discuss empathy without knowing the specific roles of feelings and needs is like building a car without knowing how the engine works. Understanding needs in particular, as defined in this book, is critical to grasping the concept and practice of empathy. Feelings serve as valuable information, as internal data about needs. In and of themselves, feelings don't mean anything until we assign meaning to them. But if we know how, we can use our feelings as guides for constructive action.

By capitalizing on these human elements instead of dismissing, tolerating, or trying to "manage" them, we celebrate our humanness and expand our possibilities and those of the organizations in which we work. We can create a world where needs matter, building a foundation for a moral economy that adds value to the world and the people we serve. This focus on feelings lights a pathway to needs awareness and meeting more needs rather than making our feelings the end goal. Ultimately, feelings provide valuable information for our choices in the future. When we aren't aware of our feelings and the needs connected to them, we are likely to repeat choices that will not meet as many of our needs as we'd like.

Two Innovative Roadmaps

Many books and models exist on developing more successful business relationships, increasing productivity in our work-related communications, and

By understanding and using our feelings and needs in service to our humanity, we can replace fear, guilt, shame, and anger and create the foundation for a moral economy.

resolving conflict. This book is the first to examine these connections through two processes that many are coming to understand as powerful and innovative: Nonviolent Communication (NVC) and its counterpart for workplace application, Integrated Clarity (IC). I developed the IC concepts and framework so others could experience the excitement and awe I felt when I first applied NVC with my business clients.

While less known in the business world than other venues, NVC is renowned internationally as a communication and peacemaking process. In excess of 240 certified trainers work on five continents in more than seventy-five countries and are particularly active in Europe, with half a million people worldwide receiving NVC training every year.[7] The basics of NVC are presented in this book within the framework of IC and are explained in more detail in Rosenberg's book, *Nonviolent Communication: A Language of Life.*[8]

As for Integrated Clarity, I remember Marshall Rosenberg calling it the "missing link" to applying the power of NVC to organizations. I was thrilled when he and I coauthored a chapter for the second edition of *The Change Handbook,* a practical guide edited by top organizational management consultants and academicians. This "definitive resource on today's best methods for engaging whole systems"[9] chose to highlight IC as one of its nineteen in-depth chapters. Our chapter, "Integrated Clarity—Energizing How We Talk and What We Talk About in Organizations," has generated wide interest, from a global European-based finance company to an international nonprofit based in India to universities, businesses, and nonprofits in the United States.

The Empathy Factor offers concrete practical strategies for developing and maintaining a completely different level of high-functioning human connection that energizes and drives what the organizational research identifies as the most successful teams and organizations. Only within the last decade or so has the quality of empathy attracted the attention of workplace researchers and leaders as a valuable area of study and practice in increasing productivity in organizations.

For the most part, in the language of businesses and organizations, empathy is often misunderstood and confused with completely different concepts, such as sympathy. A *sym*pathetic connection occurs when people relate the feelings and thoughts that others share to times when they, themselves, experienced those feelings and thoughts. Sympathy can also create connection between people, but it's different from empathic connection, where the focus is solely on the other person.

As you'll see in Chapter Two, *em*pathy is what I consider one of the most important skills we can learn for workplace and team success. Understanding where another person is coming from is a practical and effective basis for collaborating within a team, connecting with customers, and getting our jobs done. Understanding our own feelings and needs serves as this foundation. Thus the thinkers and doers can still think and do; they just add another dimension of connection to the process that increases success. Connect-Think-Do is not only more effective than Think-Do, it's also more rewarding and energizing.

Empathy is one of the most important skills we can learn for workplace and team success.

When we share in another's internal experience, we're both connected to our shared humanity. But this connection may not happen automatically—and often doesn't. In fact, many times the person *having* the feelings doesn't understand them. Thus we have the value of a model of communication and consciousness that helps all parties concerned build understanding by connecting those feelings to needs. The process also illuminates how to take responsibility for getting these needs met. This level of personal and interpersonal understanding releases a tremendous amount of energy and creates an exciting and active collaboration that makes practical sense in today's accelerating business world. It has a profoundly positive effect on workplace morale. Couple this improvement in personal communication with the IC process of working together to clarify and meet the organization's or team's needs and the needs of the customer; then, as the examples throughout this book show, you witness a measurable surge in growth as seen in the economic and social value created.

Later chapters explicitly define and dissect this process and support you in developing the skills to create and maintain high-functioning connections—what I call your "personal connection power." A step-by-step empathy work process flow shows you how to connect on the three levels previously described: intrapersonal (with yourself), interpersonal (with others), and organizational (with the entire organization or team).

The model of Integrated Clarity is illustrated in the following diagram.

Fig. 1-1. Integrated Clarity® Framework

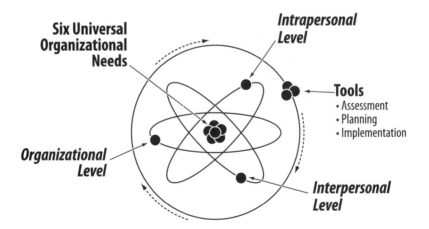

© 2011 Elucity Network, Inc. as developed by Marie R. Miyashiro

Connecting Versus Manipulating

From the particular kind of empathic connection presented here, a natural power emerges that Rosenberg calls power *with* people, not power over people. With connection also comes a natural profit—profit *with* people, not profit from people. Instead of learning techniques and developing skills to get someone to do something you want, you discover that connection in its purest form is a powerful end in itself, not a means to an end.

This new and heightened sense of connection leads people to do what you want not out of fear, guilt, or shame, but because it brings them meaning and joy to share in a mutual purpose. Therein lies the significant difference between the two-dimensional think-and-do workplace and the connect-think-and-do workplace. When empathy and connection precede the thinking and doing, results many view as remarkable unfold, as you'll see in Chapter Two.

The question may be lingering in your mind: How do you run organizations or get the job done without getting people to do what you want or what management wants? This may seem impossible. And in a two-dimensional world, it is. Why is it taking so long for the research and stories that validate empathy to be legitimately and equally received in the workplace along with thinking and doing?

Thinking and doing is out. Connecting, thinking, and doing is in.

Like the Square in Flatland, we cannot understand with the mind alone what is by nature an aspect of a more expanded but less visible dimension. All the evidence in the world will go unrecognized until we first have our own personal experiences with the third dimension and then have some means of consciously articulating it.

By exploring this third dimension of empathy through the principles and practices of NVC and IC in the following pages, you will not only understand it with your mind, you will experience it in your body. And by experiencing it, a new natural power will unfold in you and from you, to be directed at will to those around you, your workplace, and any other organization or team you choose. You will discover that you are more frequently creating what you would like in your work life, rather than being the recipient of what someone else wants for you. At the same time, collaborating with others, meeting your customers' needs, and serving a larger societal good are likely to increase.

Both NVC and IC are easy to learn, almost simplistic in their basic forms. You can use both right away without any business degree or management experience. I am confident that at least one big idea or many small ones in this book will resonate with you and move you to take action that will catapult you into the Spaceland of greater possibilities.

✳ ✳ ✳ ✳

Read on. Chapter Two provides a taste of what those possibilities might be for you, your team, and your organization.

TWO

Capitalizing on the Human Element

"Increasingly, today's most successful companies are bringing love, joy, authenticity, empathy, and soulfulness into their businesses; they are delivering emotional, experiential, and social value—not just profits."[10]

—Wharton School of Business in recommendation of the book
Firms of Endearment: How World-Class Companies Profit from Passion and Purpose

Buckminster Fuller often referred to the principle of the trim tab.[11] A trim tab is a mini-rudder attached to the large rudder of a ship. How is it useful? In order to turn the ship, the rudder must be redirected. However, the rudder is a large flat plane that meets with a tremendous amount of resistance from the water pressure around it when it's moved. In fact, if the rudder is turned too much too soon, it can break. As a small end piece, the trim tab is easy to turn in comparison to the larger rudder because of its size. Once it turns even a little bit, it breaks the flat plane of the rudder and creates a vacuum of low pressure into which the big rudder can then easily turn. The point is that a relatively small change can redirect a huge ship that would otherwise require a tremendous amount of effort to turn.

If we think of an organization or team as the ocean liner and the people involved as the rudder that sets its direction, then empathic connection becomes the trim tab. The empathy factor can drive strategy, team productivity, marketing, product and program development, sales, and eventually, profit and success. How? It's linked to collaboration, innovation, and managing changes in the market and workplace.

Similar to a trim tab, empathy can facilitate interpersonal collaboration and the connection of individuals to organization-wide initiatives so innovation, growth, and change can happen more easily and fluently. It's the catalyst that fuels the future we want to see.

Speaking to collaboration, on October 2010 John Chambers, chairman and CEO of technology giant Cisco, told a conference group of the Association for Federal Information Resources Management that the next generations of virtualization software would forever link collaboration with improved portability, manageability, and compatibility of everyday technology applications in the workplace.[12] It's easy to think of technology as impersonal and our workplaces as distinct "silos," separate from each other. However, with the advent of new virtual technology that invites collaboration, such as cloud computing, Google documents, and other web-based sharing of resources, the most highly collaborative people will very soon be those most valued in the workplace. The skill of empathy is a critical element of collaboration, and it's becoming more important because it involves an understanding of needs. Meeting needs is crucial for organizational success.

The common denominator in key current organizational research is a connection to needs at multiple levels within the organization and with its key audiences or customers. With a needs awareness, this common denominator becomes apparent. Without it, the organizational research looks like a variety of unrelated findings. I believe learning empathy as a workplace skill and supporting it as a business best practice stands out as the one focus area that can drive everything from productivity and profit to morale and meaning in the workplace.

Before we get into the mechanics of creating empathic connections as a

Empathy stands out as the one focus area that can drive everything from productivity and profit to morale and meaning in the workplace.

workplace practice in the next chapters, I'd like to share with you some of the research that reinforces the confidence I feel about the critical nature of empathy in organizations.

For many years, I've been enthusiastic about Kimball Fisher's *Leading Self-Directed Work Teams: A Guide to Developing New Team Leadership Skills*. Among many work groups, it's a standard for empowered work team training. Fisher presents the results of studies involving more than seven thousand work groups and firms as well as organizational case studies and quantitative data. The research points to three consistent attributes associated with the most successful work groups and work environments. In these, the leaders:

1. have the ability to create strong mutual respect between the workers and the leader.
2. assure that the job gets done.
3. provide leadership in getting problems solved.[13]

When I first read this list, I was relieved and gratified. The connection piece is listed as the first attribute, while the doing piece is listed second. Someone had actually researched and documented this in a clear and direct way that I had not seen before.

Within the next decade, a mountain of research would build to support the efficacy of having and developing qualities of connection such as trust, respect, compassion, and empathy in the workplace.

Emotional Intelligence, the Empathy Factor, and Trust

Psychologists Peter Salovey and John D. Mayer first introduced the idea of emotional intelligence in 1990.[14] Then, in 1995, Daniel Goleman published *Emotional Intelligence,* which expanded interest in the topic. In 1998, he wrote an article in the *Harvard Business Review* titled "What Makes a Leader?" In this article, Goleman calls emotional intelligence "the sine qua non" (an indispensable element) of leadership and lists empathy as one of its five components. He defines empathy as "the ability to understand the emotional makeup of other people" and the "skill in treating people according to their emotional reactions."

He delineates three reasons empathy is so important: the increasing use of teams ("cauldrons of bubbling emotions"); the rapid pace of globalization with its possible misunderstandings of cross-cultural communication; and the growing need to retain talent.[15]

In an article titled "What's Empathy Got to Do With It?" Bruna Martinuzzi, founder of Clarion Enterprises Ltd., a company specializing in emotional intelligence and leadership, further affirms the benefits of empathy. "Indeed, empathy is valued currency," she states. "It allows us to create bonds of trust; it gives us insights into what others may be feeling or thinking; it helps us understand how or why others are reacting to situations; it sharpens our 'people acumen' and informs our decisions."[16]

A Gallup Study completed in 2008 asked followers which qualities they most wanted from their leaders. The expected descriptors—vision, purpose, drive, ambition, wisdom—were largely absent. Instead, the qualities people most want from their leaders are trust, compassion, stability and hope, honesty, integrity and respect.[17]

Research indicates that when trust is high, retention tends to be high, which saves an organization both time and money.[18] This study was conducted by the Center for Creative Leadership (CCL®), an international institute devoted to leadership research and training. On another note, the Center conducted a survey in 2002, asking managers to evaluate what worked best when leading organizations through downsizings and other periods of difficulty. Kerry Bunker, a senior program associate for leadership development at the Center concluded: "Effective leaders seem better at blending the softer leadership skills— trust, empathy and genuine communication—with the tough skills needed to keep an organization afloat during difficult times." Results of the survey showed that leaders who best managed their organizations in times of change were proficient in "honest, proactive communication." They "listened well, demonstrated sensitivity and were willing to articulate clearly the rationale and necessity for change despite the pain those changes might inflict."[19]

Empathy engenders trust, insight, and understanding important for both internal and cross-cultural communication.

Thus empathy proves its worth in building bonds of trust that are beneficial across the board for demonstrating effective leadership.

The Empathy Factor, Meaning, and Customer Satisfaction

Dev Patnaik, author of *Wired to Care: How Companies Prosper When They Create Widespread Empathy*, focuses on how a corporate culture of empathy helps a company thrive because empathic connection with the consumer drives product development and innovation. Not only that, but it creates something very difficult to cultivate in the workplace— personal meaning for the work being done. The empathic connection to the consumer gives workers a reason to get up and go to work in the morning to meet their own needs for contribution and meaning. Patnaik and Pete Mortensen cite numerous case studies from Nike, IBM, Microsoft Xbox, Harley-Davidson, and others to illustrate how using empathy can lead to better products, more employee engagement, more valuable customer feedback, and increased revenues.[20]

Empathy is equally relevant for end users in social sectors such as government agencies, nonprofits, and universities as it is for business customers. Consider the following example of the power of connecting empathically to the market we serve.

In the 1990s, I worked with an association that represented forty-three thousand members. At the time, it was one of the largest government employee groups in the United States. The association was hosting a series of several dozen meetings statewide for members in different locations over a period of several weeks. Critical decisions were to be made in these meetings. Management was worried because turnout in the past had been lower than what they wanted.

Which staff person would coordinate and attend which meetings? The management team prepared a list of the meetings in chronological order because this made the most sense for their staffing process. During a series of informal focus groups we conducted with members, I noticed how confused members looked and how much effort they were putting into deciding which meeting to attend. Their eyes scanned up and down the list, then across. Members weren't interested in the date. First, they wanted to know the location because this was the critical decision element for them. But this information was accessible only by sorting through the more than three dozen meetings scheduled and organized by date. So I recommended that management reorganize the list according to location instead. The three events in region A, for example, were listed together under a readily visible heading, and so on. This reformatting coupled with increased communication about the needs of members that would be met by attending resulted in the largest turnout for meetings of this kind in the Association's five-decade history, a three- to fourfold increase. At one meeting, chairs had to be brought in from other rooms to accommodate the crowd. Other meetings reported similar exponential increases in turnout.

This experience led management to a big aha! Managers realized the value of communicating from the point of view of the member rather than management—with a simple, effective, and empathic solution that yielded significant results.

Consideration of the needs of others is an empathic quality that we can develop by using NVC. Let's look at other ways of being that help us connect with others for more effective outcomes.

Ways of Being

The groundbreaking book *Good to Great: Why Some Companies Make the Leap . . . and Others Don't* by Jim Collins has changed the way leaders and consultants view organizations since its publication in 2001. It presents key findings, not just about what to do but how to *be* as a leader or an impassioned workforce, based on a study of 1,435 Fortune 500 companies conducted over five years. One of these critical findings describes what Collins calls a "Level 5" leader in the companies that outperformed their competitors and the market over a sustained period of time, even in industries that were struggling. Of this type of leader, Collins says, ". . . it is important to note that Level 5 is an empirical finding, not an ideological one. Humility + Will = Level 5. Level 5 leaders are a study in duality: modest and willful, humble and fearless."[21] These are not business practicalities to do, but instead ways to connect with ourselves and others.

How are these leaders developed? Collins suggests "the right circumstances—self-reflection, conscious personal development." He states that some of the leaders in the study had "significant life experiences that might have sparked or furthered their maturation," such as cancer, World War II experiences, strong religious belief or conversion.[22] Again, we see that the human aspects that come from self-connection and self-awareness serve as the foundation for actions at work.

> *High-performing companies have leaders who are self-aware and possess certain qualities that enable them to connect with others.*

Passion, Purpose, and Values

The Hedgehog Concept is what Collins dubbed a laser-like focus that requires reflection on what you're passionate about, what you can be the best at, and what drives your economic engine. Why "Hedgehog"? Collins ingeniously named his concept after this little creature that can do only one thing well—roll up in a ball with its spikes out for protection. Hedgehogs don't run and don't even see particularly well, but they sure know how to roll up into a ball!

When I read the piece about passion, I was excited because at that time, eighteen years into my career, I had been looking for more empirical evidence that confirmed the power of feelings in the workplace. When I facilitate a group and the people start discussing what they're passionate about, I can feel a palpable energy when they get out of their heads and into their passion. For many people, conversations about how they want to contribute to others through work and the meaning they derive from this can be a personal sharing they enjoy and don't have opportunities to engage in as often as they would like.

Collins stated that less than one half of 1 percent of the companies in his research qualified for the criteria of "great." Many were what he considered to be very good companies, but what distinguished the best of the best? They were fanatical about the elements of the Hedgehog Concept. Even though many of the companies in the *Good to Great* research have experienced major upheavals in recent years with the global economic downturn, Collins's findings remain seminal in the study of organizational success.

So are these companies great places to work? Yes and no, said Collins. They are great places to work for people who share the same values. For example, if you're not a smoker, working at R. J. Reynolds would be like listening to a dentist's drill every day. He writes that the companies that were crystal clear about who they were—I call this concept organizational *Identity*—actually repelled people who didn't match their values. They're so consistent and clear about who they are that it's easy for people to determine if they fit or not and to choose companies where they would like to work. The benefit for these companies, of course, is they attract people who are more likely to fit in with their values. This, in turn, increases the likelihood that employees can fulfill their passion and purpose for work.

> *Companies that exceed market performance are "fanatical" about their purpose and clear about their values.*

Engagement and Empowerment

Both Collins and Fisher contend that the idea of managing employees is passé. If we have to manage somebody, he or she is not a fit for the job. We want people who are self-motivated, can garner for themselves what the company or team is about and decide how they can contribute to the team, and then go and do what needs to be done. William Bridges *(Managing Transitions: Making the Most of Change)* has talked about de-jobbing for a long time and so has Fisher. Great companies un-box their people and give them freedom in their roles. Employees who are in alignment with the company's identity, purpose, and passion will take their oars and happily row.

A stellar example of this passion can be observed in the development of Pixar Animation Studios. The company attracted enthusiastic people of genius and talent because of its commitment to and focus on innovation and excellence in animation. You can't argue with the results, which include but are by no means limited to twenty-four Academy Awards, seven Golden Globes, and three Grammys. Add to that $6.3 billion in earnings worldwide[23] and you have what many call outrageous success—largely due to identity, purpose, and passion. Yes, doing and creating were necessary, but these values and qualities of *being* fueled the fire.

In the boom years of Google hiring, it was common for applicants to go through a dozen—yes, twelve—interviews to meet everyone they would work with on a regular basis. At Starbucks, interviewers might ask if an applicant wants a cup of coffee before the interview. They aren't being polite. They want people fanatical about drinking coffee.

Organizations that incorporate into their thinking, planning, and doing the empathic connection that generates employee empowerment experience such far-reaching results as the following, cited in the Collins and Fisher research:

- 45 percent lower costs[24]
- 250 percent improvement in productivity[25]
- 100 percent increase in revenues and profits[26]
- 50 percent cut in accidents, absenteeism, and sickness[27]
- 3.42 to 18.50 times increase in the general stock market value [28]

People want to be empowered and have passion and purpose for the work they do. I've found in working with groups all over the United States and also in India and with companies from Japan that one of the most powerful and intimate topics people can talk about

in the workplace is how they want
to contribute. It's quite personal
to them; they desire to make a
difference. They want to get up in
the morning and do something
that counts. It's a need that people
want to fulfill. When they don't have
that opportunity at work, it starts
a cycle of frustration. Then sometimes managers judge them as being
unmotivated, when in fact, Deming said that most interpersonal issues
in an organization are not personal. They're systemic. Something in the
system is putting these people at odds instead of their personalities.[29]

People want to be empowered and have passion and purpose for the work they do and feel frustrated when they don't have this opportunity.

To encourage engagement and contribution to happen naturally,
people want to know where the organization or team is headed, why it's
going there, and how they can help. The more explicit an organization
can be about its identity, purpose, and direction and every employee's
role in advancing the cause, the more people will self-select and self-
direct. The more they self-select, the more passion and energy the
company in general will have from their efforts. The more passion it has
in combination with other key factors, according to Collins, the more
profitable it will be.[30]

Speaking of profit, the IC process considers profit as one leg of a
three-legged strategy under what I call the organizational or team need for
Energy. Peggy Holman, one of the editors of *The Change Handbook* and
an organizational consultant, told me she found this to be one of the more
exciting aspects of our process. She liked this new way to look at profit as
a means to an end rather than the goal itself. People want to engage in a
meaningful purpose that results in profit, which in turn fuels their work.

Fortuitous events unfold for companies that make a commitment
to focus on what Stephen Covey calls the "important but not urgent"[31]
questions of who do we want to be and how do we want to be together.
One of the key elements is to operate from a commitment paradigm,
where people act from self-motivation, and not a control paradigm,
where people act out of fear, guilt, or shame. The aim is a balance of
authority and accountability.

Let's use Pixar as an example again. In his blog for the *Harvard Business Review*, Tom Davenport analyzed how organizations build their capacity for sound judgment and decision making. He states that Pixar makes "better decisions" in part because the company's managers give its directors a great deal of autonomy, and the directors, in turn, seek feedback from the entire production crew. Another reason for its success is Pixar University, which not only educates but engages Pixar's people in the company's purpose and passion.[32]

The more explicit an organization can be about what Integrated Clarity terms the organizational needs of **Identity, Life-Affirming Purpose,** *and* **Direction** *as well as every employee's role in fulfilling them, the more people will self-select and self-direct.*

Self-Awareness and Strategic Conversations

Increased individual and organizational self-awareness help people engage with others and the organization as a whole in more productive ways that meet more needs and goals. Leading books in the field of organization development endorse contemplation, self-reflection, conscious personal development, and individual coaching, for example.

In addition, many may be surprised that academia recommends consideration of feelings and needs along with mental disciplines. The Harvard Business School Executive Education Program included a course called Leadership in a Time of Turbulence and Change. The course description read that change happens by influencing people's feelings with truths, not analysis and data. A course for executives at Northwestern University's Kellogg School of Management offered by writer, physician, and spiritualist Dr. Deepak Chopra has a similarly nontraditional description. It states, "In *The Soul of Leadership*, you will gain an increased awareness of your own and others' needs and a deeper understanding of your leadership potential to make a profound change in the way you lead."[33] Once again we see the importance of that third dimension that adds depth to thinking and doing.

Helping to increase self-awareness and healthy interaction, the movement called Appreciative Inquiry has gained a foothold throughout the organization development field. Appreciative Inquiry is based on sociological studies that reveal a human tendency. If you and I meet and I tell you all the things you're doing wrong, you tend to increase the error. If I meet with you and say, "Tell me about a time when you did something exceptional that was similar to this," and I help you access your own intelligence about it, you gain in confidence and competence.

Along with a high degree of self-awareness among its members, healthy organizations have high rates of oral tradition and social interchange versus reliance solely on written documentation. They tend to use the Socratic method of inquiry where questioning one another is seen as support versus doubt. These companies hold many interactive and collaborative strategic conversations and dialogues as part of their structured strategic planning. They practice participative management, engaging the whole system and particularly the worker at the level of implementation.

Effective leaders tend to have a high degree of self-awareness, and healthy organizations have high rates of social interchange, including interactive and collaborative strategic conversations.

Pulling It All Together in Integrated Clarity

I considered much of the organizational research as I developed the process of Integrated Clarity. Again and again, I found compelling evidence for capitalizing on and celebrating the human element, for maximizing focus on feelings and needs in the workplace rather than ignoring, managing, or diminishing them in some way or subsuming them to the intellect or the mind.

I concluded from the work of these researchers and teachers and my own consulting experiences that organizational effectiveness and vitality begins with a state of self-awareness. Success is not driven by what we do, by our actions or behaviors. Rather, it's driven by *who we choose to be* as a group and as individuals and the kinds of empathic connections we create. From that core of who we are moment to moment, all our actions flow. Determining and honing this driving force of an organization is the foundation of Integrated Clarity.

But how do we actually "do" self-awareness? What are the actual mechanics of becoming self-aware?

NVC shows us step by step how to become self-aware as individuals. IC shows us how to become self-aware as a team or organization. These processes include clarifying and meeting both individual needs and six universal organizational needs, using Nonviolent Communication as a tool and Integrated Clarity as a framework.

In 2005, I had dinner with my former boss, Jim Hayes, to discuss Integrated Clarity. I had worked for Hayes in the early 1980s at Time, Inc., where he was regarded in the highest esteem and still is to this day. He went on to become publisher of *Discover* magazine and then publisher for eight years of what has long been considered one of the foremost business publications in the world, *Fortune* magazine. Over a sushi dinner in Phoenix, we talked about the IC concept of organizations having needs— the foremost of which I call *Identity*.

Organizational success is driven not by what we do but by who we choose to be as a group and as individuals moment to moment and the kinds of empathic connections we create.

Basically, *Identity* is the core makeup of the organization and answers the questions "Who are we?" and "What are our values as a collective group?" In strategic conversation, the IC process begins with people in the organization inquiring into who they are as an organization and then expressing this identity in their consumer markets, the people they serve. Hayes surprised me by confirming that an organization's understanding of its own identity was so critical in his mind to the organization's future that, "if it took one year for the organization to clarify its identity, it would be worth it."

This was greatly reassuring to me given Hayes's traditional business bent. Traditional strategic planning sessions do not take the time to ask "Who are we?"—a form of connecting to members' internal sense of organizational self. Most jump right in and begin with "What do we do next?"—a shortsighted form of two-dimensional thinking, planning, and doing in a three-dimensional world.

How is it relevant to us whether or not an organization is clear about its identity? Why does it matter whether an organization has needs? What role and legitimacy do feelings have in the workplace? What difference does it make if we know what our own feelings and needs are?

If we work for an organization that's conflicted about its needs and values, and if we aren't crystal clear about what needs and values are important to us in our work, chances are, our productivity is suffering along with our morale. More interpersonal conflicts are likely to occur between people in the workplace, more frustrations may be simmering due to productivity lower than what most want or a higher than comfortable frequency of miscommunication. In addition, depending on our own personal values, we are probably experiencing more dissatisfaction in our workday experiences.

On the flip side, when these organizational needs are met and people needs are met through work, a kind of "humanistic company" develops as described in the University of Pennsylvania's Wharton School of Business book *Firms of Endearment: How World-Class Companies Profit from Passion and Purpose*:

> "What we call a *humanistic company* is run in such a way that its stakeholders— customers, employees, suppliers, business partners, society, and many investors—develop an emotional connection with it, an affectionate regard not unlike the way many people feel about their favorite sports teams. Humanistic companies—or *firms of endearment* (FoEs)—seek to maximize their value to society as a whole, not just to their stakeholders. They are the ultimate value creators: They create emotional value, experiential value, social value, and of course, financial

value. People who interact with such companies feel safe, secure, and pleased in their dealings. They enjoy working with or for the company, buying from it, investing in it, and having it as a neighbor."[34]

That describes the connection that takes place with the outer world when an organization is transformed by creating a satisfying and fulfilling environment within.

After I developed IC, I began suggesting to my clients that they pause before making strategic decisions to ask questions that open doors:

- "Who are we?"
- "How do we continuously articulate which universal human needs of our customers we are passionate about meeting?"
- "How do we measure and monitor our connection to this purpose in daily operations and decisions?"
- "How do we measure and monitor our ability to fulfill this purpose with the people we serve, our customers?"

The framework of Integrated Clarity includes answering questions around six basic organizational needs I call *Identity, Life-Affirming Purpose, Direction, Structure, Energy,* and *Expression.* These needs are fully explained in Chapter Four and referenced throughout this book. When my clients first answer questions around *Identity, Life-Affirming Purpose,* and *Direction,* strategies about what to do seamlessly flow from that clarity. For this reason, we have come to call these Source Needs. Then, what we call the Leveraging Needs of *Structure, Energy,* and *Expression* of the organization's unique place in the market and world fall into place to support those strategies.

The results? People report more fulfilling internal and external connections and appreciation, not to mention revenue and growth. Members of an organization gain deep understanding of one another's feelings, needs, and requests in the service of shaping a collective

When we first answer questions around the organizational Source Needs of Identity, Life-Affirming Purpose, *and* Direction, *strategies about what to do next seamlessly flow from that clarity.*

strategy. One that can be implemented with self-motivated commitment and empowerment versus a hierarchy of control and command.

Proof Is in the Productivity

I began to see levels of results I had not seen previously through applying Nonviolent Communication within the framework of Integrated Clarity. My clients were being transformed by the process of needs-based strategic conversations as opposed to traditional strategic planning.

CITY OF PORTLAND, OREGON

A management analyst for the city of Portland, Oregon, applied the principles of IC to her department immediately after a half-day NVC/IC workshop. She reported a year later that her department was experiencing increased productivity at a rate she had not seen previously. She felt grateful for the ideas she had learned because her personal level of satisfaction with her workplace had improved, as well.

INTERNATIONAL COUNCIL OF FINE ARTS DEANS

Dr. Ron Jones, president of the Memphis College of Art and former dean of the University of South Florida's College of The Arts and former president of the International Council of Fine Arts Deans, reports that this professional organization "was in a steady decline in membership and organizational focus until the board of directors and department chairs participated in a facilitated strategic conversation with the principles and practices of IC at its core. Membership numbers, revenues, and other key indicators are now stronger than ever."

ARIZONA DEPARTMENT OF TRANSPORTATION

The principles and practices of NVC and IC that nurture high-functioning human connections offer practical ideas, not theoretical ones. They were applied to develop an innovative and highly successful three-year program for businesses as part of a $220 million transportation construction project in Arizona—the largest single contract awarded in the state's transportation construction history.

Teresa Welborn, assistant director in the Communications and Community Partnerships division for the Arizona Department of Transportation (ADOT) explained: "This business outreach program was built around connection and empathy in a way that was groundbreaking for the businesses in the project area. The businesses benefited tremendously from this approach and became partners with the project team and advocates of the construction instead of adversaries. ADOT, the public, and the contractor benefited because this public project moved forward with support from the businesses and community and completed six months ahead of schedule, within budget and with a group of new ADOT supporters."

Once we understand that high-quality human connections are the fabric of high performing teams and organizations, everything we know and understand shifts to a more productive level. A human resources director for a small business of three hundred employees said, "Some processes focus on people issues like improving morale or communication, while others focus on strategic planning and business aspects. What's exciting about Integrated Clarity is that it addresses both at the same time."

Once we understand that high-quality human connections are the fabric of high performing teams and organizations, everything we know and understand shifts to a more productive level.

As you can see by the research, that dual focus is practical, effective, and needed for a company or team to function at its highest capacity.

Do Try This at Home

Since I began using NVC/IC in my work, I've been pleasantly surprised and inspired by how many of my clients tell me that learning these concepts in their workplaces is also affecting those they love at home in a way that all find more satisfying and connecting.

For example, the IC process has been doubly beneficial for Ken, the owner of a small metal fabrications shop, who called me one day. I asked what kind of impact the principles and practices we'd discussed had on his intent to become more connected with his machinists.

"It's working great at work, but you should see what's happening with my relationship with my seventeen-year-old daughter. We're talking!" He and his daughter finally began to share a mutually enriching connection through his practice of some elementary aspects of a needs-based awareness and NVC language.

Make Time for Transformation

Aside from its personal benefits, I hope I've shown that empathy in the workplace can be beneficial for meeting the needs of employees, the organization, and its customers. You'll see more examples of its benefits in the ensuing chapters. Most important, you'll discover ways to develop this skill and how to use it. However, I also want to be clear that implementing the IC model is a journey, an exploration of NVC and needs-based principles applied to the workplace to achieve concrete results. It's a cycle of making observations, adjusting strategies, and taking responsibility to meet our own needs and the needs of our organization or team, while at the same time being focused and driven by the needs of our customers.

This practice creates transformation from the inside out, which leads to both individual and organizational evolution toward increasing levels of harmony and success. A common thread weaves throughout the work of Integrated Clarity, Jim Collins *(Good to Great),* William Bridges *(Managing Transitions),* and Kimball Fisher *(Leading Self-Directed Work Teams),* and the wealth of other research documented here. The concepts presented by all these approaches aren't just ideas to fill our heads; they're practices to embody and live.

Although the process of Integrated Clarity is easy to learn, it's not a quick fix. It's simple to understand but challenging to live because of our habituated ways to the contrary. Our language is embedded with the constructs of blame, guilt, control, shame, and separation. NVC offers an opportunity to change our habits in the workplace and anchor them permanently with communication that can meet the needs for respect and effectiveness more often. I want to emphasize the importance of having patience with yourself as you learn and forgiving yourself when you slip up. No one is perfect and we can all be triggered, especially when under stress or experiencing health issues. Be easy on yourself. You are transforming entrenched patterns and some of them are subtle. Remember that by changing the next words you speak, you are actually changing the way you think and the way you see the world. It will take a while, but your bright new world will be well worth your time and effort.

Incorporating IC and NVC into your organization and your daily work activities requires a change in habits of communication, creating empathic connections throughout the organization that become integrated over time.

Bridges says that change is an external event but transition is an internal experience.[35] For example, just because I've received a new title at work and I've moved into a different office doesn't mean I've fully integrated that new role on the same day. It's a similar process when we're learning a new skill.

Putting the concepts in this book into practice in your organization requires the following five phases of learning for integration that produces results:

1.   Reading and understanding the concepts

2. Engaging with the concepts and questioning or seeing where they are already working in your own life, organization, or team
3. Continuing to test the concepts by practicing the process personally
4. Making adjustments to strategies to hone your results
5. Observing and appreciating what's working, enhancing that, and creating more of it

Although it does take time to transform our habitual ways of relating and operating, NVC and IC are the simplest, fastest ways I know of to learn and practice empathy as a professional skill. Empathy is innate to all of us, but NVC and IC articulate how to deepen and develop empathy and integrate needs-based awareness at the individual and organizational levels. Make time your friend and allow this process to unfold. I think you'll find it gratifying.

I invite employees and managers alike to join me in an exploration of who they are, what they value, and how they want to express those values in the workplace and in their consumer markets. Embarking on this work holds the promise of a workplace with a bright future of increasing vitality and prosperity.

* * * *

Chapter Three explains the basic principles and application of the NVC process, and Chapter Four describes the Integrated Clarity model and how to apply a needs-based awareness to the workplace. Together, these processes can help you develop your own connection power and facilitate workplace breakthroughs into the third dimension. There you'll discover a world of meaningful empathic connections, increased possibilities, and more fulfilling outcomes.

THREE

Basic Principles of
Nonviolent Communication

*"It turns out that if you change how people talk, that changes
how they think. . . . All this new research shows us that the languages
we speak not only reflect or express our thoughts, but also shape the very
thoughts we wish to express. The structures that exist in our languages
profoundly shape how we construct reality. . . ."* [36]

—Lera Boroditsky, professor of psychology, Stanford University
and editor in chief of *Frontiers in Cultural Psychology*

Research on how the words and language we choose affect our experience of reality brings to the fore the relevance of the Nonviolent Communication model. I like to say that NVC is the language of empathy. It's also known as Compassionate Communication.

Marshall Rosenberg is known for saying, "The next words you speak could change your life." I've extended this idea to, "The next words you speak could change your business." The previous chapter established the power of empathy and compassion to improve workplace productivity as validated in organizational research. In this chapter, you'll discover a step-by-step process for building your empathy muscles. We begin with how to practice empathy within ourselves as well as with others. In the next chapter, we'll look at additional specific applications for teams and organizations.

What *Is* Empathy?

Two points strike me in reviewing the research about empathy.
First, I see no widespread agreement on how to define empathy and
compassion. While the primary focus of this book is how empathy is
defined and practiced using NVC, in this chapter, I mention additional
sources and definitions when I think they add to our understanding for
workplace application.

Second, I am struck by the fact that none of the research or books
on empathy I have reviewed articulated a concrete way to actually
engage in and practice the empathy process. The tips I did find for
demonstrating empathy were along the lines of truly listening to
people and showing respect and interest in others, or putting yourself
in someone else's shoes and feeling what they are feeling. These are
valuable pieces of advice. They did not, however, outline a specific
process flow for empathy—giving the mechanics of how to actually
demonstrate empathy as a repeatable, step-by-step process. Nor did they
address the deeper issues underlying conflict and pain or say how to
resolve them through empathic connections. In fact, the very definition
of what empathy is varies from research to research. One author refers
to empathy as "the ability to reach outside of ourselves and walk in
someone else's shoes, to get where they're coming from, to feel what
they feel."[37] Another definition of empathy is ". . . the ability to identify
and understand another's situation, feelings and motives."[38] A *Gallup
Management Journal* article, "What Leaders Must Do Next," provides
this tip for leaders: "The way you talk has to include empathy. Ensure
that you convey an understanding of any hardship [a decision] may be
placing on the employees."[39]

Is There a Difference Between Empathy and Compassion?

Dr. Tania Singer, director of the Department of Social Neuroscience
at the Max Planck Institute for Human Cognitive and Brain Sciences
in Leipzig, Germany, says yes. In an interview by The Center for
Compassion and Altruism Research and Education, part of Stanford
University's School of Medicine, Singer described what she believes

are the distinctions between "emotional contagion," empathy, and compassion. Following is a paraphrase of these main distinctions:

Emotional contagion: This is a basic response level, such as when one person yawns, others yawn, or when one baby cries in a nursery, others start crying, too. Research shows that all animals and humans are hard wired with this instinct.

Empathy: Emotional contagion can evolve into empathy when we begin to distinguish between what we are feeling and what others are feeling but recognize we are separate from them and that their pain is not our pain.

So, while I may feel your sadness, I understand it's your sadness and not mine. Feeling an empathic connection doesn't necessarily mean I'm motivated to help the other person, but empathy is a precursor for "empathic concern," or compassion.[40]

Compassion: Empathic connection when it evolves into empathic concern, or compassion, results in a strong wish to do something to help the other person. Singer didn't mention in this interview how to transform one into the other, but I can tell you that in my experience, the process of NVC can do just that. It encourages you to guess at the other person's needs (or your own) and help them (or yourself) to formulate a request to meet those needs.

Listening

One of the most crucial elements of empathic connection is listening, as described by Stephen Covey in his book *The 7 Habits of Highly Effective People:* "Empathic listening involves much more than registering, reflecting, or even understanding the words that are said. Communications experts estimate, in fact, that only 10 percent of our communication is represented by the words we say. Another 30 percent is represented by our sounds, and 60 percent by our body language. In empathic listening, you listen with your ears, but you also, and more importantly, listen with your eyes and with your heart. You listen for feeling, for meaning. You listen for behavior. You use your right brain as well as your left. You sense, you intuit, you feel."[41]

Sometimes "doing something" for people to meet their needs may involve just listening to them with deep empathic connection, guessing their feelings and needs either silently or out loud. Two instances of my early use and practice of NVC stand out in my memory and represent the type of pivotal experiences that continue to encourage me in my practice to this day.

The Cab Driver. The first time I mustered up the courage to try this new language of feelings and needs, I was in a taxi on my way to the Atlanta International Airport. I had just spent a week in trainings with Marshall Rosenberg. I felt excited to empathize with people, to be completely focused on them, with not only empathic connection but empathic concern for who they were and what their life was like.

Empathizing with the cab driver seemed like a logical starting point. It was low risk for me in that I'd almost certainly never see this person again, and I knew our dialogue would come to an end when we arrived at my destination. I don't recall how the conversation started, but I do remember that right away I made an observation and guessed out loud to him about what he might be feeling and what his needs might be. I translated his words and story back to him as pleasant feelings and needs met or unpleasant feelings and needs unmet: "When I heard you talk about your daughter, I'm guessing you felt quite proud and have a need to support her." "Yeah, yeah. That's right," he'd say, and he'd continue, adding more details. He talked about his family and about owning his own cab and business.

At first, I was a stranger to him and he was guarded talking to me, as he would have been with any other fare. But the more I empathized, the more he became animated. I was surprised at how much I was enjoying getting to know him in this way. It didn't matter if I guessed wrong. He'd set me straight, and in doing so, our connection grew during the short cab ride. He went from what I'm guessing was his usual work face to a big beaming smile. He made eye contact with me constantly through the rear view mirror. He sat more upright. His voice became more lively.

Finally, he asked me what I did for a living because he'd never had anybody ask the questions I did. I told him I was a communication and strategic planning consultant. I don't think he quite got what all that meant but he said he enjoyed our talk. As I left, he gave me a big hug and said he had never had a conversation like that before. Interestingly, I think I might have said fifty words at most over the course of the entire ride. But to him, we were now old friends.

The Iraq vet. The second instance I'll always remember took place in an airplane. On the flight back from facilitating a strategic planning session in Florida, I noticed a man rush into the plane just as the doors were closing for takeoff. He was tall, broad shouldered, tanned and fit, about mid-thirties. He wore a short-sleeved T-shirt and his eyes were bloodshot. When he walked, he swayed from side to side and bumped several people sitting on the aisle. Some of them appeared irritated. When he took his seat in the row across from me, I detected what smelled like alcohol. He began speaking in a volume louder than what a couple of people around him were comfortable with. One of them moved to an empty seat in another row with a few heavy sighs and body language I interpreted as disgust.

Within a few moments, the man got up and walked toward a couple of flight attendants preparing to review safety procedures. He wanted to order an alcoholic beverage and one of the attendants told him to return to his seat for takeoff. During this time he was facing away from me and I could see the back of his T-shirt. It had the firefighter's Maltese cross emblem on it and the words "Iraq" and "firefighter" along with some other words. I became instantly curious and wondered if he was just back from the war in Iraq. Since the war had begun only a few months earlier, I had yet to speak to anyone who had been deployed there. When he returned to his seat, I mentioned his T-shirt and asked if he had served in Iraq. He said he had, and we began a conversation as I expressed my curiosity and gratitude for his service. I began guessing his feelings and needs with him. He answered and seemed to be enjoying our dialogue but was also cautious. At one point, he asked if I was a reporter. I chuckled and explained that I only wanted to understand what it was like for him.

He started opening up not only about Iraq but about a stint in Afghanistan for three years before that. He was a paramedic, but instead of saving people, he mostly pulled dead bodies out of the rubble after an attack. He talked about how they stacked the bodies. I asked if this was a difficult job for him, and he replied that he eventually got used to it. He told me about having been in South America for a while where he got into trouble talking to a news reporter—hence his questions and caution about me. He said he was on his way to Phoenix to stay with his mother for a while. Then, this big, strong guy began to cry—and not just a little. He wept and asked for a few minutes to himself. I sat there looking out the window, guessing his feelings and needs and simply imagining what he might be crying about.

After a few minutes, he started speaking to me again and apologized for crying. I said I was very moved by it. He reached into his pocket and pulled something out, then said he wanted me to have it. When I reached out to receive what he had in his hand, I could see it was a round military patch with a removable Velcro backing. It had an outline of Afghanistan on it in three colors, which divided the country in thirds of black, red, and green. On the top, it said, "Bagram Combat Prison Patch." On the bottom, "Operation Enduring Freedom 2004." In the middle, above a lightning bolt emblem, was stitched "Black Ops." He told me he wanted to forget Afghanistan and to please take the patch. I accepted it and thanked him. He slept for the rest of the ride until we landed.

I walked out with him, thanking him for his service and courage. He told me not many people say that to him and he was grateful to hear it. One of the passengers who had seemed irritated with him earlier was walking with us and thanked him too, having realized what he had been through. The veteran was in good spirits, laughing and joking. We said goodbye, and when I last turned around to see him, he and a woman I assumed was his mother were embracing in a long hug, the man bending over to hold her and put his head on her shoulders.

I imagine that the gift of the patch represented the gift of us sharing his pain together. I think of him from time to time when I look at the patch. I'm grateful he was able and willing to connect, and I sometimes wonder if what he shared with me was ever shared with anyone else before or after that time.

His actions that day serve as a gift to me today because I think of him as my emotional hero. This man, whom others initially perceived as an irritant or as demonstrating "inappropriate" behavior, was actually a real life combat hero. When I recognize that others may be judging me, I think of him and his courage and empathize with myself that those who have judgments of me are only expressing their own unmet needs and pains in the best way they know how in the moment.

This story illustrates how deep empathic connection can enhance a relationship with a person who at first glance may appear to be totally uninterested in these kinds of connections. Further, in practicing NVC, the intention to connect determines the quality of the connection regardless of how adept we are with the empathy process presented in this book.

Empathy in Action in the Workplace

Empathic resonance and connection are not enough in the workplace for productivity improvement because what leads to improvement is action. Connect-Think-Do. All three are necessary for effective changes.

I define empathy as the intention to create an emotional connection through human needs, which we explore next. This idea of universal human needs is central to empathic connection and the kind of productivity, engagement, and meaning empathy can give rise to in the workplace. It's not just sharing feelings or putting oneself in in someone else's shoes, although this is the *foundation* for empathic concern that leads to action. Later chapters discuss how empathic action in the workplace can fulfill individual needs based on requests and organizational needs based on strategies. This concept relates back to the Connect-Think-Do steps we discussed in Chapter One. All three are necessary for effective changes.

Can Empathy Be Learned?

Yes. While basic levels of emotional resonance and empathy are natural to us as humans, the more developed levels that result in actionable empathy benefit from cultivation. That's the purpose of this book. NVC is the simplest and fastest way I know of to develop basic and higher forms of empathic connection and empathic action as a learned skill, not just a vague concept. This four-step process addresses and explains every communication and interpersonal aspect I can think of or have encountered in my twenty-nine years of studying and teaching interpersonal, team, and corporate communications in the workplace. William Ury, bestselling author of the business book *Getting to Yes* and co-founder of Harvard Law School's negotiation program, says, "NVC is the most important process you'll ever learn."

The steps of NVC can be grasped in a few minutes and, with consistent practice throughout your organization, can lead to the kind of productivity improvement, profit increases, and leadership and team success the previously referenced research identifies. Skill at developing empathic connection requires continued practice, but the reportedly significant personal gains along with the business advantages make that practice worthwhile. True empathy is not a mental construct; it's an emotional and whole-body experience that can be learned. For this reason, NVC practitioners don't really "teach" NVC as much as we share it in a way that others may experience it for themselves.

> *True empathy is not a mental construct; it's an emotional and whole-body experience that can be learned.*

Introducing NVC: The Lunch Date Exercise

Here is one way I like to introduce the basic components of NVC with workplace teams.

Imagine. . . . It's 11:15 AM. You call Bob, a business associate, and ask if he'll meet you for lunch at Tobey's Grill at noon to discuss a project you're both working on that is of high priority. He agrees. You finish up what you're doing and roll into Tobey's parking lot at 11:55. You go in and get a table for two and begin checking out the menu. You look at your watch. It's 12:10. No Bob. You pull out your iPhone and start playing with a few apps. You look at your watch again. It's 12:25. Still no Bob.

When I present this scenario to a group of business people, I ask the participants, "What might you be feeling in this situation?" Typically, they first name feelings such as "irritated," "frustrated," or "annoyed." Time and efficiency are often valued in our work settings. Along with the identified feelings, someone might include comments such as, "He's rude," or "He's disrespecting me." At this point, I help the group make a distinction between what they are thinking and what they are feeling by asking, "When you tell yourself 'He's disrespecting me,' what might you be feeling?" They usually think for a moment and then someone says, "Hurt. I feel hurt that he's kept me waiting."

As we go through this exercise, I draw a chart that looks something like this:

Fig. 3-1. The Lunch Date Exercise — Feelings and Thoughts

SITUATION	MY FEELINGS		MY THOUGHTS
Bob said "12 p.m. lunch is OK at Tobey's Grill."	Irritated Annoyed		"He's rude."
12:25 p.m. No Bob No messages	Hurt		"He's disrespecting me."

More feelings are added as people continue imagining this scenario.

"Worried. I'd be worried wondering if Bob was okay or if something had happened to him."

"Relieved. What if I thought Bob was a pain in the neck, and I really didn't want to meet with him?"

"Happy that I have twenty minutes to myself for the first time all week!"

"Nervous. What if Bob doesn't like the idea I propose for our project?"

So now our chart looks like this:

Fig. 3-2. The Lunch Date Exercise—More Lunch Date Feelings and Thoughts

SITUATION	MY FEELINGS		MY THOUGHTS
Bob said "12 p.m. lunch is OK at Tobey's Grill."	Irritated Annoyed		"He's rude."
	Hurt		"He's disrespecting me."
12:25 p.m. No Bob No messages	Worried		"Is he OK?"
	Relieved		"He's a pain!"
	Happy		"I can relax."
	Nervous		"I hope he likes my idea."

As participants look at the chart, a couple of things start to stand out for them. They notice that a wide range of feelings came up— everything from "happy" to "hurt" to "irritated." So first they recognize that the exact same situation can result in many different feelings. Second, they see that their thoughts are not their feelings.

Thoughts are things we tell ourselves in our heads. Feelings are sensations we experience in our bodies. For this reason, if someone says, "I feel disrespected" or "I feel like he shouldn't have said that," I might respond with, "When you think you're being disrespected, are you feeling hurt?" or "When you think he shouldn't have said that, are you feeling irritated?" Most of us aren't conditioned to distinguish between these two internal processes. The ability to make this distinction is one of the keys that make NVC so powerful for business application. Why? Because seeing the situation for what it truly is, without our thoughts of interpretation, evaluation, or judgment obscuring it, allows us to assess both the situation and how we feel about it more accurately. In other words, we can see the situation more clearly because we are able to separate our feelings and thoughts about it from the situation itself.

Thoughts are things we tell ourselves in our heads. Feelings are sensations we experience in our bodies. Most of us aren't conditioned to distinguish between these two internal processes.

Based on the chart we've created, I point out to the group the logical conclusion: the situation is *not* the cause of our feelings. If this were true, then we would have the same feelings for the same situation all the time. We can see from the exercise that this is not true—that people experience many different feelings given the exact same situation. We can also easily imagine that the same people could have different feelings about the same situation on a different day. In fact, someone's feeling might change from irritation to worry or relief within a few minutes.

Following is a list of universal human feelings that we might experience in the workplace. (A list is also provided in the Appendices.)

Fig. 3-3. Feelings Inventory for the Workplace

SAD	TIRED	CALM
Ashamed	Burned Out	Absorbed
Blue	Distracted	Awed
Brokenhearted	Exhausted	Blissful
Depressed	Fatigued	Comfortable
Disappointment	Flat	Confident
Discouraged	Frazzled	Content
Disheartened	Hopeless	Fulfilled
Fragile	Indifferent	Loving
Helpless	Lethargic	Peaceful
Hurt	Off Center	Relaxed
Lonely	Restless	Secure
Miserable	Weary	Serene
Numb		
Vulnerable	**WORRIED**	**FRIENDLY**
	Alarmed	Appreciative
GLAD	Anxious	Cordial
Delighted	Concerned	Fondly
Eager	Disturbed	Grateful
Encouraged	Guarded	Open
Excited	Nervous	Receptive
Happy	Overwhelmed	Sensitive
Hopeful	Panicky	Social
Inspired	Scared	Tender
Optimistic	Shocked	Trusting
Proud	Suspicious	Warm
Relieved	Tense	Welcoming
Satisfied	Terrified	
Thrilled	Wary	**EXCITED**
		Adventurous
MAD	**CONFUSED**	Amazed
Agitated	Cautious	Creative
Angry	Conflicted	Curious
Annoyed	Doubtful	Energetic
Bitter	Hesitant	Engaged
Disgusted	Puzzled	Exhilarated
Enraged	Reluctant	Fascinated
Frustrated	Skeptical	Free
Furious	Torn	Inspired
Impatient	Troubled	Interested
Irate	Uncomfortable	Intrigued
Jealous	Uneasy	Invigorated
Pessimistic	Unsettled	Passionate
Resentful	Unsure	

© 2011 Elucity Network, Inc. as developed by Marie R. Miyashiro

Integrated Clarity® List adapted from Nonviolent Communication™

So, if the situation, or Bob not showing up, isn't the cause of our feelings, what is?

In NVC, we acknowledge that the root of our feelings lies within us, not in the situations or people around us. Our feelings are connected to our own internal needs. By identifying and articulating our own needs, we take responsibility for our feelings. Needs, as defined here, are not desires, wants, or wishes. These are *universal* human needs in that every person has the same basic set of needs, although different needs may be more active in us from one moment to the next. This fact fundamentally unifies us in our shared humanity.

In NVC, we acknowledge that the root of our feelings lies within us, not in the situations or people around us. Our feelings are connected to our own internal, universal human needs.

Fundamental and Workplace Needs

Rosenberg developed a list of basic shared needs based on the work of Chilean economist Manfred Max-Neef, known for his human development model of Fundamental Human Needs. Max-Neef's work is related to the hierarchy of needs model developed by Abraham Maslow, the founder of humanistic psychology. This psychological perspective emphasizes personal responsibility, free will, and self-actualization, or achieving one's full human potential. Rosenberg studied with noted American psychologist Carl Rogers, another influential figure in humanistic psychology.

Because I bring NVC to organizations, I have adapted Rosenberg's needs list for people in the workplace. The workplace list organizes needs into eight categories that the organizational research shows produces results above the norm. These results include both extraordinary work products for the team and organization as well as increased satisfaction for employees and customers. The following tailored list serves as a needs vocabulary and points to areas of focus that optimize team and organizational functioning and experiences. (As with the feelings list, a needs list is also provided in the Appendices.)

Fig. 3-4. Needs Inventory for the Workplace

RESOURCES
PHYSICAL NEEDS
Air/Food/Water
Comfort, Ease
Consistency
Equipment, Tools
Health
Movement, Exercise
Privacy
Respectful physical contact
Rest/Relaxation
Safety, Security
Supplies
Time, Efficiency

COMMUNICATION
MENTAL NEEDS
Awareness
Clarity, Direction
Data, Research
Decision Making
Discernment
Education, Training
Information
Reflection
Stimulation, Challenge

AUTHORITY
EMPOWERMENT
Autonomy
Choice
Co-creation of strategies
Collaboration
Discipline
Freedom
  (emotional, spiritual, and physical)
Individuality
Solitude

ACCOUNTABILITY
INTEGRITY
Authenticity
Contribution
Effectiveness, Progress
Feedback, Tracking
Honesty
Humility, Self-reflection
Morality
Punctuality
Quality
Self-worth
Sincerity

INTEGRATION
INTERDEPENDENCE
Acceptance
Appreciation
Clarity
Closeness
Community
Compassion
Connection
Consideration
Cooperation
Emotional Safety
Empathy
Harmony
Inclusion
Intimacy
Love
Reassurance
Respect
Support
Trust
Understanding
Validation
Warmth

SELF-EXPRESSION
CREATIVITY
Creating, Generating
Growth, Progress
Learning, Mastery
Meaning
Play, Fun, Laughter
Teaching

SELF-ALIGNMENT
NATURAL ENERGY
Beauty
Equality, Mutuality
Harmony, Peace
Inspiration
Order
Purpose, Meaning
Respect

MARKING OF TRANSITIONS
CELEBRATING BEGINNINGS
Ceremony/Ritual
Delight
Enjoyment
Excitement
Healing
Humor
Passion

ACKNOWLEDGING ENDINGS
Accept learning
Accept limitations
Acknowledge regrets
Grieve dreams unfulfilled
Mourn lost relationships

© 2011 Elucity Network, Inc. as developed by Marie R. Miyashiro

Integrated Clarity® List adapted from Nonviolent Communication™

When this kind of needs awareness is encouraged in the workplace, I have seen two dynamics occur. First, interpersonal conflicts diminish. Why? Because the perceived wrongness of others can be translated into the expression of our own needs. Consider the following example.

I was presenting the preliminary results of our online organizational assessment for one of our clients to a team of consultants on a project I was leading. One of them became focused on the specific wording in the survey statements and asked several questions, expressed confusion and doubts, and took more time than any of the other consultants were wanting to take on this issue. Sensing he had needs that were being triggered by seeing our assessment tool, I asked how many surveys he'd seen in which he was happy with the wording. He said, "Not many." At the end of the meeting, he expressed embarrassment that he took the focus away from the debriefing of the results. Later, I learned from him that his father was a market researcher and an expert in surveys. I was guessing my colleague felt passionate about the wording in surveys and had a need for quality, accuracy, or professionalism that was tied to his relationship with his father. I also sensed he had a preconceived notion of how he wanted to see those qualities represented in surveys.

Whether this was true for him or not, guessing the possible feelings and needs going on for him was a productive way for me to channel the thoughts I had about his behavior. I was able to stay connected with him instead of hearing his comments and questions as criticism, blame, or judgment, which would have created separation between us. In distinguishing my own thinking and needs from his evaluations, I was able to see him more clearly and also take in his suggestions more fully. Based on his comments, we immediately made an adjustment to the survey design that I liked and think is producing more actionable information for our consulting with clients. Had I heard only criticism, I might have spent my energy defending, justifying, and explaining (which I did initially) and missed the opportunity for process improvement and change as well as a valuable professional and personal connection with this colleague whom I hold in high regard.

Triggered Feelings Mean Unmet Needs

Back to the lunch date exercise. At this point, I hand out the complete list of needs to the group. I ask them to guess what needs might be met or unmet for each of the feelings we'd already listed in the chart. Without much thought or effort, the chart ends up looking like this:

Fig. 3-5. The Lunch Date Exercise — Feelings, Thoughts, and Needs

SITUATION (Observation)	MY FEELINGS	MY NEEDS	MY THOUGHTS
Bob said "12 p.m. lunch is OK at Tobey's Grill."	Irritated Annoyed	Consideration	"He's rude."
	Hurt	Respect	"He's disrespecting me."
12:25 p.m. No Bob No messages	Worried	Safety	"Is he OK?"
	Relieved	Comfort/Ease	"He's a pain!"
	Happy	Quiet/Peace	"I can relax."
	Nervous	Collaboration	"I hope he likes my idea."

Now it's clear to the group. The causes of our feelings are more closely related to our own needs than to the situation or to Bob. The situation acts as a trigger, a stimulus that activates our awareness of whether our needs are met or unmet. In NVC, we refer to the stimulus as an "observation"—a concrete, verifiable fact that provides a description all would agree on. The power of this observation is the absence of evaluation, interpretation, or judgment. In our lunch date exercise, notice how only the observable facts are listed. It's a fact that Bob agreed to meet at noon at Tobey's. The facts are also verifiable that at 12:25 PM. Bob had not arrived and neither had any messages from

Bob or anyone else about why he wasn't there. Described in this way, all would be in agreement. To say, "Bob is late," however, would not be an observation but a judgment that some may not agree with. In many cultures or cities, arriving ten or twenty minutes after the agreed-upon time is considered to be "on time." And in some places, you are "late" even if you arrive at the agreed-upon time because others have arrived a few minutes before this time ready to go. Because of such variables, the Indian philosopher J. Krishnamurti commented once that observing without evaluating is the highest form of human intelligence.

Observing without evaluating is the highest form of human intelligence. (J. Krishnamurti)

Making an observation is the first fundamental step in the NVC process as well as in the business world. There's power and competitive advantage in being able to see something for what it is, as a pure observation. From this place, we can develop more choices and strategies because of the decreased interference of judgments. Think of it like a television transmission signal. If you can receive the signal without distortion, you see and hear the information with clarity. This clarity was a key reason I became excited about the potential of widespread use of NVC in the workplace, even though it's more widely known in the peacemaking and social justice arenas.

For example, the travel website company Travelocity made an unsuccessful attempt in 2005 to broaden its core business. Instead of making judgments and assigning blame, then CEO and president, Michelle Peluso, stuck with observations. In an interview at the time, she explained: ". . . We don't punish each other for making a bad decision or taking a risk. . . . When you don't succeed, there are great lessons to learn—learn them and move on. . . . [We made] sure the employees who were working in those areas understood that we learned an enormous amount from what they had done and we could incorporate that into accelerating the core business."[42]

Evaluations, interpretations, and judgments can act as powerful decision-making tools in the workplace. But when we unconsciously mix them with our feelings and needs, we don't do justice to either our feelings or needs, or the business facts. So, we don't want to stop making evaluations, interpretations, and judgments. We just want to separate them and be clear about when we are making them as distinct from when we are making objective observations. When we mix the former with the latter, what we say is more likely to be heard as criticism by the person receiving our message.

In addition, our needs get obscured by our judgments of the other person. We tend to focus our attention on the external situation and blame instead of objectively make requests that could meet our own internal needs. Thus we miss a precious opportunity to connect with our own unmet needs and then, out of this connection, do something about it that can be more productive and fulfilling, even life changing. Sometimes I refer to this as "projecting" our own unmet needs onto someone else. When we do this, most of us are doing it out of unconscious habit. This act can be highly separating if the person receiving the message doesn't have the skills, awareness, or desire to understand the judgments as an expression of the sender's unmet needs. This kind of separation among team members or between employees and customers becomes an obstacle to productivity, as examples throughout this book illustrate. Rosenberg calls being triggered by feelings we experience as unpleasant a gift because it's an opportunity for each of us to recognize that an unmet need is calling for our attention, whether it's ours or someone else's.

Evaluations, interpretations, and judgments can act as powerful decision-making tools in the workplace. But when we unconsciously mix them with our feelings and needs, we don't do justice to either our feelings or needs, or the business facts.

The Process of Self-Empathy

In NVC, this process of connecting with our own needs as they're triggered by something we see or hear is called self-empathy. It works like this: I pay attention to what is going on with my feelings. As soon as I notice that something I have seen, heard, or thought triggers feelings:

1. **I make a pure observation,** such as, "He rolled his eyes three times while I was presenting my report" versus an interpretation, judgment, or evaluation, such as "He's unsupportive."

2. **I identify what I'm feeling,** and if I'm not sure, I start guessing at what I'm feeling. A pleasant feeling indicates my needs are being met; an unpleasant feeling indicates my needs are not being met in the moment. With the eye-rolling observation mentioned above, I might be feeling irritated or concerned.

3. **I connect these feelings to my needs,** and if I'm not sure, I guess at what needs of mine might be met or unmet. In the observation above, my need might be for trust, respect, understanding, or to be seen as competent, for example.

4. **I can make a request of myself or others** once I've connected to my needs. In the eye-rolling situation, if my need is to be understood, I might say something like: "I want to be sure I'm being clear in presenting my report findings. Are there three people who would be willing to tell me what they've gotten from my presentation so far?"

Figure 3-6 presents a flow chart of this self-empathy process.

Fig. 3-6. Self-Empathy Process Flow Chart

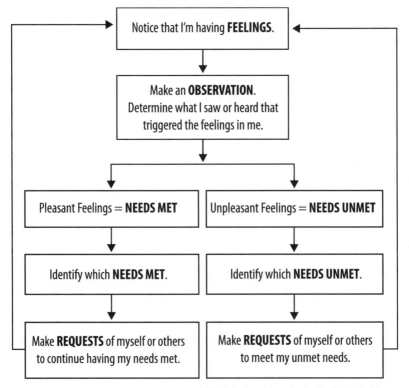

© 2011 Elucity Network, Inc. as developed by Marie R. Miyashiro

Observing without evaluating what is going on in the moment makes us uncommonly powerful in our workplace settings by increasing our clarity about our available choices. People respond much more favorably when they know you intend no criticism of them, as you can see from the following story.

Several years ago, I met with an upper-level management team of fifteen people. I was presenting what I thought I had been hired to do in the hopes this would lead to further discussion and participation in the strategic planning process. A minute or so into my talk, I noticed that about a third of the people at the conference table were engaged in some activity other than listening or looking at me—reading and signing documents, checking and responding to emails, working on their laptops, and the like. Some of them were the key decision makers, directors of divisions. This behavior had been going on since before I began speaking when the group was conducting other business.

I continued to speak for another few minutes, thinking they were finishing up some items and would soon be listening and looking at me. I was able to empathize with their possible feelings and needs behind choosing to do what they were doing instead of listening to me. Had I not been able to give them this empathy—to imagine their overload of work, their frustration or caution about a new consultant—I likely would have interpreted their actions as criticism of me or what I was saying. I might have jumped to the conclusion that they thought I wasn't competent, they didn't like my approach, just weren't interested, or any number of interpretations.

After a couple of minutes, I noticed my observations had not changed; some members of the group were still engaged in activity other than listening or looking at me while I was presenting (step 1). I noticed I felt uncomfortable, uneasy (step 2) and that I had a need to be understood and to contribute to them (step 3). I thought: "Well, what can I do now? This isn't a productive use of my time or theirs." While I was unsure what to say to this group that I had met only once before, I was certain continuing was not worthwhile for the group as a whole. So I decided to be transparent about what was going on for me and said something like this: "I notice that some of you are doing things other than listening to or looking at me. I have something to share with you that I think you will find of value. But right now, I'm not at all sure how to go about sharing it with you. Do you want me to continue?" (step 4)

All the typing and page turning stopped. Every head turned toward me and several directors took off their reading glasses to look my way. The people in the room who were watching this interaction between me and those who had not been listening seemed to be holding their collective breath. You could have heard a pin drop.

Finally, after about five seconds of silence, which can be an eternity in a meeting in some circles, one of the directors said, "Well, what is it that you want to share?" From that moment on, everyone listened and we engaged in a collective discussion with all participating at some level. Ironically, the information I wanted to share was about needs consciousness—both individual needs through NVC and organizational and team needs through my process of Integrated Clarity.

At the end of my twelve-month contract with this group, two events occurred that I found affirming. First, the group requested an additional month of work from me to complete discussion on a few action items. This extension was considered most unusual and required a special exemption from the highest levels of the organization. I was moved that the group members thought enough about our work together to engage in an involved contract extension request. Second, one director who had been the most skeptical about my work with the team told me that when he saw me stop in the meeting and heard me say what I did, he became sold on my approach. He told me I was the third planning consultant they'd brought in, and he was expecting to be disappointed, as he had been with the other consultants. But he said he was impressed by what I did and gained respect for me. I asked him how his need for respect and authenticity had been met by my actions. He replied that in their industry, people don't make themselves vulnerable like that. So when I did, he knew I was being real with them, and it was a relief for him to see. He also thought it was a powerful moment for them as a group. Months later, he told me how beneficial NVC had been to him in his role as a volunteer deacon at his church as well as with his seventeen-year-old son.

Years before this event, I heard consultant Judith Orloff Faulk, a colleague of business consultant Marshall Thurber, say, "Vulnerability is the safest place to be." Thanks to the specific NVC process, I was able to access the mechanics of empathy in a stressful moment in this conference room and to be vulnerable in a way that was still perceived as professional. The four-step process was easy for me to remember, and having had a minimal amount of practice, I was able to do it on the fly. This, in large part, was due to my intention. I didn't have any desire in me in the moment to make them "wrong" for not listening. I was purely open to finding what would work for all of us. I believe this is what they were sensing and assessing in the few seconds before someone spoke. Out of context, what I said could have been heard as a criticism or manipulation. But I had no attachment to wanting them to respond or be any particular way with my request. It was a true request out of my curiosity and valuing of our time rather than a demand camouflaged as a request.

Intention is key. An intention to empathically connect coupled with the NVC process flow of empathy results in empathic connection that can lead to more effective collaboration.

We know we have made or heard a demand instead of a request when there's a consequence for a "no." The consequence can be irritation, judgment, or other forms of indicating that a "yes" is what was really wanted. I had decided before I spoke those words that if this was not of value for them, I would bow out of the contract. Why force a mountain to move? I value this work and value working with people who want this information. In being willing to lose the contract, I was free to be with them in a nonjudgmental way—a way in which I could connect to their feelings and needs rather than interpret and judge.

If our intention to connect with someone's feelings and needs, to walk in someone else's shoes, is to get that person to do something we want, it's not empathy or true connection. It's what I'd call manipulation. Empathy is a pure state in which we empty ourselves completely in order to experience what the other person is experiencing. Self-empathy is a process in which we pause and empty our own thoughts to connect with our own feelings and needs. When we engage in empathy and self-empathy, we are open to what will come from this connection and cannot predict with certainty what the outcome will be. We simply stay true to our intention to connect empathically.

Intensity of Feelings Is a Clue

Another way we can keep
feelings from affecting our
personal business productivity
is to be aware of the intensity
of our feelings in relation to the

*With self-empathy, we pause and
empty our thoughts to connect
with our own feelings and needs.*

triggering event. If an event is relatively minor in the scheme of our lives
or work but our response to it is on a considerably larger scale, we can
guess that the need is vital and active for us because it's being triggered
at the slightest opportunity.

Suppose, for example, I'm explaining a particular situation to a
colleague because I know it would be helpful for her and she's asked
me to give her suggestions, and she keeps checking her mobile device
for messages. She's obviously distracted and I might guess she's
uninterested, just as the executive team appeared to be at first glance.
The interaction with my colleague represents an opportunity for
introspection so I can understand my own needs better and request
what I want, either from myself or her. The behaviors of others simply
trigger something that's already active inside of me. If I have thoughts
of blame ("She's disrespecting
me."), I've missed an opportunity
to connect with my own needs by
projecting them onto her. If, on
the other hand, I'm able to guess
what her feelings and needs might
be, then I can hold my needs and
her needs at the same time and in
so doing, maintain our empathic
connection.

*If an event is relatively minor
but our response to it is on a
considerably larger scale, this
indicates we have an active
unmet need that is key for us.*

As I act on more strategies to take care of this need, I find the
frequency and intensity of these unpleasant feelings diminishing. When
my needs are often and fully satisfied, I tend to have a higher tolerance
for behaviors that might otherwise trigger me. The higher my tolerance
without cost to me or others, the more valuable a team member I am

because I can work in a diverse number of settings and with different types of people.

For example, part of my job is to work with business owners, managers, or employees who are angry or frustrated over a particular situation. It's common for them to raise their voice or choose words that many others might hear as "yelling" or "rudeness." Because of my NVC practice, I don't take their actions as commentary about me or the projects I'm representing. I'm able to translate their actions into guesses about their feelings and needs.

People who practice NVC have a wider bandwidth of ability to work with others who are experiencing a diverse range of intense feelings. The objectivity that comes with both self-empathy and empathy for others is a valuable quality in the workplace for internal teamwork as well as for customer service.

Practicing self-empathy and empathy for others allows us to work with people experiencing intense feelings without being triggered ourselves—a valuable ability for teamwork and customer service.

The Process of Empathy for Others

Empathy for others is the process of translating the judgments or reactions other people send in our direction into what we guess they might be feeling and what met or unmet needs they might have. Judgments can be perceived as negative ("You're incompetent.") or perceived as positive ("You're the best salesperson we've ever had.").

Empathic connection is built around guessing someone's feelings and needs rather than knowing them because we can never fully know what others feel or need unless they tell us. We can only imagine. Have you ever told someone, "I know how you feel," only to have them say, "You have no idea how I feel." Or, "I understand," only to hear, "No, you can't possibly understand what it's like for me." Because the primary purpose of empathy is connection, we want to be aware of words or statements like these. They could cause a break in our connection to others and interfere with being present to whatever is alive in them in the moment. When we say, "I," we take the focus off them and put it back on ourselves. For this reason, an empathy conversation is "you" focused.

Empathy for others while maintaining self-empathy requires a balance, a dance if you will, between listening to the other person and empathically expressing what's going

The process of empathy teaches us to guess what others are feeling and what met or unmet needs they might have. We guess because to say we "know" or "understand" is less connecting.

on for us in service of maintaining our connection with the other person. This balance will be further addressed as we discuss applications of empathy in the following chapters. For now, let's return to the basics.

In essence, the empathy process between people is similar to self-empathy except that instead of guessing our own feelings and needs, we guess the feelings and needs of others. We can do this out loud with the other person or silently to ourselves. In the case of my executive team meeting, because the situation involved people I was meeting for the first time and who worked in an environment where direct, honest discourse was not common, this process of empathizing with others happened internally and silently. Here was my process once I noticed that something had triggered my feelings:

1. **I made a pure observation:** "He's reading and signing papers instead of listening to and looking at me," versus an interpretation, judgment, or evaluation such as, "He doesn't like my presentation," or "He's being rude."

2. **I guessed at what he might be feeling.** Having made the observation above, I guessed that he was feeling overwhelmed with paperwork or cautious that another consultant was hired or irritated by these weekly management meetings.

3. **I guessed the needs behind the feelings:** progress, clarity, hope, understanding . . .
4. **I made a request of others** in the meeting once I connected to my needs and guessed at what they might be feeling and needing: "Do you want me to continue?"

Figure 3-7 shows a flow chart for the empathy process with others.

Fig. 3-7. Empathy Process Flow Chart

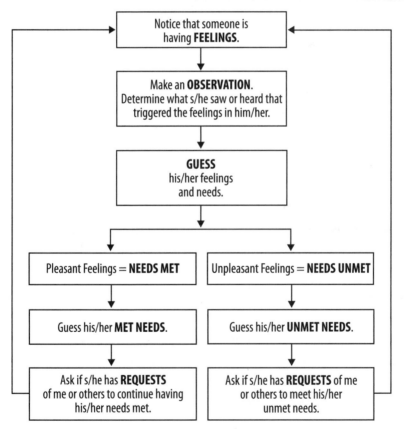

© 2011 Elucity Network, Inc. as developed by Marie R. Miyashiro

The fourth step of making doable, concrete requests crystallizes the power of NVC to create and support change in the workplace. We'll discuss this more in the next chapter on applying NVC in the workplace. Empathic connection with respect to the workplace can effectively drive strategy, marketing, sales, product development, and success.[43] In my experience, people who are practiced in self-empathy spend less time being triggered by what others say or do. They are more able to clearly observe key business issues and spend their time and resources on developing strategies to address them.

For example, IBM was in crisis in the early 1990s. Lou Gerstner, chief executive officer of IBM, implemented "Operation Bear Hug, a culturally appropriate name for an empathy program at one of the least emotionally demonstrative companies in the Fortune 500."[44] This was a listening, not a selling, series of meetings with customers for IBM's top fifty managers to hear about their customers' concerns. This organized listening process resulted in immediate resolution of many customer issues and highlighted new market opportunities, as well.

People practiced in self-empathy spend less time being triggered by others, can more clearly observe key business issues, and spend more time and resources on developing strategies to address them.

Silent Empathy

The idea that we can empathize without speaking is a useful concept for the workplace. When we're fully present to someone else's experiences by guessing and connecting to their feelings and needs, or even to our own feelings and needs, a deep empathic connection forms even when we don't say a word. The construct of feelings and needs helps us translate the concept of empathy into a concrete, doable process. That, in my experience, is the beauty and power of NVC.

I heard the following story from Kathleen Macferran, Center for Nonviolent Communication certified trainer. She was in an airport with about thirty minutes until her plane was scheduled to board. An acquaintance of hers was upset and asked Macferran if she would be willing to listen to her for the few remaining minutes. Macferran wanted to accommodate her request and also realized she wanted to eat before the flight. So they agreed that Macferran would listen while eating.

Listening while she ate, Macferran just looked at the woman. She didn't say a single word. But internally, she was actively engaged in the process of listening and then guessing the feelings and needs of the speaker and her own feelings and needs. *Oh, she's feeling this and maybe her need is that. . . . I'm noticing I'm a bit anxious and want to trust we can both get our needs met in this limited time.*

After about ten minutes, the woman who was speaking stopped and exclaimed, "That was the best empathy I've ever received!" She thanked Macferran and felt completely heard and satisfied. Her discomfort had been transformed by the presence of someone silently connecting to her feelings and needs with the intention of being present to her experiences.

Opportunity for Feedback and Change

Self-empathy and empathy create opportunity for feedback and change not only when our feelings are unpleasant but also when they are enjoyable. Praise is the flipside of the criticism coin. Praise can mask our own met needs the same way our judgments mask our unmet needs.

When we praise someone, we're mixing our met needs with an evaluation of the person. A positive evaluation is not as valuable as an observation of what was heard or seen coupled with how we feel about it and the needs it met. "You gave a great presentation!" does not provide as much information as, "When I saw the verbatim comments our customers made (observation), I was relieved (feeling) because it confirmed (need) how we were hoping they would react to the new product." Translating positive evaluations is an equally important opportunity to connect with and understand what needs of ours are being met. Now the presenter can be sure to include more verbatim comments in the next presentation, having heard the value this brought to at least one person.

The chart in Figure 3-8 shows the value of the empathic process in relation to what we tend to call praise and blame:

Fig. 3-8. Comparative Value of Praise, Blame, and Empathy as Workplace Feedback

Positive Evaluation About Presentation	Value	Empathic Connection About Presentation	Value
"You gave a great presentation!"	Low to Medium	**OBSERVATION:** "When I see the verbatim comments ... **FEELINGS:** "I feel relieved ... **NEEDS:** "because it confirms my market research."	High

Negative Evaluation About Presentation	Value	Empathic Connection About Presentation	Value
"You don't know what you're talking about!"	Low	**OBSERVATION:** "When I see you interviewed 200 customers out of 3,500 ... **FEELINGS:** "I feel uneasy ... **NEEDS:** "because I want more reassurance that we talked to enough people."	High

© 2011 Elucity Network, Inc. as developed by Marie R. Miyashiro

When we are clear with others about what we observe, how we feel, and what needs of ours are being met, others can learn from the objective feedback. They can learn what to keep doing to meet the needs of others as expressed through praise translated into feelings and needs. Conversely, when we express our praise as feelings and needs, we learn what needs are important to us—needs that might otherwise go unnoticed until triggered by a pleasant feeling. When we focus on these needs, we can create more strategies to keep these needs met, knowing how important they are to us.

When we're clear with others about what we observe, how we feel, and what needs of ours are being met or unmet, others can learn from the clarity of the objective feedback.

NVC is useful for the workplace for another reason. My experience consulting for all kinds and sizes of organizations and teams has revealed that the feelings of stakeholders—from customers to employees to board members—are generally unconscious, misunderstood, and in many instances, running the show. NVC can bring them to the surface and into the light of understanding. The following story illustrates this point.

A team leader at a Fortune 50 defense contracting company received feedback from several of his direct reports that he "micromanaged." They said things like, "You call me three times a week for a status report on a project when you and I have already agreed that I would give you a monthly update." Or, "You reply to emails that are directed to me and you are copied on before I have a chance to reply and address a situation that I'm accountable for."

In an executive coaching session, the team leader realized a link between this type of behavior with his team and a childhood circumstance. His mother had become ill when he was young, and circumstances forced him to assume many of the responsibilities of an adult as a child. He met his needs for safety and continuity with the strategy of controlling the details of his life. This worked well for him as a child and even in the early stages of his career. But now he could see how this pattern and specifically the needs he sought to meet by controlling the details were hindering him as a manager. By identifying these needs, he could now develop strategies to meet them that also met his team members' needs for autonomy and trust.

The manager remarked that, for the first time, he knew what to do instead of what not to do. As Rosenberg says, "You can't do a don't." It's only partially helpful to know what to stop doing. It's more helpful to know what to start doing in its place.

Throughout this entire process of NVC, the consciousness and awareness of needs is pivotal. Needs consciousness serves as the structural foundation for creating empathy as a step-by-step practice. Naming needs empowers us to connect with them. Connecting with them fuels our ability to develop more strategies to meet our needs. The naming of things can be a powerful action. When China regained authority over Hong Kong from the British, one of the first actions the new government took

Naming needs empowers us to connect with and then make requests to meet those needs.

was to change notable street names from English to Chinese. This was to meet the needs for expression of authority and the new order. Social justice movements understand the power of a name and especially naming things for themselves.

The Power of Language

Returning to the lunch date exercise, once people grasp the power and simplicity of separating judgments from feelings and needs, someone almost always asks why we tend to be more judgmental with our communications than we might be intending. The answer may have to do with the way our English language is constructed. To reiterate a segment of the quotation that begins this chapter from Lera Boroditsky, professor of psychology at Stanford, ". . . the languages we speak not only reflect or express our thoughts, but also shape the very thoughts we wish to express."[45] For example, research shows that English sentence structures focus on agents of causality, whereas in Spanish and Japanese, they do not. "Such differences between languages," states Boroditsky, "have profound consequences for how their speakers understand events, construct notions of causality and agency, what they remember as eyewitnesses and how much they blame and punish others."[46] English speakers, as it turns out, may be more likely to judge, blame, and punish others because our language predisposes us to this way of thinking. NVC provides a way to change this tendency so that more harmony results in the workplace, which supports productivity.

I like to tell a story about golf and the Japanese language, but first, a preamble. Having grown up in a bilingual home in Hawaii where English and Japanese were spoken, I speak a little Japanese. If I tell you I'm a good golfer (evaluation), you're probably left with more questions than a picture of how I actually play. If I tell you I'm an accomplished golfer, this is still a judgment but at least it points to some kind of empirical achievement. However, what if I tell you I qualified to play in three national United States Golf Association amateur championships? And what if I say that in 1997 I became one of the first women in Hawaii to advance to the match play section at the U.S. Women's Mid-Amateur Championship? Those are observations of fact that give you information without interpretations.

The English language predisposes its speakers to judgment and blame. NVC can help us change this tendency.

Now that you know what kind of golfer I am, I'll tell the story. In parentheses, I've identified the four parts of the NVC process within this story.

When I hit a tee shot, a long ball to begin a hole, someone might remark in English, "Great shot!" He has taken an objective event—the golf ball flying through the air (observation)—and placed his subjective experience of inspiration (feelings) on top of this event by calling it "great." What happens if I know I hit the worst tee shot for me that I've hit for the whole round, or for ten rounds? Now, when he says, "Do that again!" (request), he and I are in conflict. He has labeled the shot "great" out of being inspired and possibly wanting to be supportive (needs), and I don't think it was great at all and would like to hit it differently on the next hole.

When the same golf shot flies through the air in Japan, however, the Japanese language accounts for it differently. The Japanese say, "Subarashii" instead of "Great shot." Loosely translated, "subarashii" means splendid, wonderful, marvelous. But this word also has an inherent feeling component, as many words in Japanese have, and the word can be more fully translated as, "I feel beautiful inside (watching the ball sail through the air)." Being a contextual language, Japanese does not turn an objective event into a personal judgment as often as English does. No conflict arises between the person who enjoys the beauty of the ball flight as an internal experience and me as the ball hitter. When people who speak English as their primary language hear this about the structure of English, they're often relieved and their need for consideration of others is more fully met. I sometimes hear: "Oh, that explains some of it. I didn't realize how judgmental English is. It's not just me after all." Long before I read the Boroditsky research, I knew that Japanese was less judgmental than English, and many people who spoke Spanish in my client workgroups told me the same thing about the Spanish language.

A Natural Ability in an Unnatural System

The ability to be empathic is something we're all born with. It is genetically encoded in us as social beings. I like to say this work is less about learning empathy and more about remembering it. Rosenberg calls empathy a natural response. He says that many people who've never even heard of NVC engage in the NVC process naturally. Therefore, Rosenberg's work is actually about thoughtfully and carefully articulating a natural process rather than inventing a new one. Author and business strategist Dev Patnaik says we are "wired to care" in his book of the same name.[47] He explains in an article titled "Innovation Starts with Empathy" that "as sophisticated as our neurological systems for detecting the feelings of others might be, we've created a corporate world that strives to eliminate the most human elements of business. Companies systematically dull the natural power that each of us has to connect with other people. And by dulling our impulse to care, corporations make decisions that look good on paper but do real harm when put into practice in the real world."[48]

In *The Age of Empathy: Nature's Lessons for a Kinder Society*, Frans de Waal, professor of psychology and director of the Living Links Center at Emory University, states that "empathy is an automated response over which we have limited control."[49] In other words, it's our nature to care about and for each other. Why, then, is empathy considered such a foreign concept in business and a "soft" attribute of leadership?

Like fish adapting unconsciously to their water world, Rosenberg reminds us we've been operating within a system of domination hierarchy for several thousands of years. It's difficult for us to see the effects of this "habitat" unless we purposefully stop to consider them. The system places most of the control of resources and power in the hands of a relatively few people. As such, this system limits the autonomy and choices of many people in order to meet the needs for order and stability. Granted, without some kind of system in place for social order, chaos could reign and with it the kind of pain and turmoil we see when countries tumble into a government-less confusion. However, the system unintentionally encourages disconnection from our feelings and needs so order and stability can be maintained and rules can be put into place that we follow without question. Anyone who has managed to graduate from high school or college or has stayed out of jail has in some way followed rules that our system has set. But what about those who go to college because "it's the thing to do" and they would much rather do something else? And what about those who manage to stay out of jail but become alcoholics or drug addicts to tranquilize their rage or despair over their loss of autonomy or meaning in life? Because our society is more rules conscious than needs conscious, many people end up disconnecting from their needs, either consciously or unconsciously. Trouble then brews below the surface.

Yes, revolution can happen when people become feelings and needs literate. One of our most basic needs as people is the need for autonomy, to choose the way we live—and the connection to needs germinates requests and strategies for change. But change can be beneficial and is sometimes necessary.

Organizations and teams are struggling to balance the needs of people with the needs of the whole system. Where to begin? We can start by learning a language of empathy that combines universal people needs and universal organizational or team needs. We can address this struggle with the understanding that all needs matter and with the goal of meeting them across the board. Thus we can achieve progress in a way that meets the needs for respect, harmony, and effectiveness.

Making Empathy Actionable

Reviewing the research on empathy in the workplace through the NVC construct of feelings and needs makes it more accessible because we can put what the research reveals into an actionable format. Take the results of a Center for Creative Leadership survey, for example.[50] Two distinguishing characteristics were associated with those leaders who were found, according to the Center's criteria, to be the best in managing their organizations through change. I have listed the research finding first and then translated it into the doable components of NVC.

1. *"They were skilled in honest, proactive communication."* How do we *do* "honest, proactive communication"? By connecting with our feelings and needs and communicating them through the four-part process of Observations, Feelings, Needs, and Requests. This way, we demonstrate an authenticity that is more likely to be perceived as "honest." By being present to what is going on inside of us moment to moment, or as we say in NVC, what is "alive" in us, we are more likely to be proactive, to be aware of something that needs our attention or action.

2. *"When they did communicate, they listened well,
    demonstrated sensitivity, and were willing to articulate
    clearly the rationale and necessity for change despite the pain
    those changes might inflict."* How do we "listen well?" The
    quality of the experience of being listened to increases when
    the listener is guessing the feelings and needs of the speaker
    as a way to stay present with the speaker throughout; it's a
    practical way to "walk in the other person's shoes"—either
    out loud with the speaker or silently. Articulating clearly
    "the rationale and necessity for change" means spelling
    out what needs are being met by the changes being made.
    In this way, even if people disagree with the strategies, the
    needs consciousness is still maintained.

In the next chapter, we will discuss how teams and organizations
also have universal needs, which are separate from but interconnected
with the needs of people. NVC makes empathy actionable in addressing
individual needs and can be woven into the process of addressing
organizational needs.

Creating Empathic Connections in the Workplace

Initially, people are often skeptical about using NVC in the workplace
because they mistake empathy for softness or permissiveness. However,
it's vital to realize that deep empathic connection and true compassion
are not about being nice. Instead, they're about effecting change and
getting results through making requests out of our shared connection.

Ike Lasater understands the
skepticism that many people
initially have about instituting
NVC in the workplace, but he has
seen it overcome many times by
the effectiveness of the process. An
attorney who learned the power of
NVC from Marshall Rosenberg,
he began offering NVC mediation

*Deep empathic connection and
true compassion are not about
being nice. Instead, they're about
effecting change and getting
results through making requests
out of our shared connection.*

trainings in Poland, Australia, and the United States. In his book *Words That Work In Business: A Practical Guide to Effective Communication in the Workplace,* Ike has this to say: "In our workplaces, we often create an illusion of separateness and formality that then reinforces our beliefs in this regard and thereby results in our acting in more confining ways. In workshops I have seen over and over again that when people do their own self- and silent empathy work at a deep level, they realize that they are not limited by what they can say in the workplace. I think what they begin to see—even those who come to a workshop absolutely hopeless about being able to apply Nonviolent Communication in a work setting—is that people are people, whether they are at work or elsewhere."[51]

When we view people and our workplaces through the lens of needs consciousness, we can choose to operate from our own humanity and in concert with the humanity of others. In the next section of the book, Making Empathy Actionable, we delve into the practical applications of the key ideas listed below. In creating empathic connections in the workplace, we can keep the following in mind:

1. *People are always acting in service of their own needs.* Even when the expression of their unmet needs triggers pain or discomfort for us, their expression still has more to do with their own needs than with criticizing or harming us. We may really dislike or disagree with their strategies to meet their needs, but this doesn't diminish the idea that people are acting in service of their own needs.

   In turn, *how we hear what they express* has more to do with our own needs. Their words act as triggers for our needs, bringing up pleasant or unpleasant feelings; but they are not in and of themselves the cause of our feelings. When we can guess at their feelings and needs behind their actions, it creates an empathic connection between us. When we guess at our own feelings and needs, we are engaging in self-connection or self-empathy. The process of self-empathy makes it possible to take in what we see or hear that could otherwise be difficult to receive. For leaders and team members, this is a critical skill. For this reason, it's explained more fully in the first chapter of Part II—Chapter Five: How to Increase Self-Productivity.

2. ***Conflicts occur at the request or strategy level, not at the needs level.*** For example, if a team of five people wants to find a conference site for a retreat, they would likely be in immediate conflict if they each began naming specific retreat sites. One person might suggest Resort A and someone might then say, "I don't like Resort A because they don't have direct flights there," and so on. But if the team begins with a needs consciousness—with needs built around the specific intentions and programs of the retreat— they are likely to be in greater agreement. For example, one person might suggest a destination because of the need to have it accessible by direct flights. Another might suggest value in terms of costs and benefits. Yet another might suggest a setting in nature because of the outdoor exercises that are part of the retreat. In this way, the needs checklist will point to a number of specific retreat sites. These sites are strategies to meet the needs checklist. Because we're mostly conditioned to focus on strategies first and don't operate from a needs consciousness, more conflict exists in the world and our workplaces than is necessary.

> *Our focus on determining strategies before considering needs creates more conflict in the world and our workplaces than is necessary.*

3. ***We can never fully understand what another person is experiencing or has experienced. We can only imagine or guess.*** As mentioned previously, the act of guessing or imagining what others might be feeling and what needs might be connected to those feelings creates more empathic connection than thinking we know or understand what they're going through. For this reason, saying, "I

understand" or "I know how you feel" can actually weaken that connection unless the other person tells you directly. Guessing how someone feels or silently guessing how the person feels and the needs connected to these feelings without assuming you know is likely to be perceived as more empathic.

4. **Every feeling is new in each moment, even if we have the same name for that feeling.** The way I feel sad or excited about something today may feel very different a few seconds from now. Feelings are constantly changing within us and others, as well as the connection to needs related to these feelings. Therefore, it's important to come to each moment fresh, without assumption or attachment and without comparing one feeling to the next or one behavior to another. Comparing one person's behavior to someone else's or to that person's at a different time can be difficult to hear. "I wouldn't have done what you did to me," is more of a separating energy than an empathic one. An empathic approach might be guessing, "Are you hurt and wanting some acknowledgment about how you like to be treated?"

5. **We cannot put our energy into empathic connections unless enough of our needs are filled first.** For this reason, executive coaching of customer service team members, managers, and leaders as well as retreats and other support programs for employees and managers are critical and cost-effective. If a critical mass of people in an organization or on a team has significant numbers of unmet needs, much of the research previously cited indicates that work productivity will not be optimal.

6. **Form empathic connection before education, explanation, or justification.** Connect-Think-Do. Have you ever been in a meeting where someone's goal in listening to you was to be able to respond with what he or she wanted to say? In NVC, telling someone something that might be of value for that person without first asking or knowing if s/he is interested

is called "education." It's "explanation" when we listen to the content or situation but not the context—the feelings and needs under the expression. And when we defend something at the content level, it's called "justification." Any form of educating, explaining, defending, or justifying before someone feels heard or understood, creates more separation than connection in my experience. Therefore, I like to ask people if they would find value in me explaining something before I begin sharing the information with them. When they're not ready to listen to what I have to say, they likely have needs for understanding, expression, more information, or the like. This is a clue for me to connect with their feelings and needs. When they're ready to listen to me, they might pause and stop speaking in such a way that I notice they're now open to hearing what I have to say. Many times I've had people say, "Now I'm ready to listen to you."

7. *In an empathic connection, the speaker assumes the burden of communicating rather than giving the listener the burden to understand.* For this reason, asking, "Have I been clear?" is more connecting than "Do you understand?" I've been told by many people I've worked with that "Do you understand?" or "Is this clear to you?" provokes memories of thinking they had no choice but to answer "yes" as children—with their teachers or parents, for example.

In my work with a division of GTE, the basic premise of the communications training I developed for customer service representatives echoed many of the key principles of NVC, including this one. Creating connection with the customer began with placing the burden of communication on the customer service professional and not the customer. So if the customer was unclear about something, it was never because they didn't understand. It was because the service representative wasn't clear enough. The training emphasized the value of taking every opportunity to suspend judgment or evaluation of the customer. Any labels, such as "whiner" or "difficult," "angry," or "upset" customer, only serve to create separation from the very people with whom we want to build connection and upon whom the business success depends—the customer.

8. ***Empathy is not sympathy.*** In the process of being empathic, we fully focus on others by guessing what they're feeling and their needs, met or unmet, rather than sharing our experiences of similar situations. "Are you feeling worried because you have a need for progress in the new project?" is more connecting than saying, "Oh, that's nothing. You should have seen how many times we had to go back to the drawing board on *our* project." Have you experienced this situation yourself, where you were sharing something that happened to you and the other person began talking about him- or herself? You likely experienced an energetic pull of attention away from you and your experiences, which can weaken or break connection.

9. ***Connecting to feelings and needs is powerful. But the true power of empathy comes from the strategies and requests for change (when needs aren't met) or continued behavior (when needs are met).*** Empathy is really about strategies in action and meeting more needs, not just feeling better or feeling heard. Connecting to feelings and needs is a practical and actionable path to productivity for

> *Empathy is really about strategies in action and meeting more needs, not just feeling better or feeling heard.*

this reason. The empathic connection results in concrete and tangible actions that contribute to the needs of individuals and the collective organizational needs.

10. ***In the workplace, empathic connection to ourselves (self-empathy) and others (empathy) takes place in the context of universal organizational and team needs.*** These needs

of the group, perceived as a shared reality, structure the quality of our connections to one another within our workplace settings. We build our organizations, and then they shape us with their identity, purpose, and values.

✳ ✳ ✳ ✳

Having introduced the four steps of Nonviolent Communication and the principles of the empathic process, we'll move on to Chapter Four to begin exploring the idea of universal organizational or team needs and how having a needs consciousness can support developing profitable and effective strategies for organizational and team success.

FOUR

Applying Needs-Based
Awareness to the Workplace

"For, in the end, it is impossible to have a great life unless it is a meaningful life. And it is very difficult to have a meaningful life without meaningful work. Perhaps, then, you might gain that rare tranquillity that comes from knowing that you've had a hand in creating something of intrinsic excellence that makes a contribution. Indeed, you might even gain that deepest of all satisfactions: knowing that your short time here on this earth has been well spent, and that it mattered."[52]

—Jim Collins, *Good to Great: Why Some Companies Make the Leap . . . and Others Don't*

D o you experience alignment and resonance with your team or department? Are you connected to others and your organization in a way that energizes and fulfills you? In the same way that NVC makes understanding our relationship with ourselves and others more accessible through a needs-based awareness, Integrated Clarity makes understanding our relationship to our organizations and teams more accessible.

Organizations can be complex systems. If we don't have some kind of map of the entire system and how it works, we have no frame of reference to help us make sense of the whole and our part in it. Likewise, if we don't fully understand the purpose and direction of an organization, we might feel alone or think we're isolated and have an unmet need for shared reality and purpose with others.

The more people are added to an organization—even a relatively small team—the more distance in space and time is created between all the people in the system. If you and I are conversing, we experience no lag time between what you say and what I hear. But if you have a conversation with another team member and I'm not there to hear it firsthand, it might be hours, days, or never that I catch up with the information in that discussion that might relate to me. The more people in the group or organization, the more complex the relationship system becomes. This complexity grows not arithmetically, but geometrically, like this:

> **2 people** = **3 distinct relationships** (2 intrapersonal ones with ourselves + 1 interpersonal relationship with each other)

> **3 people** = **7 distinct relationships** (3 intrapersonal + 3 interpersonal dyads + 1 whole group)

> **4 people** = **15 distinct relationships** (4 intrapersonal + 6 interpersonal dyads + 4 interpersonal triads + 1 whole group)

Thus a team or department of fifteen people has hundreds of possible groupings of relationships. When I share this concept of complexity with work teams, people feel some sense of relief about why more complications and considerations arise within teams than they expected.

Without a framework to comprehend all these relationships, we will likely feel alone and disconnected from the whole—and perhaps even from ourselves. We can consider three levels of relationship or communication in an organizational context: the first level is the relationship we have with ourselves, the second is relationships we have with others, and the third is the relationship we have with the whole system—our organization or team. The third level is also where the organization holds its other critical relationships with external customers and clients.

Fig. 4-1. The Three Levels of Communication Within an Organization

© 2011 Elucity Network, Inc. as developed by Marie R. Miyashiro

The following chart explains these levels and how Integrated Clarity can be used within each level to facilitate better communications and meet needs.

Fig. 4-2. Applications of Integrated Clarity Within the Organizational Dimensions

LEVEL	DESCRIPTION OF RELATIONSHIP	APPLICATION OF INTEGRATED CLARITY
Intrapersonal	Our thinking – what we tell ourselves	Journaling, one-on-one mentoring, executive coaching (to help discover thoughts/feelings/ needs), self-inquiry and contemplation
Interpersonal	What we tell others, what we think we hear others telling us	Facilitation, mediation and conflict resolution, confirming what is said is what is heard, personnel reviews, team processes, and operational communications
Organizational	What we think the organizational data is telling us	Strategic conversations that provide a framework for planning; Organizational Needs Dashboards, widespread, whole system processes

© 2011 Elucity Network, Inc. as developed by Marie R. Miyashiro

It's important for people within an organization to begin at the intrapersonal level and become aware of their own needs and find ways to meet them. For example, if team leaders have core needs that are repeatedly triggered, the internal pain of unmet needs makes it difficult for them to be present with and for others. Likewise, leaders who are tuned in to the needs of others in their group will be able to address others' needs and thus improve productivity. Here's a case in point.

I was helping a business management group develop a way to meet that was more effective and efficient. Every one of the fifteen people in the group had told me their meetings had been exhausting and frustrating. Typically, their weekly team meetings were at least two hours long, and it was not uncommon for them to extend into three-hour marathon sessions with different people wanting to discuss their own areas and concerns. Worse yet, these meetings were held first thing Monday morning!

As I was facilitating the meeting, I noticed one woman wasn't speaking. I checked with her to see if her silence was triggered by something I was doing (thus also taking care of my own need to be clear). "I notice you haven't been speaking as much as I'm used to hearing you, Nancy, and I'm curious. Is it something about the way I'm facilitating that's keeping you from contributing?"

Nancy explained that it was the five-year anniversary of her husband's death and she was having feelings about that. The group then listened to her and just sat with her for about five minutes. After that, she fully participated and became energized and smiling. Several team members commented that they too felt energized having contributed to a team member in a way that was meaningful for both of them. Had I, as the facilitator of the group, ignored her, silently judged her, or worse, criticized her for not providing input, we all would have missed an opportunity to develop stronger team connections and energize individual productivity.

Over and over, I see energy for productivity and contribution unleashed in people when there is a level of connection at the feelings and needs level. Group members learned that by recognizing and acknowledging one another's feelings and needs, they could shorten their meeting times and also make the meetings more meaningful and effective. Much of what made the meetings longer than anyone wanted was team members' lack of clarity in expressing their feelings and needs about customer or operational data they heard and saw. Further, when they became clearer about how to do this and make powerful requests to increase their interpersonal and team productivity, the requests contributed to strategic planning for the whole system. Strategies became altogether different because they were now needs based instead of a disconnected series of solutions and strategies that weren't necessarily connected to critical organizational needs.

(Name has been changed.)

It's exciting for me to see how such a simple act of recognizing individual needs can transform a situation. As you read this chapter, you'll also come across situations in which recognizing and meeting interpersonal and organizational needs can make a huge difference. So often, we are blind to these underlying driving forces.

Why So Many Communication Problems in Organizations?

I like to begin my work with team members and leadership groups talking about how organizations as we think of them today are relatively young as social innovations. The Industrial Revolution in Europe and North America arose in the late eighteenth and early nineteenth centuries—only a couple of hundred years ago. And think of the changes that have happened since then! Understanding how to work in organizational settings remains in its infancy. People are often surprised by this. We assume that somebody "should" know how to make it all work or that we ought to know this ourselves, which is one reason some people experience more frustration than they would like in their workplace experiences.

People also express surprise when they hear another reason why work processes and communication among different people or teams can be difficult. We all grew up in completely different kinds of families, the original "organizations" in our lives. A particular demonstration of respect in one family may hold completely different interpretations in another family. Let's look at an example of how that might play out in an organizational setting.

I conduct confidential interviews with key employees or managers when I begin an assessment process to help organizations or teams determine action steps. Once I spoke with a newly hired manager at a nonprofit, and he voiced a complaint: "Every morning I come to work promptly at eight o'clock. A few minutes after this, my boss [the executive director] comes into my office and starts discussing the plan for the day."

At this point, I notice he appears to be irritated or disturbed and looking at me as though I ought to know why he's displeased. I continue to listen, unclear about what's troubling him. To me, what he's just described seems like a predictable scenario in many office settings.

Then he says, "Don't you get it? She never says 'good morning.' She just comes in and starts talking about what she wants to get done."

Okay. Now I'm clear about what bothers him. He pauses and looks at me. So I say, "It sounds like it's important to you to exchange 'good mornings.' Have you told her how important this is to you and asked her if she'd be willing to say 'good morning' to you before you begin discussing work issues?"

"No," he replied. "What she does is rude. She should know better."

Now, internally, I'm guessing his feelings and needs. I like to silently empathize with people I'm meeting for the first time in the workplace until I get a sense that they are open to verbal empathy or until I feel more comfort with them. In my experience and as discussed in earlier chapters, empathizing without spoken words can still be transformative and powerful. Initially, I guessed he felt hurt and had a need for respect in hearing her say, "good morning."

Having now heard he is unwilling to ask for what he wants because of his thinking that "she should know better," I'm also guessing he feels cautious about asking for what he wants and has a need for connection and to be understood.

While I felt disappointed that he was unwilling to explore with me the possibility of requesting a "good morning" from her, I was satisfied that he had clarity about his choices. Because this irritation occurred for him first thing in the morning every day at work, I guessed he would leave his job within three months to meet his need for peace of mind and respect. He left after four weeks. In doing so, he chose to meet his needs with strategies that involved working elsewhere. But by leaving without ever having made his request, he eliminated an opportunity for the executive director to contribute to him in a way that could also have been a gift for her.

This exchange falls into the category of interaction with others, and it clearly demonstrates how people can't respond to your needs if they don't know what they are. Likewise, people can't respond to an organization's needs if they aren't clearly defined. Perhaps we tend not to define our needs because we've been trained to believe needs and feelings are unprofessional and don't belong in the workplace. The fact is, all people have feelings and share universal needs, and organizations have needs that if unmet can contribute to their demise. Therefore, it's to our advantage to bring these feelings and needs into awareness where they can be addressed. However, it's equally important to have an understanding and ease with the process and language of NVC and IC, or people might interpret your actions as a technique rather than sense your underlying intention for meaningful connection.

The language of NVC and framework of IC create an awareness of both individual and organizational needs and engender both personal and group responsibility to meet those needs.

When used with knowledge and skill, the language of NVC and the framework of Integrated Clarity create an awareness of both individual and organizational needs and also engender personal as well as group responsibility to meet those needs. In my experience, transparency of needs leads to requests and strategies to meet those needs.

Needs and Requests, Not Demands

The model of Integrated Clarity helps organizations develop cultural characteristics that are needs based and empower people within the workplace to respond empathically to their own needs and those of others, especially team members and customers. It's not a "my way or the highway" mentality; it's "let's build this highway together." It's simply more effective to use the language of needs and requests rather than demands. Why? Because when we think someone is demanding something of us, we subconsciously (if not consciously) activate the demand-resistance cycle, a natural human response rooted in our need for autonomy.

Requests or strategies can be received as demands when people in the organization believe they will be blamed or punished if they don't comply or meet performance expectations. Demand-resistance cycles are highly nonproductive and drain organizational resources.

We subconsciously (if not consciously) resist demands, creating a decline in productivity. The language of needs and requests is less likely to activate the demand-resistance cycle and has a much higher likelihood of improving productivity.

While we can never tell if a request is really a demand until we see the reaction to our, "no," providing the need behind the request increases the chance it will be heard more as a request than a demand. Note the different energy between: "Have that report completed and handed in by four this afternoon" [request without need explained] and "I don't have the statistics from your sales initiative [observation], and I'd like that information for my talk tomorrow [need]. Does it work for you to have it to me by four this afternoon [request]?" Whenever people *perceive* there will be a consequence for saying no to a request, it likely becomes a demand in their thinking. That consequence could be as simple as raised eyebrows or a deep sigh of exasperation, or it could be as serious as the threat of losing their job. More common, it might be the fear of feeling embarrassed if the "request" is made in front of others in a way that doesn't meet the need for respect. The intention behind the words is often more critical than the words themselves. This explains why we can hear the same words from different people with completely different responses. Their intention, our history with them, and our own history separate from them all contribute to what we think we hear in the workplace.

Of note, the more history of trust and connection we have with others, the more likely we are to hear their "demands" as requests. I experienced this in my own family.

> My father was raised in a rough and tumble neighborhood during the plantation days of Honolulu, Hawaii. As an adult, this translated into being a man of few words. But because of this, when he spoke, his words held great meaning for him. He wasn't comfortable with pleasantries and politeness. Like other Asian and Hawaii natives I grew up with, he thought too many polite words were suspect—a sign of non-authentic connection. In his world, you said what you wanted and you spoke your mind directly. This constituted an expression of respect, not the "please" and "thank you" that might be empty habit or come from a desire to "look good."
>
> So after visiting with my parents, when I was getting ready to back out of the driveway, my dad would walk me out to the car, stand by my car door smiling, and always say, "Don't hit my car," which was parked behind me. I knew this was his way of saying, "I love you. See you soon." I learned not to get so caught up in words, but to hear the intention behind the words.

The bottom line? Performance produced through fear, guilt, shame, or punishment is less productive, generative, and sustainable than actions given freely from a connection to people and organizational needs.

Self-Empathy Can Bring Empowerment and Choices

The idea on all three levels of communication—intrapersonal, interpersonal, and organizational—is detachment. You let go of the drive to get the other person to do, be, or say something you want. You might be thinking, "But what if something really *has* to be done and I have to demand it?" You may want to consider empathizing with your own feelings (worry) and needs (accountability) before you make requests of others.

In connecting with ourselves first, two likely scenarios unfold. First, out of a connection to our needs, we may discover more choices than the idea that something "has to be done." When I work with managers and employees, they often come to different solutions when feeling more ease around their unmet needs than when they are feeling unsettled or hurried. When we connect with the need behind the thinking of the "should," empowerment and a sense of choice follows. For example, if a customer service representative chooses to follow guidelines instead of giving the customer what he is asking for, she can acknowledge to herself that this is her choice because she values the stability (need) the job provides in her life. She can also acknowledge to herself that she does not have the authority or access to resources to do what is being asked of her and that this is part of the agreement she made in accepting the job description. Instead of a sense of futility, this kind of acknowledgment about her choices can lead to the recognition of what she does and does not have choice over. For example, she could be more willing to ask someone who does have authority and access to resources if there's a way to meet the customer's request.

Connecting with our own feelings and needs allows for the kind of awareness foundational to best practices in change management. One of the fundamental guidelines to facilitating change in organizations is helping people experiencing the change to distinguish between what they can change and what they cannot change. In this way, people put their energy and resources into areas where they are empowered and have authority instead of in areas where they are most likely to exhaust themselves with little return on their efforts. As mentioned in

Chapter Two, William Bridges describes change as an external event and transition as an internal process. Connecting with our feelings and needs is a powerful and structured way to engage in this type of internal process.

Second, we are less likely to perceive our requests as demands when we are able to give ourselves empathy for our own unmet needs. Further, we are more likely to be able to frame our request and choose our words from a needs-based awareness—both our needs and theirs. The energy of "have to" dissipates. We hear this every day in the workplace and it might sound something like this: "I know it's four o'clock on a Friday [observation]. I'm disappointed [feeling] that I didn't come to see you earlier in the week about the sales figures I'd like for my presentation Monday morning [need] to the strategic planning group [organizational need for *Direction*]. Are you willing to consider pulling those numbers for me this weekend [request]?" Notice, the request is not about an action in the future. The request is about a willingness in the present moment. Further, the willingness isn't about doing the work. It's about considering doing the work. In this way, the person making the request holds the other person's needs in mind when making a request to meet his own needs, too.

What if in this situation you get an answer such as, "I don't have all the data from my field sales force yet." In this case, you might guess that the person is feeling nervous or anxious about not having the statistics you want. Because the needs behind what was just said are not clear, your response might be to ask, "Are you uncomfortable because you'd like the full picture of sales before you share the data?" If the person's response is something like, "Yes, I wouldn't want you to present an inaccurate picture," you might reply with, "Would you find value in additional staff helping to obtain the data?"

Finally, if at times a demand is necessary rather than a request, be transparent about it. Explain why you think you don't have much choice about what you're asking for and remain respectful of the other person's choice. Remember that any time we get someone to say yes out of fear, guilt, shame, or blame, there's a price to pay in terms of this costly shortcut. Lower productivity results when people do what we want because we demand it and they are afraid of the consequences rather than out of a desire to contribute to a shared purpose or transparent need.

The president of a company I was working with related to the relevance of this point. He had been learning about the NVC process and needs-based awareness when he heard about an employee-manager situation in his own firm. The firm's five-year receptionist was known for being prompt, and she routinely took on duties outside her job description, such as washing the dishes in the lunchroom, before she left the office. People were satisfied with her job performance. Then, three times over the course of several weeks, she arrived at work later than usual because of an unexpected series of family issues. Instead of having a conversation with her about what might be going on in her life to create these circumstances, her supervisor called her in for a performance discussion. He wrote a formal letter of reprimand for her personnel file and gave her an ultimatum that unless she could begin work on time, she would be put on notice for termination. The receptionist complied, and her promptness was no longer an issue. However, the dirty dishes piled up in the sink until the group needed to create a new procedure to address the situation.

Consider how this situation might have turned out had the supervisor used the NVC process of empathy. When he talked with her, he might have said, "I've noticed that three times this month you've arrived after your agreed-upon starting time, which is unusual for you. I'm used to your prompt arrival so I'm guessing that something might be going on in your life that's preventing you from getting here on time. Are you open to discussing how I can support you [her need] and also have the phones and front desk covered [his need]?"

Because some (perhaps most) people are unaccustomed to saying no when asked by their supervisor about having such a discussion, I suggest that all supervisors or people with structural power and authority confirm the comfort level of the other party. In this way, the discussion occurs from a place of authentic willingness rather than fear. The results of the conversation are likely to be quite different based on both parties' level of willingness.

At this point, it would be up to the receptionist to say how she was feeling and explain the situation (even if she didn't want to provide personal details) and request what she needs. Ideally, she would have felt comfortable enough with her supervisor to go to him and explain the situation when it first came up and request that someone cover for her because she couldn't make it to work on time given family circumstances. That way, the front desk would have been covered, issues of guilt and blame would have been avoided, and chances are, the receptionist would have continued to do the dishes.

Using NVC in Team or Project Meetings

The single greatest waste of time in a meeting is people responding to what they *think* they heard without checking out what others really meant.

WAIT!

Productivity can be increased and time saved if participants would all consider the acronym WAIT—Why Am I Talking? Raj Gill, Center for Nonviolent Communication certified trainer and a professional coach, explains the acronym and gives additional relevant interpretations.

I learned of the acronym WAIT (Why Am I Talking) when I was in the coaching program with The Coaches Training Institute in 2000. I was made aware that I was doing much of the talking in my coaching sessions (a painful experience) and that I needed to listen more to what the coaching client had to say. I put the acronym WAIT on my phone, which served as a reminder to keep my mouth shut and focus more on the listening than the talking.

In 2001, I began learning NVC and found WAIT to be quite helpful for building my empathy practice. I incorporated the acronym into my learning guide that I offer to participants in workshops or practice sessions, explaining it this way:

W.A.I.T!

What Am I Thinking? Pause for a moment and become aware of how my thinking about a situation in which I feel triggered influences my words and actions.

Why Am I Talking? How is what I am about to say going to contribute to the quality of connection? Might listening be where I want to place my attention?

What Am I Telling myself? The reality of what is happening (observation) can sometimes be quite different from what I tell myself—"my story."

In the intermediate level NVC course, I add *WAIT—What's Alive In Them?*

I so love it when I hear people using this acronym to remind themselves to be in the present moment and become more conscious of their words and actions.

So hurry up and WAIT.

(Raj Gill is listed in Contributors to This Book.)

Most of us aren't at all clear about what we want back from the group when we speak. Meetings would be expedited if we first give our purpose for speaking, say what we want to say, then make a request to the group about what we want in response. We then relieve the listeners of trying to figure out what we want from them. Requests that are concrete, doable, in the present moment, stated in the affirmative (others can't *do* a *don't*), and based on connection to needs, increase the likelihood that the request will be met in the desired way.

The following is an example of a meeting led by Kathleen Macferran. Notice her consideration of Observations, Feelings, Needs, and Requests.

In March 2008, I facilitated a meeting of faith-based community leaders in Washington State. Coming together for the first time, these leaders wanted to explore creating an organization to support inmates being released back into society.

Prior to this meeting, I pondered the idea that it's my *being*—my orientation to life—rather than my *doing,* that ultimately has the greatest impact in organizations I serve. I decided to approach my role as facilitator primarily as the creator of a context that would allow life-serving possibilities to emerge organically. I used what I'd learned in NVC as an internal map and framework from which I could draw clarity. Participants weren't expected to learn NVC. They could show up in whatever ways were habitual for them.

I shared with the group four values or intentions I hold when I facilitate and asked if the individuals agreed with these values and if they wanted to add others. We worked from this list for the meeting:

1. Every person has a voice at the table.
2. Every person has the experience of being fully heard.
3. Every person is clear what s/he is contributing before speaking and knows what s/he wants back in relation to what s/he said.
4. Every person makes requests to help meet those needs (what the person wants back).
5. Every person sets the intention to stay connected to his/her Life Source. (A value added by the group.)

I referenced those values throughout the meeting when I wanted feedback. For example, I'd say, "I'd like to check and see if anyone senses not having a voice at the table." Or I'd make an observation. For example: "I'm noticing that out of the last five people who've spoken, four of them have been men. I hope this information is helpful in gauging how we're holding to the values we've set for the way we communicate."

A priority for me in coming from a place of *being* versus *doing* was to model a quality of presence and respect that I hoped to see among all participants. I imagined that the quality of listening and speaking that's a hallmark of NVC would allow connection, cooperation, and trust to grow quickly. In fact, participants appreciated the depth of understanding they experienced when

I reflected the feelings and needs present in the room. They soon started to reflect feelings and needs to each other spontaneously or when I requested that someone reflect back what they heard from a speaker before we moved on to other responses.

I wasn't as concerned about the format as I was about the exchange of meaning. Much of what is said in meetings is not heard or acknowledged. For example, when one of the participants said the same thing for the third time, other participants began rolling their eyes, sighing, sitting back in their chairs, putting down their pens. . . . I suggested to the group that when someone repeats something, it might be because s/he doesn't have a sense s/he has been heard. I turned to "John," who had just presented the same idea three times and asked if he sensed he'd been heard in the way he wanted. He replied, "No, not at all." I then asked if participants would reflect back what they heard. Two people did this. I checked with John to see if that was what he wanted them to hear. He said, "Yes," and we were able to continue with the discussion.

My intention was to make the needs (the underlying values, such as respect) visible as much as possible in the meeting, trusting the strategies proposed in relation to those needs would then be more effective and elicit focused discussion. I also supported participants in making strategies specific and doable, a framing I use for NVC requests, as well.

One participant spoke with great passion about his idea but concluded with no request. I said, "Wow, sounds as if you'd like something back from this group. What do you want?" He thought for a moment then yelled out "green cards!" That was a specific and doable request, and it elicited specific responses. Here's why.

I had given all the participants a set of cards—green, yellow, and red—which allowed them to respond to what was happening in the meeting nonverbally. Green cards meant the holder was resonating with and excited about the idea. The request for "green cards" was a shorthand way of checking out with the group who supported the idea, who had questions and/or found the idea within the range of his/her tolerance (yellow cards), and who had concerns that extended beyond his/her range of tolerance that needed to be addressed (red cards).

Within two seconds of the "green cards" request, all of us had a read on the room. We could then go to the two red card holders and find out what needs of theirs would not be met by the proposal currently on the table. I asked how they felt about it and what request they had to change the current proposal so it took care of their unmet needs. In only a few minutes, we had a proposal that was within a working range of tolerance for all participants. The proposal then became our strategy, which specified doable actions within a certain timeframe.

One key concept of the NVC process enhanced the meeting's effectiveness more than I could have predicted: our third value that every person knows what s/he wants back in relation to what s/he said. I was surprised it was so immediately effective in a group of people who weren't "trained" in making requests and hadn't even considered the concept of knowing what they wanted back before they opened their mouth.

Internally, I was looking for a request from each person who spoke. I supported speakers in creating a request by saying, "I'm guessing you'd like something back from the group in relation to what you just said. What is it you'd like?" or "That sounds like a proposal to me. Would you like to turn it into a proposal the group can respond to, or would you like support from me to do that?" Proposing action that could be taken in the present moment produced a palpable energy and momentum among the participants. This clarity was further enhanced and extended by agreement on specific requests for strategies that needed further resources.

I gave the group feedback in the form of observations and also asked for what participants saw or heard that led them to draw the conclusions they drew. Observations contributed clarity and led to individuals taking responsibility for their own interpretations and conclusions.

For example, when we were working on the wording of the mission statement, a group member objected that one paragraph was non-inclusive. When I asked what specific word or phrase gave the impression of non-inclusivity, the participant gave the phrase "to those determined to be in need." He was then given the opportunity to offer a different phrase that would capture the original intention yet convey the value of inclusion. The participant suggested using the wording "to all in need." His need behind his suggestion was clear, he took responsibility for his interpretation, and he was able to propose a change that took all needs into account.

In the six-hour meeting, we created mission and vision statements and a name for the coalition and also determined how the group would make decisions and who got the floor to speak. We even created committees and began to identify specific action items. At the closing, we celebrated the effectiveness of the meeting, which merged action, connection, and collaboration.

(Kathleen Macferran is listed in Contributors to This Book.)

Working for Shared Reality About Organizational Needs

IC provides a process for collective conversation. It promotes collaboration and shared responsibility by putting into practice two key principles—that all needs matter and all voices can be heard—in service of something bigger than ourselves as individuals.

I'd like to clarify the term "organizational needs." Although you will see the terms "organizational needs" and "an organization's needs" in this book, they are used for the sake of brevity. Organizations as living systems of people have needs. Organizations as legal or philosophical shells have no needs. It's the people in them and their collective shared reality about who they are, why they exist, and where they are going together, etc. that give life to their collective needs, their organizational needs. These are universal because every organization has these same needs. The distinction is critical because one of the ways the domination hierarchy justifies its power over people is to declare, "It's company policy," or "The group decided," and similar statements. In this way, people absolve themselves of the responsibility for their own choices based on their own needs, such as job security, for example. When this individual responsibility is attributed to a group, the dangers of making choices that are not life serving become more prevalent. In worst-case scenarios, such as decisions made under the aegis of the Third Reich, individuals claim (and often believe based on the alternatives of death or imprisonment) that the organization (or government) decided and they have no choice in the matter. The IC model aims to give as many people as possible a voice within teams and organizations. Therefore, when you read "organizational needs" or "an organization's needs," keep in mind that they mean the collective needs of the people who make up the organization. On a related point, while we may attribute a collective personality to organizations or, for that matter, nations as distinct cultures, all our relationships with any collective group are in actuality a collection of relationships with individuals.

Do organizational needs conflict with individual needs? Thankfully, no. Strategies may conflict, but needs never do. For example, an organization's strategy to begin the work day at 7:30 AM may conflict with an employee's need to get more sleep, but the underlying organizational need to service customers and complete the necessary work does not. In this case, the employee can take responsibility to develop a strategy for more sleep that still meets the organizational needs. Or, the company can find a job for this employee that meets his or her need for ease in the morning and find another employee whose needs are served by starting and ending earlier in the day.

The needs-based awareness model is effective for integrating people from differing backgrounds and levels of power and giving them incentive to work together in the service of common organizational needs. From the beginning of my career working with a diverse cross-section of clients such as telecommunications companies, real estate developers, unions, university professors, employees, consumer groups, nurses, teachers, engineers, accountants, mechanics, and more, I've helped people navigate in organizations where an imbalance of structural power exists. Now I use the IC/NVC model to make organizational needs more apparent so everyone shares the same vision and values, and individual needs such as autonomy, respect, and contribution are also met. The organization becomes values and principles based instead of policy and procedure based. Workers then tend to be values and principles based and self-motivated instead of management controlled, as well as purpose and achievement oriented and aware of others and the whole system. As a result, the entire organization operates from a "power *with,*" not "power over" model that energizes and propels the kind of success documented in earlier chapters and reflected in increased profits, higher productivity, and improved morale.

Once the values of both the individuals and the team or organization become more explicit, this creates more opportunity for choice by both parties on whether they want to align. Many employees and employers have inherent conflicts not because of their personalities, but because their intrinsic values are so divergent.

When organizational needs are made apparent and the organization is principle rather than policy based, workers are more likely to be self-motivated and purpose and achievement oriented.

While we all share universal individual needs, the primacy of some over others is key to team alignment and integration. If you value creativity and autonomy, then your values may be irreconcilable with those of a team that inherently values order and predictability. As pointed out in Chapter Two, if a manager is frequently "managing" an employee, the problem is likely to be a system issue—a conflict of values or an uneasy fit—not a people issue.

The IC Framework

Normally, I'm called into an organization to help with strategic planning. Often people are unprepared for the transformative results that the IC/NVC model can deliver. Raymond Tymas-Jones, Ph.D., dean of the College of Fine Arts and associate vice president for The Arts at the University of Utah, wrote to me after experiencing training in the tools of NVC and IC: "The training has enormous potential to revolutionize the College to achieve greater accomplishments in arts education." Likewise, Wallace Wilson, director of the School of Art and Art History at the University of South Florida, felt that the training was "vital to us and our future" and would be "remembered as a major turning point in [the department's] history!" The keys to continuing success are deepening and strengthening a new organizational culture based on the NVC model of communication and the IC needs-based framework.

The four steps in the IC framework are shown in the following chart, which compares the NVC process between individuals with an adaptation of this process for organizations.

Fig. 4-3. The Four Steps of the Integrated Clarity® Framework

A needs-based approach to workplace productivity

Individual People Orientation Nonviolent Communication (NVC)	Whole System Orientation Integrated Clarity (IC)
1. Make Observations. • What am I seeing or hearing? • Objective, concrete, factual	**1. Identify Data.** • Observations that can be analyzed, compared, measured: metrics, dashboards
2. Identify Feelings. • Feelings vs. non-feeling judgments or evaluations about observations and business data	
3. Connect Feelings to Human Needs. Universal needs that all people share, such as respect, learning, purpose, and autonomy	**3. Connect Data to Organizational Needs.** **Source Needs** **Leveraging Needs** 1) Identity 4) Structure 2) Life-Affirming Purpose 5) Energy 3) Direction 6) Expression
4. Make Requests to Meet Our Needs. *Examples of a request:* "Would you be willing . . . 1) to tell me what you heard me say?" 2) to complete this report and have it on my desk by five o'clock?"	**4. Develop Strategic Intentions.** In organizations, requests are strategies. Strategic planning and implementation on a whole system level are intended to meet organizational needs that people in the system perceive and monitor.

This chart illustrates the two parallel processes of meeting individual and organizational needs. Identifying feelings is the common portal to both individual as well as larger system needs. Our feelings point to the needs met or unmet in both cases. This illustrates the importance and utility of identifying feelings.

Again, these processes are not about feelings per se. They're about connecting to needs and making requests of individuals or developing collective strategies to meet more needs. They're about incremental change to meet more needs.

Non-Feelings and Non-Data

The chart that follows provides clarity on the difference between feelings and non-feelings (#2 in the Four Steps) when using NVC and the difference between data and non-data when using IC (#1, Identify Data). Why are these distinctions important? Because in interpersonal communication, a non-feeling is a thought, evaluation, judgment, or criticism that will likely create separation and resistance. In organizational communication, a non-data statement is also a generalized evaluation—either positive or negative. Such a statement isn't specific enough to be helpful and is likely to create resistance.

To reiterate, I'm not saying that evaluations and interpretations aren't important or necessary in the workplace. The key is distinguishing them from our feelings and needs as discussed earlier. In this way, our ability to use both becomes more empowered. In NVC language, we don't experience "negative" or "positive" feelings. All feelings are information about needs. We experience pleasant or unpleasant feelings. We think positive or negative judgments.

On the interpersonal level, think back to the employee who considered his director "rude" because she didn't say good morning to him every day before discussing work-related topics. Had he been able to separate his observation (she doesn't say good morning) from his judgment (she's rude), he may have been able to make a request to meet his need and stay in a job that he otherwise might have enjoyed.

All interpretations, judgments, and evaluations are expressions of our own unmet needs. If we think someone is rude, we have a feeling about that (e.g., hurt, sad, angry) because we have an unmet need (e.g., acceptance, connection, respect). The chances we'll make a request of the individual to meet our need are low because we've boxed the person into our judgment.

If this employee could have realized his own need for respect and connection—and even considered that his director had a need driving her behavior (e.g., productivity)—he likely could have released her from his judgment box. He may even have said something like: "I sense you have a need to get things accomplished, and I understand that. But would you be willing to exchange a 'good morning' each day before we jump in?" That way, she knows he understands her need to be efficient—or she may answer with another need of hers that would help him understand her better.

In the Non-Feelings and Non-Data chart that follows, you can see other examples of where judgment and blame can creep in. Feelings or data mixed with evaluations often stimulate resistance.

Fig. 4-4. Non-Feelings and Non-Data

Non-Feelings

Accepted	Insulted	Pressured	Unwanted
Approved	Intimidated	Pushed	Unworthy
Ashamed	Inadequate	Put down	Used
Attacked	Invalidated	Rejected	Victimized
Betrayed	Invisible	Ripped off	Violated
Blamed	Isolated	Ridiculed	Worthless
Cheated	Left out	Stupid	Useless
Cornered	Let down	Teased	_____
Criticized	Manipulated	Threatened	_____
Distrusted	Misunderstood	Trampled	_____
Dumped on	Neglected	Tricked	_____
Guilty	Overpowered	Unheard	_____
Hassled	Overworked	Unimportant	_____
Ignored	Patronized	Unseen	_____

Non-Data

- *"Third-quarter performance was poor."* Rather, use specific numbers to describe performance. E.g., "Third-quarter sales were down by 10,000 units (or $100,000)."
- *"You're late."* Rather, use observable measures without judgment, such as "You arrived 20 minutes after the time we agreed upon."
- *You're doing great!" Keep it up."* In the absence of specific observations, the listener doesn't know what behaviors to "keep up." If you say, "I like seeing you reach 70 percent of the goal in half the time," it's clear what you're praising.
- *"Customers are happy."* How is "happy" measured? What level of "happy"? What percentage of/how many customers? Rather, say, "Ninety percent of our customers indicated on the survey that they would buy our product/service again."

Ways of Expressing Non-Feelings

When you say:	Followed by:	You are usually expressing:
"I feel . . ."	like . . .	
	that . . .	thoughts
	it . . .	evaluations
	as if . . .	judgments
	you . . .	criticisms
	I, she, he, they . . .	

Note the difference between feelings and non-feelings, which aren't feelings but judgments. Knowing the difference can contribute to more success in our empathic connections. Real feelings in organizations are important in that they're the accessible and reliable indicators of whether human needs are being met. Feelings are critical in decision making, relationships, and energizing the workplace.

The simple yet challenging act of making observations absent of judgment is the foundation to a vital and coordinated workplace free of blame and able to respond strategically to changing markets and conditions. This happens because identifying the pulse of the people

(people's feelings and needs) and the pulse of the organization (its data and organizational needs) focuses the organization on making requests and developing strategies that are most likely to get all needs met. This is a learn-by-exploring, observing, and adjusting approach that current organizational research validates and encourages.

Think about your everyday conversations and begin to translate them into feelings and data. For example, you could translate "I'm feeling hassled today" into "I feel frustrated and nervous because I don't think I can finish all three of my assignments today." Or translate "I feel attacked because you said you didn't like my proposal" into "I feel confused because you didn't give me reasons for not liking my proposal." In terms of data, you could translate "Her report left something to be desired" into "Her report didn't include statistics from Diversity in Human Resources." Or instead of "I liked the way you ran the meeting," you might say, "I appreciated the way you asked everyone to take turns speaking to ensure everyone had a chance to speak. It helped me understand all aspects of the situation."

This process of communication is about intention and being honest and transparent with professionalism. It takes only one person to engage in it to create a connection. Once you've connected, it changes the dynamic to one of understanding and cooperation. It also encourages productivity, which comes from the ability to identify needs—met or unmet—and to make requests on the individual level and on the organizational level to create strategies to meet unmet needs.

The Importance of Connection and Feelings

Connecting with people on an empathic level can have quite a dramatic effect on your company's bottom line. In *Megatrends 2010*, Patricia Aburdene tells the story of Greg Merten, former vice president of Hewlett-Packard, who also managed HP's huge inkjet division. He wasn't interested in connection. He was task oriented and not at all empathic. Then Merten was jolted into realizing the power of empathy the hard way. His teenage son—a people person—was killed in a car accident. This event completely changed how Merten approached his work. He dedicated himself to becoming empathic. Now wanting to create connection, he became people oriented, focusing on conversation and community, trust and understanding, forgiveness and suspending judgment. Merten was an inspiration to his team, others in the company, and those who worked with him to build new company sites, creating breakthroughs in productivity that added hundreds of millions of dollars to HP's bottom line.[53] He proved what IC and NVC claim, that it's more effective to profit *with* people than to profit from people.

Here's another reason for getting in touch with how you feel. Jonah Lehrer, a neuroscientist and author of the book *How We Decide,* states: "The process of thinking requires feeling, for feelings are what let us understand all the information that we can't directly comprehend. Reason without emotion is impotent."[54] In fact, Lehrer points out that people whose emotional brains are damaged can't make decisions![55] This information ties in with Gardner's "multiple intelligences" and Goleman's "emotional intelligence" mentioned earlier in this book, enhancing the relatively new view of our multifaceted brains. Lehrer explains that, used in appropriate measures given the circumstance, our emotions add wisdom to pure logic.

Using Integrated Clarity in the workplace, we incorporate an awareness of feelings throughout the process of determining organizational needs and developing strategies to meet them. Feelings can act as barometers, signposts, and beacons to guide the process, but feelings are not the point in and of themselves. They lead to the discovery of needs, and when we identify needs, we can make requests (individual) or establish strategies (organizational) to meet those needs.

> *"The process of thinking requires feeling. . . ." People whose emotional brains are damaged can't make decisions. (Jonah Lehrer,* How We Decide*)*

Dian Killian, Ph.D., Center for Nonviolent Communication certified trainer and director of the Center for Collaborative Communication has considerable experience using NVC in business situations. In the story that follows, Killian explains how an awareness and expression of feelings and needs helped one of her coaching clients with a business presentation.

When people think about Nonviolent Communication, or Collaborative Communication as I like to call it, they often associate it with conflict resolution. I have found, though, that NVC is equally effective, if not more so, when applied to "everyday" organizational situations such as meetings, presentations, proposals, negotiations, client services, needs assessment, strategic planning, and feedback or reviews. By practicing NVC in these "mundane" situations, conflict is less likely to develop because from the very beginning, a greater level of shared perspective, engagement, and interest is established between people. There's also more mutual respect and connection, which creates an environment where courage and candor (two qualities often sought in companies) can truly be expressed.

One of my coaching clients works for a large, international corporation. Kevin had a presentation coming up of a proposal he wanted upper management to adopt, and several of his peers were also presenting proposals. When talking with him about it, I heard him say several times how crucial his proposal and its successful adoption were. I heard a level of urgency in both his words and his voice. I doubted this urgency would support a successful presentation of his proposal. Kevin also told me how much he wanted his ideas to be heard, even if they weren't adopted in the end. He simply wanted confidence that his viewpoint had been understood. He had had previous experiences with senior management where decisions had been made without benefit of the "big picture" of his "on-the-ground" knowledge.

I invited Kevin to take a moment to consider why the project really mattered to him. If it was adopted, what needs might be met for him, his clients, and his organization? He spoke with passion about what he saw as the client's experience and how much his project would help the company. He wanted his idea adopted because he saw a reoccurring problem regarding delivery, and his proposal would resolve the situation, adding value and building confidence. He wanted effectiveness and contribution, and relief for his clients; he also wanted to build trust with them as someone responsive and competent to address their concerns.

Once Kevin was aware of his needs on a core level, I noticed he was much calmer. This, in itself, was a first step. Unexpressed anxiety can turn up in unexpected and undesirable ways when communicating with others—and easily come across as pressure or aggression. If we're acting from a place of urgency (which, at its root, is based on fear), this also affects our ability to be levelheaded and clear-sighted, especially when already under pressure. Now that Kevin was aware of his core needs, the success of his presentation was no longer about *him* or his performance—it was about his deep desire to contribute to the well-being of his clients and improve the lives of others. That core desire was there all along, but by naming it, he became even more motivated and focused on giving his presentation, and he relieved himself of much performance anxiety.

I then suggested we role-play, with me playing the part of the supervisor. After brief formalities, Kevin proceeded to role-play and present data—statistical information, his assessment of the situation, what intervention he advocated, and why. I quickly found myself overwhelmed with the level of detail and became disengaged. My mind flashed to how many presentations like this (accompanied by detailed PowerPoint slides) the supervisor heard each week. I doubted this would be inspiring or compelling for the supervisor or anyone else in the meeting. Where had the life and passion gone that Kevin had accessed just a few minutes before when describing his drive for the project? This passion was not in his head or the facts he'd accumulated; it was articulated in his voice and the very way he spoke about his ideas.

I paused the role-play and asked Kevin how he was feeling when he imagined his project being adopted. "Excited" was the first word that came to him—and then "inspired" and "energized." I asked him to start the role-play again, this time naming how he was feeling about having the conversation with the supervisor (pleased, grateful) and about the project itself and its objectives. I also asked him to name the needs that were met for him. Rather than, "Since

2008, we've had X capabilities for X clients, with X percent of turnover . . . blah, blah, blah," he began: "I appreciate everyone attending this meeting because I am very excited about an idea I want to share with you that will support our clients and boost their satisfaction and trust in our product."

While coaching him to integrate feelings and needs throughout his presentation, I also reminded Kevin about making connection requests (to pace the conversation) to make sure he was being heard and understood. Connection requests, such as checking what others have heard can sound like: "I want to see if I'm getting this across. Can you tell me the gist of what you've heard?" Another version of this question, which Kevin used during his presentation, is: "I want to check if I'm making this clear, so I want to pause and see if there are any questions or comments so far." These "checking in" skills are natural to us as human beings—yet we often can forget to sufficiently slow down a conversation to maximize understanding and connection. Because Kevin particularly wanted to know that his ideas were being heard and understood, these kinds of questions were especially crucial.

Connection requests can also focus on hearing a response from the other person—getting a "weather report" on the ideas presented. For example, Kevin said, "I'm wondering what your response is to what I've presented so far. . . ." and asked, "What's your sense of this?"

By integrating these practices in his presentation, Kevin knew that he'd been heard by his supervisor and was able to see how his ideas were being integrated and adopted. By checking in with others, he also fostered a sense of collaboration and invited others' ideas and insights, thus supporting their engagement and "tweaking" the project to make it even more effective. In giving a presentation grounded in his passion (his feelings and needs), he presented himself as someone who knows what's happening "on the ground" and is alert to his customers' concerns. He also stood out as a leader and a visionary—someone others *want* to listen to and involve.

(Dian Killian is listed in Contributors to This Book. Although this was an actual situation, her client's name has been changed.)

How to Use IC in the Workplace

Integrated Clarity works across the three dimensions of an organization—intrapersonal, interpersonal, and organizational—by developing a needs-based awareness that engenders responsibility to meet those needs. The process is one of inquiry—of self and others.

IC can be used in the following three ways to improve relationships, increase operational efficiencies, and expand profits.

1. **Assessment tool.** Initially, IC works as an assessment tool to discover what's working and what's not working in all three dimensions of an organization or team. You can find an abbreviated IC assessment in the Appendices. Assessments measure the degree to which people and organizational needs are met so recommendations can be established.

    One of the reasons IC is so effective is that it doesn't ignore people needs and focuses only on business needs. It combines the two and can be applied at any level of a business, nonprofit, or association.

    The more people's basic needs are met, and the more harmoniously people work together and align with organizational needs, the more solid and successful the company can be.

2. **Planning process.** Next, IC becomes a series of conversations in which the organization's six universal needs are discussed: *Identity, Life-Affirming Purpose, Direction, Structure, Energy,* and *Expression.* The specifics of each need are determined in light of the group's unique organization, e.g.: nonprofit, service business, corporation, college or university, or professional association.

3. **Implementation tools.** Finally, IC provides the means for implementing what was discovered in the conversations. Various tools and techniques of application are presented in Part II of this book. Throughout all discussions, NVC is employed as a communication tool focusing on feelings, needs, and requests.

Distinguishing Between Needs and Strategies

For both individuals and organizations, it helps to distinguish between needs and strategies. It encourages us to develop strategies to meet specific needs rather than create them for reasons other than those that are needs-based such as comparisons like, "that's how XYZ company does it." Many company policies (strategies) are established and followed even though no one is sure what need they're meeting. And if they do meet a need, perhaps that need can be met in better ways, as one executive found out.

Phillip, second in charge of a large research team, was surprised by an epiphany when he began discussing his wish for people to show up at 8:00 AM when the company opens. His previous strategy had been to shoot off emails to key people telling them to do something about this problem. Somehow his emails were never effective. Later feedback at an IC retreat revealed that Phillip's team members perceived him as "mean" or "angry."

Phillip's epiphany came when he realized that his need was not for people to observe the policy but for connection. He liked to come in and connect with others—even go to coffee with a colleague. Knowing this, he could plan to meet his need for connection, beginning with telling people what was going on with him. Immediate understanding was established between Phillip and his team when he openly shared his need at the IC retreat.

Phillip's ability to distinguish between strategies and needs then became a valuable tool to create more quality connections in his work relationships and more meaning in the workplace.[56]

(Name has been changed.)

Where Is IC Used?

Conversations to determine needs can be held with any group or individual within an organization, such as in:

- one-on-one executive discussions

- performance reviews
- conflict resolution or mediations
- meetings with company-wide management teams
- small-group employee trainings
- work-group discussions
- large-group meetings
- board and committee chair meetings
- combined communication and strategic-planning retreats

Usually these discussions are first held with management team(s) or individuals and then extend to work groups, departments, teams, committees, or the board. To provide a few examples, IC/NVC can be used *intrapersonally* for executive coaching or self-inquiry (such as was done initially with Phillip) or *interpersonally* for mediation, team processes, and personnel reviews. It's used *organizationally* for conversations around strategy and planning and to establish a Needs Dashboard for the organization to determine how well needs are being met by monitoring data. (See Part II, Chapter Seven for a discussion of the Organizational Needs Dashboard.)

Six Universal Organizational Needs

Before we consider the six universal organizational needs in detail, you can see an overview in the diagram on the next page.

Defining the Source Needs of *Identity, Life-Affirming Purpose,* and *Direction* provides the foundation and guiding principles for the Leveraging Needs of *Structure, Energy,* and *Expression.* The term "Source" intentionally refers to the connection people within the organization form with a larger, causative force that sources and inspires their collective efforts. Source Needs are the "what" of an organization. Leveraging Needs are the "how."

Following the diagram is an explanation of each organizational need and then a case study that shows how one organization gained clarity regarding their needs and the dramatic effect this clarity had on the group as a whole.

Fig. 4-5. Integrated Clarity® Six Universal Organizational Needs

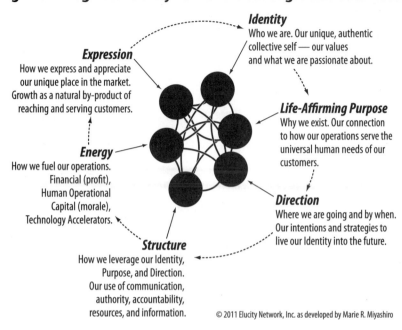

Identity
Who we are. Our unique, authentic collective self — our values and what we are passionate about.

Expression
How we express and appreciate our unique place in the market. Growth as a natural by-product of reaching and serving customers.

Life-Affirming Purpose
Why we exist. Our connection to how our operations serve the universal human needs of our customers.

Energy
How we fuel our operations. Financial (profit), Human Operational Capital (morale), Technology Accelerators.

Direction
Where we are going and by when. Our intentions and strategies to live our Identity into the future.

Structure
How we leverage our Identity, Purpose, and Direction. Our use of communication, authority, accountability, resources, and information.

© 2011 Elucity Network, Inc. as developed by Marie R. Miyashiro

Source Need #1: Identity

First, I invite businesses or teams to define *who they are* rather than decide *what to do next*. Groups have found it helpful to delineate *Identity* upfront because all policies, decisions, and actions flow from that understanding. To help us determine *Identity,* one approach we use comes out of Jim Collins's "Hedgehog Concept,"[57] a seminal research finding he introduced in *Good to Great.* The three questions we ask are depicted by the diagram on the following page (see page 118).

Another crucial aspect of *Identity* is articulating the organization's or team's unique core values and principles, which eventually become expressed in everything the organization does. We don't establish these as much as we define what is already true and part of the organization's "DNA." The work then becomes to maintain a team's or organization's integrity as a collective whole, which means each person involved is aligned with its values. Otherwise, the character of the organization erodes over time. Each has a unique identity. Even branches within the same organization or franchise have slightly different characteristics while still sharing the values of the whole.

Thus it's not only helpful to define those values, but to hire people who are aligned with them and monitor that alignment over time.

Fig. 4-6. The Three Circles of the Hedgehog Concept[58]

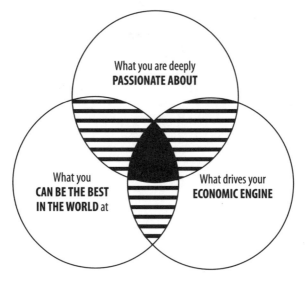

Good to Great by Jim Collins. Copyright © 2001

When I visited the Swedish furniture store IKEA for the first time, I was amazed at how even the building architecture from half a mile away screamed its unique progressive identity and values. Upon entering, I saw signage that made the whole shopping experience immediately clear to me. I saw a store map, instructions on how to get and use their unique shopping carts and bags, and even instructions for how to stack my items at the checkout stand so the barcodes were face up. I did an informal interview of about twenty employees, and each in his or her own way could tell me the key values of the company—which related to what many called "something about socialism," how all employees and bosses are equal, and that everyone matters equally.

When I asked what they'd heard or seen that indicated these values, they made comments such as, "Well, my manager does all the same things I do, like stacking boxes," or "At the holiday party, every employee had a wrapped gift with his or her name on it." Even the parking lot attendant, who had worked there for only two weeks, articulated something similar. This is an example of organizational *Identity* at its purest.

Source Need #2: Life-Affirming Purpose

Why does your organization exist beyond the desire to make money? What need does it fulfill in society? What is it doing for people? How does it enhance life? When the focus within the organization is on what its product or service is doing to benefit its customers or clients, a natural inspiration takes hold. This purpose then guides the actions of all employees. Even if their jobs don't directly impact the customer, they are supporting the final outcome, the fulfillment of needs. The more aligned with this purpose everyone is, the more productivity on the job tends to result. It's not just a matter of the social sector; workers having clarity about how the organization meets human needs. My experience is that people in every type of organization, including commercial enterprises, long for a connection to meaningful human purpose related to their efforts.

When I worked with Horizon Moving Systems, a United Van Lines company, for example, I found the company wasn't just about moving furniture or cargo. In one of our sessions, employees had no trouble

When the focus within the organization is on how its product or service benefits its customers or clients, a natural inspiration takes hold.

explaining that their jobs always related to some life transition for their customers—perhaps a death or divorce, or a new job or new family. They saw themselves as people who helped others during difficult times of transition. One of the van drivers even quoted statistics about moving being one of the most stressful events in a person's life. The employees genuinely enjoyed being a support system for these customers. The company adopted a new positioning statement, "Moving Customers Through Life," with adaptations for specific customer groups, such as "Moving You Through Life" and "Moving You Through Business."

The information we collect from employee groups and leadership teams through our 10 Minutes to Clarity® Organizational Needs Assessment, shows a positive relationship between employees who find personal meaning in their work and productivity and workplace satisfaction. The more meaning, the higher the level of productivity and satisfaction.

Questions to clarify an organization's *Life-Affirming Purpose* include:

- How do we continuously articulate which universal human needs we are passionate about meeting?
- How do we measure and monitor our connection to this purpose in daily operations and decisions?
- How do we measure and monitor our ability to fulfill this purpose with the people we serve?

Source Need #3: Direction

Where does your organization intend to go? What results do you want to manifest—and by when? It's easy to get caught up in plays that may not be moving the ball toward the goal if everyone isn't completely clear where the goal posts are. Strong intention, a clear layout of the playing field, and a vivid picture of the goal will get you there.

Questions to determine strategies for *Direction* that fulfill your *Life-Affirming Purpose* in keeping with your *Identity* include:

- What are our critical intentions regarding each organizational need and our people needs?
- What results do we seek to create? (What would it look like? Sound like? What would we be feeling?)
- What are our "Big Hairy Audacious Goals" (BHAGs)—from *Built to Last* by Collins and Porras?[59] (Do we have a

clear finish line for all to see, a goal that energizes us to take action, and one that's slightly outside our comfort zone but doable?)

Examples of organizational *Direction* in action are collective efforts in political elections and visions of scientific achievement such as landing humans on the moon. These endeavors are inspiring and have clear, observable, easily understandable projected outcomes. Walk into the office of any CEO who has clarity about the organization's needs, and you'll see pictures, words, and other symbols that inspire continued focus on a vision of the organization in the future.

Leveraging Need #4: Structure

Every organization needs structure, but what does that entail? Is it merely a top-down pyramid of authority? The kind of structure referred to here is the kind that grows out of clarity around Source Needs, not transplanted structures from other organizations. While best practices and benchmarks from other organizations can serve as a healthy starting point, ultimately the structure will be as unique as and unique to the Source Needs of the organization. Intention-driven *Structure* governs function—the first law of biomechanics. How we build our organizations dictates how well those organizations can operate from their Source Needs.

Integrated Clarity builds on Kimball Fisher's concept of empowerment as a base for what I call organizational *Structure*:

- Authority (who decides what),
- Resources (financial, technological, human),
- Information (which is power in organizations), and
- Accountability (who is responsible for what and by when).[60]

Communication shapes *Structure*, as well. If you want to build a participative workplace environment but implement it with the language constructs of the domination hierarchy embedded in our unconscious communication, you'll likely be less successful than you want to be. NVC, as a language of needs and empathic connection, supports an empowerment paradigm. For this reason, it's a key element of this universal organizational need of *Structure*.

Questions to ask include:

- How do we create perfect balance between authority and accountability? (Does someone have more accountability for an outcome than authority over that outcome? Does someone have more authority over an outcome even though the accountability rests with someone else?")
- How do we develop and measure or monitor access, use, and productivity of critical information and resources?

Leveraging Need #5: Energy

Energy in this context is partly the natural energy arising from alignment with the organization's identity and its connection to its purpose and people, both internally and externally. Energy also means the fuel that gives the organization its drive and is defined as a triumvirate of profit, workforce morale, and technology.

- Profit (or "cash flow in" for the social sector or nonprofits) fuels operations and is a key element of *Energy*, a Leveraging Need because of the leverage financial resources can provide for operational initiatives.
- Workforce morale constitutes a key impetus behind productivity. The unique combination of NVC, which focuses on the needs of individuals, with meeting the six universal needs of organizations creates an energetic synergy. I started calling workforce morale "human operational capital" as a way to clearly indicate the value of investing in employee morale and the return on this investment in terms of productivity that the research shows.
- The third component—technology—is becoming steadily more crucial, providing time- and money-saving innovations that propel organizational or team progress.

By framing financial profit as part of the three-pronged need of *Energy*, the human factor and technological considerations all hold equal weight as elements that can propel an organization or team into growth. In this way, money is not a need unto itself but instead is in service to the energy an organization requires as a living system.

An important clarifying point about corporations, both for profit and nonprofit: their boards of directors have a fiduciary duty to support *reasonable* financial profit, not necessarily *maximum* financial profit. The idea of *Energy* as an organizational need allows for other forms of profit beyond the financial. For example, emotional profit and connection with the customer and employees, increased social value and social profit in terms of how a company is viewed through the lens of ethical capitalism, and so on.

Leveraging Needs #6: Expression

Once an organization understands its Source Needs of *Identity*, *Life-Affirming Purpose*, and *Direction* and creates the *Structure* to support these and the *Energy* to drive it, its *Expression* takes shape. *Expression* is the celebration of the organization's unique position in the marketplace and the world. All branding, sales, marketing, and service flow from this identity, purpose, and organizational values. *Who we are* comes through with laser focus and *how we can meet your needs* is broadcast with clarity. Growth is not the goal but instead comes as a natural by-product of serving universal human needs through the authentic Source Needs of the organization.

The customer or client is the ultimate beneficiary of an organization that operates from a needs-based mindset. To contribute to life, to serve human beings is the sole reason for organizations and groups to be born, grow, and evolve. Whether it is capitalistic market pressures or the collaborative inspiration of a sharing economy, human needs drive it all.

The following case study tracks a simple but organization-changing insight from an IC strategic planning session. The pattern you see here is similar to results that appear in the organizational research outlined earlier.

CASE STUDY: THE INTERNATIONAL COUNCIL OF FINE ARTS DEANS (ICFAD)

In the 1990s and into 2005, the International Council of Fine Arts Deans experienced stagnation of growth in membership, and high turnover was associated with deans at fine arts schools within universities, from which the group draws its membership. ICFAD's president at the time was Maurice Sevigny, dean of the College of Fine Arts at the University of Arizona. For the first time, he included task committee chairs in a board of directors' retreat, inviting the group to clarify ICFAD's vision and mission in a newly participative way that focused on organizational needs.

Since 2005, I've worked periodically with the International Council of Fine Arts Deans, Sevigny, and its president in 2010, Ron Jones, to define and meet their six organizational needs. The Integrated Clarity process is built on an adaptable whole-system change framework that integrates the work of Jim Collins, Kimball Fisher, William Bridges, and current organizational thinking from other leaders in the field. It involves a series of strategic conversations, the results of which are implemented over a timeframe that averages about four years according to Collins's extensive research.[61] Why so long? The strategies are first developed in a series of discussions; they are then implemented and tested; and finally, they're refined over time.

ICFAD began with a discussion of *Identity* and *Life-Affirming Purpose* and later addressed *Direction*. Their clarity about *Structure, Energy,* and *Expression* needs grew organically out of these conversations as the Source Needs were determined.

The strategic process began with ICFAD's executive planning team participating in the 10 Minutes to Clarity Organizational Needs Assessment, an online assessment tool that measures sixteen individual and organizational qualities known to contribute to higher levels of productivity and profit. The assessment revealed the levels at which both organizational needs and people needs were being met and helped to focus our strategic conversations for increased impact, efficiency, and meaning.

Results showed that ICFAD was meeting people needs such

as Respect, Trust, Acknowledgment, Meaning, and Learning. Organizational needs such as *Direction*, *Structure*, and *Energy* were not as strongly met. This demonstrated that the group had made progress with two of its Source Needs, *Identity* and *Life-Affirming Purpose,* since our first strategic conversation about these needs. Group members were now ready to determine strategies for how to implement these Source Needs in a unified *Direction* with *Structure*, *Energy* and means of *Expression* behind it.

After discussing ICFAD's *Identity* and using the Gradients of Agreement tool for decision making (fully described in Chapter Eight), the group arrived at the following statement of *Identity*: **"Arts Deans Helping Deans."** From this, the organization's *Expression* would organically grow. The leaders then determined their statement of *Life-Affirming Purpose* as: **"ICFAD is the organization that speaks for the arts in higher education."** This single purpose upon which ICFAD exists and every decision is based changed the structure and manner in which it operates to do what it's *Best at:* "Providing forums and services to meet the professional development and networking needs of Arts Deans and their administrative teams."

The group's *Passion* of "Coming together in the spirit of collegiality and camaraderie to share, renew, inspire, and collaborate in service of advancing The Arts" took two-and-a-half days to determine. The robust, highly dynamic, and highly sophisticated dialogue was intended to bring out the wisdom of each person, which collectively creates a result greater than any one person could come to on his or her own.

The insight of "coming together" as a crystallization of "Arts Deans Helping Deans" (their *Life-Affirming Purpose)* sounds simple; but up to that time, they were modeling themselves on fairly traditional organizations, and that was about to change.

They immediately applied their new insights to the annual conference coming up in a few months. Intention drove the structure of the conference rather than the other way around. For example, instead of focusing on a structure such as five sessions of seventy-five minutes each, they asked, "What format would be most conducive to 'coming together'?" They found that the most exciting part of the conference wasn't the sessions but getting together in between sessions and for lunch or for social connections after formal sessions. Hence, they conducted more casual professional development by having a speaker over lunch, for example. They flip-flopped their conference schedule, and as a result, they received the most positive feedback they'd ever had on the post-conference survey. The conference *appeared* more like "Arts Deans Helping Deans," and conference participants found joy and power in coming together to enhance their collective identity, exchange ideas, and provide practical problem solving.

ICFAD also used "coming together" as the litmus test to keep, develop, or stop its various programs or activities. For example, the group eliminated the telephone mentoring program because of its one-on-one structure. This mentoring didn't have the camaraderie of "coming together" that the whole group had—which was confirmed by the fact that people hadn't shown as much interest in this program as other events that had the "coming together" component. ICFAD began to track "coming together" time as a quantifiable measurement.

The group had its highest annual conference attendance ever that year. Within two years of determining its purpose of "Arts Deans Helping Deans" and changing the structure and manner in which ICFAD operated, membership increased by 27 percent and continued to grow through 2010. The group dramatically improved its ability to serve its members. Numerous strategic opportunities are now being determined for future services, conferences, and benefits for ICFAD members.

The ICFAD leaders became clear on how the board, committees, staff, and members could work together and how the organization could become a mechanism for members to provide input into national policy issues. They also determined how to describe this *Structure* and its implementation at the Fall 2010 conference.

In 2005–2006 strategic conversations, the group examined its Leveraging Need of *Energy.* Its *Economic Engine* includes ICFAD's economic driver (cash flow per member) and resource driver (resources of time, money, and brand per member), which are elements determined by Collins in *Good to Great and the Social Sectors.*[62]

- Time—attracting people who contribute for free or below market rate
- Money—sustained cash flow (primarily from dues and annual conference fees, and ICFAD is now working on other sources of revenue from membership)
- Brand—the deep well of emotional goodwill and mindshare of potential supporters and how people perceive the organization's unique place in the market

In follow-up conversations, ICFAD established action steps for how to develop these resources and how to measure the results.

In early 2010, the leadership group focused specifically on the Source Need of *Direction*, creating further strategies to fulfill the organization's *Life-Affirming Purpose* in keeping with its *Identity*. The group focused on *Direction* because that was both the next logical organizational need to address and it was among the most unmet of its organizational needs, scoring in the bottom three of sixteen individual and organizational needs assessed.

As a result of determining its six organizational needs, the International Council of Fine Arts Deans has expanded, revitalized, and become a more effective and exciting resource for its members as well as an important voice in the conversation about arts in higher education. The entire process of inquiry engendered a renewed sense of direction and enthusiasm for the future of the organization.

※ ※ ※ ※

Chapter Four has explained how the awareness and language of needs can be used on the three levels of intrapersonal, interpersonal, and organizational to improve productivity and create clarity of focus that propels the success of a team, group, or organization. It has described the six organizational needs and how organizations can benefit from defining and meeting them.

Part II begins a series of chapters that provide more specifics, tools, and techniques for implementing this information in the workplace, gradually changing needs-based awareness into needs-based consciousness. In this context, "needs-based awareness" refers to being aware of needs. "Needs-based consciousness" implies a deeper and overarching philosophy that includes awareness of needs plus living and making choices out of this awareness. Awareness acts as a steppingstone for consciousness. Because Part II begins discussing how to put empathy into action, I refer to needs-based awareness as needs-based consciousness from here forward.

PART II

Making Empathy Actionable

FIVE

How to Increase Self-Productivity

*"I'm on fire because I'm recognizing in myself that the more
I meet my needs quickly . . . the more productive I am as a result.
Also I'm noticing that when I stop to think about whether something
I'm feeling is a need, it turns out that some of the things I thought
were needs were actually habits or just distractions."*

—Executive team participant in a Needs-Based Leadership
and Communication Training

Part II, Making Empathy Actionable, provides specific strategies and tools you can use to develop your empathic-connection ability and your needs-based awareness to increase productivity in the workplace and develop a deeper needs-based consciousness. This chapter begins with self-productivity because we, as individuals, are central to the three levels of communication in organizations or workplace life.

As discussed earlier, what we tell ourselves (*intra*personal level) informs and colors what we tell others and what we think they are telling us (*inter*personal level). It also affects how we interpret and act on the organizational data we receive, especially what our customers tell us (organizational level). Further, logic tells us that under most normal circumstances, we have full control of ourselves only. Finally, connecting with ourselves as the foundation for all other connections follows the Connect-Think-Do flow because we more often connect with others in a meaningful and productive way when we're first connected to ourselves. Out of this connection, new and richer strategies arise to meet more needs. Without this self-connection, we're like a radio that isn't quite tuned in to a station. Not only is our own communication garbled, but it's difficult to make out exactly what the other person is saying if we aren't "tuned in" to ourselves first.

I use the term self-productivity because it reminds me of the concept of self-care. One of the most accessible and immediate forms of self-care is self-empathy, the process we've discussed and outlined in a process flow diagram in Chapter Three (p. 60). Self-empathy involves connecting with our own feelings and needs, not as a generalized concept but as a moment-to-moment process accessible to us at any given time.

Moment to moment? How do we do this in the workplace when we're so busy? Why is it important for work productivity and productivity for ourselves and others?

Recently, I was conducting an online training for executives and managers about empathic leadership and communication skills. The group was given an exercise between training sessions. The exercise called for them to observe when they were triggered with pleasant or unpleasant feelings and to identify what observation triggered those feelings. Then they connected these feelings to needs, met or unmet.

A department director shared that he had experienced a breakthrough. By monitoring his feelings and needs throughout his workday, he gained a new level of clarity about what he could control and what was beyond his influence or his willingness to put effort into doing. His sense of feeling overwhelmed was transformed into specific actions that he recognized he had control over and the power to do. He reported that a sense of relief and increased energy resulted from this clarity.

The Benefits of Self-Connection

The first time I did conscious self-connection I was in a grocery store. Earlier in the day, I had a meeting with two other consultants. We had teamed up to develop a program for a client, and two of us were going to speak at a national industry conference for this group. During the meeting, I learned that my colleague's birthday was the same day as the conference. Suddenly—and illogically, as such thoughts often strike—I started imagining that she would be the star of the presenters and I would be relegated to the dark corners of the stage. I pictured her walking into the ballroom being serenaded with "Happy Birthday!" by hundreds of cheering people in the audience.

As I roamed the grocery aisles, I became vaguely aware of a sickening sensation throughout my body, like I wanted to crawl out of my skin. My discomfort triggered a recognition that this was an ideal moment to practice self-connection and that I was being invited into a process of self-discovery. In a flash, my unsettled feeling was accompanied by elation as I realized I had a ripe opportunity to discover an unmet need. I remember shouting with glee in my own mind, "I have an unmet need!" The intensity of the sensation told me this was an important need.

So I took the first step in self-connection. I asked myself, "What am I feeling?" Coming up blank at first, my mind scrolled through a snapshot of a printed list of guesses. Angry? No. Some variation of sadness? Nope, not it. Fear? Now I was getting closer, but I still wasn't there. Aha! Jealousy. I was feeling jealous about the future attention I imagined my colleague would receive. I was pleased that my emotional literacy was developing. I couldn't recall a time before this moment when I was consciously aware of all the components that made up my experience of jealousy. I had the bodily sensations of an increased heart rate, a powerful flow of energy, and a deadness in my senses as though I were in a bubble separate from the world. I felt the odd, jangled combination of fear, anger, and hurt all at the same time, seemingly fighting for dominance. Finally, my mind was manifesting a relentless inner dialogue. I could hear it only when I turned my awareness to it as part of the practice of self-connection: "You're not as good as she is. People like her more than you. You don't count."

Having brought the inner voice to the surface, I could now apply logic to this internal event. The ludicrousness of all this imagining became quite obvious. Her only part in it was that she had been born on the same day as the conference! This clearly was not about anyone but me. I moved on to step two in self-connection. I asked myself, "Well, if this isn't about anyone but me, what need of mine could this be about?"

I knew I had more awareness of my feelings than my needs. In fact, I had to deliberately remind myself that this process was not about what I was feeling. Feelings are just emotional energy. They don't mean anything until we attribute meaning to them. For example, physiologically, fear and excitement can have the same bodily sensations and characteristics. Sports psychologists often help athletes recondition their thoughts and sensations around fear into those of excitement. Athletes want the adrenaline rush and maybe even butterflies in the stomach because their body is preparing for peak performance. One of the worst things to experience before an important competition is a numbing flatness with no state of arousal. But these sensations should be associated with excitement of the pending performance and not fear.

The richness of this process is about needs—the universal human needs that Rosenberg identified and we've discussed in previous chapters. Not wants or desires, but needs that are fundamental to every one of us for health and well-being in the fullness of our humanity.

My entire process of self-connection happened in just a few minutes, in about the time it took me to walk from one end of the store to the other as I was looking for a particular aisle. If anyone had been watching me, it would have looked as if absolutely nothing was happening except grocery shopping. But inside, a whole new world was opening to me.

The need I connected with was appreciation—appreciation for what I *did* have to offer that was different from what anyone else offered. It suddenly didn't matter so much what the people in the audience thought of my colleague. I now recognized what I could contribute to them, and that's what mattered most. Almost instantly, that uncomfortable, edgy feeling I had experienced earlier transformed into a deep sensation in the middle of my chest. I felt grateful because my need for appreciation was met with a reinvented inner dialogue of: "I'm good enough. I have something unique to offer because I'm unique. She's good enough, and I wish her a happy birthday!"

This process resulted in two concrete outcomes for my consulting practice. First, I delivered a talk to this group that I enjoyed giving; and from the feedback I received, people found value in the topic of connecting feelings to their own and others' needs. I shared from my own experiences and vulnerabilities in a way I wouldn't have likely done had I not experienced self-connection in the grocery aisle. Second, I was willing to look at my colleague as a friend in the spirit of a deeper level of collaboration than I was able to feel previously. Both of these outcomes serve me to this day. I could see why Marshall Rosenberg celebrates the idea that pain, even when it's nominal like this one, is a gift pointing to our unmet needs and giving us the opportunity to develop strategies to meet those needs. As a means of self-encouragement, my clients often repeat to themselves something I've heard Rosenberg say: "An unmet need is a gift!"

Meeting our needs is an act of compassion and productivity combined, not just for ourselves but for all around us. When we give to ourselves in service of affirming life, we give to everyone we come in contact with, from our intimate alliances to the most casual encounter. Self-connection stands as the foundation for self-productivity, which in turn supports interpersonal, team, and organizational productivity.

Meeting our needs is an act of compassion and productivity combined, not just for ourselves but for all around us.

The Dangers of Unconscious Thinking

If we're not trained to notice our inner dialogue, it runs us. We're telling ourselves something and we're not aware of it. When this happens, we tend to directly associate whatever is happening around us with our inner experience and think it's the cause of our feelings. In the workplace, this kind of unconsciousness can lead to widespread chaos.

I now think of effective team and organizational leaders as managers of their own thoughts and feelings first and foremost. Then they can more fully take in the thoughts and words of others without confusing them with their own inner dialogue. They increase their ability to observe without distortion.

In this sense, a needs-based consciousness allows us to objectively observe reality like scientists. We can also observe the effects of our choices and actions on situations in the same way scientists observe the effect of a variable in an experiment.

The whole point of self-connecting while we're working is to increase our capacity for self-productivity and for making choices that meet our needs and those of our internal and external customers.

Effective team and organizational leaders manage their own thoughts and feelings first and foremost, thus increasing their ability to observe and hear others without distortion.

The Role of Feelings in Decision Making

As it turns out, feelings play a significant role in making choices when they aren't co-opted by thinking. Recent research in neuroscience suggests that emotions trump painstaking analysis for productive decision making. In *How We Decide*, Jonah Lehrer devotes a whole chapter to this phenomenon, aptly titled "Choking on Thought." He documents half a dozen experiments from experts such as product review leader *Consumer Reports* and researchers at Caltech and Stanford University. As Lehrer explains, this research "illuminates the danger of always relying on the rational brain. There is such a thing as too much analysis. When you overthink at the wrong moment, you cut yourself off from the wisdom of your emotions, which are much better at assessing actual preferences. You lose the ability to know what you really want."[63] When you're making decisions, Lehrer suggests that ". . . the one thing you should always be doing is considering your emotions, thinking about why you're feeling what you're feeling."[64]

And why you're feeling what you're feeling has to do with needs, met or unmet.

Methods for Self-Connection That Lead to Self-Productivity

Employees and managers with whom I work report results such as an increased awareness of choices in their workday by practicing the following methods of self-connection:

1. Journaling once a day at about the same time each day for approximately fifteen minutes about the four steps in the self-empathy process (Observations, Feelings, Needs, Requests).

2. Conducting an internal feelings and needs self-assessment on a regular schedule triggered by a reminder, such as three times a day with a meal, every time you drink water, or on the hour every two hours.

3. Conversing for ten minutes with a trusted colleague, an "empathy work buddy," during which you speak unedited for one to three minutes about whatever is going on with you at work. Your colleague then tries to guess your feelings and needs if you're not expressing them yourself, and if you are, your colleague repeats them back to you. He or she gives you empathy as a way to support your process of self-connection.

4. Focusing on connecting to someone else's feelings and needs. One of my early and constant teachers of NVC is Sylvia Haskvitz. She taught me that many people find it easier to empathize with others as a way of creating connection with themselves. I remember once, long before I learned about NVC, being in a funk about something going on in my life. I was completely focused on what was happening that wasn't working. Then, I had the insight

to stop focusing on myself and to go and do something that would be of value to someone else who was in pain. It worked. I was instantly more connected to my own feelings and needs and was able to make requests of myself and others that led to the end of my feelings of hopelessness. In addition, the person who received my support benefited from this process, as well.

5. Meditation or sitting quietly to connect with your breath and body. I find even sixty seconds can be beneficial, although many of my clients find twenty minutes a day first thing in the morning with an additional five minutes at lunch can be ideal.

Especially for application in the business world, I want to reiterate that the process of self-connection is not an exercise in vanity. It's practical. The idea is to create connection so we can make requests of ourselves and others that meet more of our needs as well as the needs of those around us. At its core, this process is about productive change and progress.

The exercises described may seem difficult to you, or when you try them, you may come up with feelings of numbness or go blank. I find this often happens with people who are used to working at extremely high paces and under tight deadlines. Remember you can start by recognizing your own feelings and associating those feelings with needs. Or simply practice experiencing the physical sensations in your body.

You can start by recognizing your own feelings and associating those feelings with needs. Or simply practice experiencing the physical sensations in your body.

The Challenge of Emotions

In *Healing through the Dark Emotions: The Wisdom of Grief, Fear, and Despair,* Miriam Greenspan discusses what she calls "emotional alchemy." She says we can transform emotions, particularly around grief and fear, into feelings such as gratitude and joy and attributes such as faith and courage. We can then mobilize these powerful qualities in the service of our work to meet others' needs. The process of self-empathy is one way to transform these "dark" emotions into productive energy.

I once worked with a retired top sales manager from Hewlett-Packard. He described himself as ex-military and very practical. Thus I was surprised when I asked him after a training session what he got the most value from and he said the recommended reading list I provided, which listed Greenspan's book—and he mentioned it in particular. I asked him why he thought that book was so important. He related that in his years of work in the corporate world as well as in the military, people's emotions were what created the most challenges for a team. He recognized that people have a wide spectrum of emotions, and that this part of our human nature naturally shows up in our work.

When I share with groups how shocked I was to hear Rosenberg, a former practicing psychologist, say that more than half of the prescriptions in the United States are for antidepressants, people sometimes reply, "Is that all?" The workplace is an extension of people's lives. If they feel crummy outside of the office, they're not going to feel any different inside the office. Recognizing this fact and empathizing with team members and officemates is important when we consider that a higher percentage of them than we might expect are using medication to cope with their feelings every day. I'm not implying any wrongness here—just an awareness and gentle acceptance of what is. Emotions affect every aspect of our workplace experiences.

Emotions Are in the Body

"I can't say this enough," states Greenspan in her book. "Feelings are in your body. Talking about feelings is not the same as experiencing them. Emotional intelligence is a bodily intelligence . . . [so] you have to know how to listen to your body. This is the skill of emotional sensitivity."[65]

In some groups I've worked with, I've given participants an exercise I created for myself. I provide them with a simple outline of a human body, and they begin their awareness of feelings and needs by first identifying sensations in their body. For example, they might pause for sixty seconds to notice where they feel tightness in their body. They might identify the jaw and mouth and how the tongue is drawn up tightly to the roof of the mouth instead of relaxing and lying on the floor of the mouth. Or they might feel tenseness in the shoulders. They would then draw a representation of this on the line drawing. How big is the area of tightness? Is it a constant sensation? Does it pulse or do something else? Is this sensation connected to other parts of the body? If they gave this sensation a name, what feeling would it be?

A participant in one of my group sessions made this astute observation: "One of the things I've noticed during work meetings is that people's faces indicate tension (e.g., clenched jaw, furrowed brows), so that even when they don't say anything, they're saying something. Perhaps I can learn to identify physical tension in myself and then ascribe a feeling to it. My dentist tells me that I've nearly worn the enamel off a couple of my teeth from grinding them. I have caught myself clenching my teeth in reaction to situations at work, but I've never stopped to wonder what I'm feeling at that moment. Aha!"

Unacknowledged feelings can create disaster not only in our interactions but in our health. Greenspan notes: "In the absence of a skilled ability to listen to the emotional language of the body, 'symptoms' arise, calling us to pay attention. As a mild stomachache over time can become an ulcer, an unrecognized grief can become a full-blown anxiety disorder or clinical depression. Denied fear makes itself known in a lowered immune system and psychosomatic disorders. Disavowed despair lives in our bodies, enticing us to act in ways dangerous to ourselves and others."[66]

In fact, not only does self-empathy support health, but it is easier to empathize with ourselves and others when we are healthy, so the two create a valuable synergy.

Unacknowledged feelings can create disaster not only in our interactions but in our health.

The Health Connection

Many books discuss the effects of diet on our well-being, but I want to mention three items in particular that hinder our ability to self-connect.

First, caffeine. Coffee and "energy drinks" are common substitutes for natural energy in the workplace. I admit I occasionally partake in this type of artificial energy. It masks my fatigue in situations such as wanting to be alert for traveling or an urgent due date. However, heavy consumption of caffeine on a regular basis exacts a cost. For many people, this stimulant can distance their physical sensations from their emotions. In Chapter Nine, I describe how I've seen this contribute to less than productive demonstrations of anger and irritation in the workplace.

Second, refined sugar. My colleague Sylvia Haskvitz is a registered dietitian. She creates natural-energy-boosting menus that are low in refined sugars at the retreats she and I conduct for work teams. We can see a direct relationship between the consumption of refined carbohydrates and refined sugars and people's ability to focus, be present with others, and discuss important business issues during the retreat.

This condition is mirrored in our workplaces. The act of empathic connection requires energy. If we are depleted or fatigued, we are less likely to be motivated to connect productively in this way. You can read more about Haskvitz's work with NVC and food in her book, *Eat by Choice, Not by Habit: Practical Skills for Creating a Healthy Relationship with Your Body and Food.*[67]

Finally, impaired health. For the three-year period during which I was writing this book, I encountered a number of health issues. I endured thyroid cancer and two surgeries, suffered fatigue from anemia and a lowered immune function, and contracted more colds and other health challenges during this time than I'd experienced in my entire life. Throughout this period, I recognized I was less resourceful with others than I wished. When I felt better, I worked on self-forgiveness and reconnecting with people as best I could. Having been generally healthy up to then, this was an important learning for me in how to cope with a full workload and stressful home life through self-connection. I've since learned that compromises to my health are important signals about how I'm not receiving or asking for enough support in my life or that fundamental issues may be out of alignment. I also learned that living with someone who has serious health issues can be a tremendously taxing experience requiring advice from experts about the dynamics of care giving. I'm grateful I was able to make choices that better supported me, and in so doing, better supported others, as well. Now that I'm cancer free and fully healthy again, I've learned what it's like for those with chronic illness, and I share a newfound empathy for them around the challenges they face every day.

I discovered personally that health contributes greatly to our empathic connection power, and in turn, taking care of our emotions through self-empathy can support health.

We don't want to wait until we're overwhelmed by symptoms before we discover and acknowledge our feelings. Exercises such as the ones mentioned previously build awareness of our feelings and needs. They serve as practical ways to increase our productivity as well as keep us healthy. As pattern interrupters, they can bring us back from the numbness of the over-thinking and over-analysis associated with busyness, being overwhelmed, and over-scheduling. They can return us to a connection with our feelings and needs that generates a natural energy for productivity rather than a hyped-up caffeinated, edgy one. We've all experienced this natural high, and when we do, we think it's wonderful. Our work becomes less of a burden and more of a joy. Our emotional and mental well-being is a gateway to productivity that can serve not only ourselves but everyone around us.

✳ ✳ ✳ ✳

This chapter has discussed how we can improve our personal productivity through self-connection, achieving a greater awareness of our own feelings and needs. The next chapter explains how we can use this awareness to help us create empathic, connecting, and productive relationships with others in our workplace.

SIX

How to Increase Interpersonal Productivity

"At Cisco Systems, a California company that creates technologies for the Internet, whenever an employee suffered a significant loss, such as a death in the family, CEO John Chambers made it a policy to contact that employee within 48 hours to offer his condolences and help. His example gave others within the organization a green light to act compassionately toward their co-workers, and employees consistently rate the company as one of the best places to work in the country." [68]

—Jill Suttie, "Compassion across Cubicles," *Greater Good*

Most of us have heard or used the expression that we "can't see the forest for the trees." In the workplace, it's often that we "can't see the trees for the forest"—or rather can't see the human beings within the structure. And when we lose sight of the feelings and needs inherent in our common humanity, we lose sight of why we're doing what we're doing and why others are doing what they're doing. Not only does purpose become obscured, but basic human compassion and connection are lost. When this happens, people suffer and morale and productivity decline. In fact, connection is so important that the concept has led Dr. Brené Brown, researcher and professor at the University of Houston Graduate College of Social Work to say: "... Connection is why we're here. It's what gives purpose and meaning to our lives. ... Neuro-biologically, that's how we're wired. ..." [69]

What is the purpose and meaning of organizations? All of them are strategies to meet human needs. The idea here is twofold. On the one hand, organizations are not like people with an inherent right to exist. They exist to meet needs that somehow benefit people. Even scientific groups that study obscure animal or insect populations exist to meet the need for human knowledge. If the need being met isn't important enough to people or it changes and no longer acts as a strategy to meet a need, people won't support the organization with resources, and it will cease to exist. Consider all the companies that have gone out of business or had to change strategies when advances in technology made their products obsolete.

On the flip side, if an organization continues to exist, it's meeting human needs at some level. Some people may not agree with an organization's strategies, such as manufacturing cigarettes to meet the need for enjoyment at the expense of the need for health. Nonetheless, the organization is meeting human needs or it would cease to exist, even if the needs being met are for profit reasons at the expense of the consumer.

While organizations don't share the same rights as people, they do share many qualities as living systems, such as life cycle development, cultural character or personality, and universal needs. One of these universal organizational needs we've discussed is a *Life-Affirming Purpose.*

Therefore, when the people in an organization lose connection with the needs they're serving—their common *Life-Affirming Purpose*—this disconnection is often reflected in the relationships they have with others within the organization. Instead of everyone working together for a common cause and mutual understanding, the network can fragment into a disparate collection of jobs with the purpose of obtaining a paycheck. When an organization is needs based, both overall and interpersonally, meaning and connection happen, strengthening productivity.

All organizations are strategies to meet human needs. Otherwise, they would cease to exist.

A Life-Changing Realization

Haskvitz says, "Bringing NVC to the business world will support systemic change quicker than any other way I have found. Empathy makes it possible to connect—humanizing workplaces and transforming our world." Following, she describes an interpersonal business situation in which insight opened the door for empathy and connection and thus more potential for productivity.

I offered an individual coaching session to Jerry, the manager of a mid-sized company who was feeling frustrated and annoyed with one of his employees.

After empathically connecting with him (reflecting his feelings back to him so he knew I understood), I asked, "What are you guessing are the feelings and needs of this employee?"

He stopped and was silent; then he had an "aha" moment. He said, "Wow, I never even considered what his feelings and needs might be."

This realization was life changing for Jerry. He noticed all the times he had labeled this person and never stopped to wonder and check in to find out what needs the employee was attempting to meet by the actions that triggered Jerry's annoyance.

In that instant, the employee was humanized, Jerry's judgments were transformed through empathy, and the possibility of connection and willingness to work cooperatively were born.

(Sylvia Haskvitz is listed in Contributors to This Book. This was an actual situation, but the name of the manager has been changed.)

Chances are we've all experienced people who are more challenging for us to get along with than others, who don't perform the way we'd like them to, or who have a different set of values than we do. We think we are being objective when we describe them as "difficult" people or that talking with them is having a "difficult" conversation. In fact, as we've been learning, these are our moralistic judgments of them, a covert expression of our own unmet needs. In the workplace, this friction can cause everything from annoyance to disaster. How can these situations be defused, or better yet, transformed? We can make observations instead of judgments or be transparent about our judgments, consider our own as well as the other person's feelings and needs, and ask for and make clear requests so both parties can have their needs met.

Translate Into OFNR

In other words, we translate what we hear into the language of OFNR (Observations, Feelings, Needs, Requests). We can do this silently if we haven't built mutual trust with this person, or out loud if it's important that we have shared clarity. Just naming feelings out loud and connecting them to needs can dissipate the energy of them if they're unpleasant or enhance their energy if they're enjoyable. For example, when we say we're stressed or sad because we have a need for more rest and play and then we talk about it, the stressed or sad feeling tends to diminish just in the act of sharing. In my experience, having our feelings heard is powerful. When we also make the connection to needs, it can be transformative because an opportunity to make requests of ourselves or others for change often accompanies the expression of feelings and unmet needs. In the case of needs met, the request might be for ways to continue supporting the needs being met or to celebrate what's working as a way to anchor this support.

So sometimes it can be productive to ask someone, "Are you feeling anxious because you'd like more reassurance?" The person might then say yes or perhaps say no and explain that s/he's worried. In response, you might ask if s/he would like to talk about it. Naming the feeling and need and lightening the load by talking about them will enhance this person's overall productivity—a priceless gift you can give a workplace colleague.

For this reason, executive and team leader coaching or mentoring have risen to the highest priorities in organizations that place a premium on productivity. Taking care of people is taking care of business.

I'm often asked how this process, which takes more time than most of us are used to, can fit into a busy workday. A manager at one of my trainings thought of empathy and connection time as a luxury, something that would be nice to do if he had time. Because Rob was telling himself that he didn't have time for this kind of interpersonal connecting process, he couldn't imagine how to even try it. Ironically, he hadn't yet understood that when we identify needs, we get to the core of what

Helping someone name feelings and needs and talk about them will lighten the load and enhance this person's overall productivity—a priceless gift you can give a workplace colleague that can take only a few minutes.

other people are saying, which can be a huge timesaver. I asked if he wanted support around this issue and Rob said yes. I suggested two ideas. First, he could give himself empathy or receive empathy from someone else for his sense of feeling overwhelmed and his need for more ease, progress, and time to meet with others. My guess is that he drives himself hard. In so doing, he denies himself time to connect with himself, which shows up in his work settings as not much time to connect with others. Second, he could just try it, see how it feels, and assess the outcomes for himself and the other party. For example, he could allocate ten minutes, and no more, to play with this form of connection in a low-risk setting. He might try it in a relationship that was not of much consequence, like an interaction with someone in a different department that he likely would not see again, or in one where he already had a high level of mutual trust.

At the end of this training session, Rob said he liked these ideas and was willing to try one of them at a meeting he had later that afternoon. He reported to the training team a couple of weeks later that he had experienced an unexpected benefit when he engaged in this process. He'd become clearer about what he wanted to invest his time in changing and

When we identify needs, we get to the core of what other people are saying, which can be a huge timesaver. We can also save time by eliminating our actions that don't address significant needs.

what he was unwilling to address because of the lack of perceived return for his time.

In the training, I had been sharing interpersonal connection strategies and helping people understand that these very same strategies work for facilitating groups and meetings. We don't have relationships with groups. We have relationships with individuals within groups. In a meeting, even when we're addressing a group of people, we're actually speaking to individuals in rapid succession. Holding the idea that we have relationships with individuals within a group instead of with a group at large is an essential principle for our Chapter Seven topic, How to Increase Team or Organizational Productivity. We are connecting to form relationships with people because we can connect with their feelings and needs, whereas groups and organizations don't have feelings and needs *per se.* Instead, the people in them perceive collective needs for themselves that we refer to as "organizational needs."

In our interactions with people in the workplace, we can train ourselves to hear the needs behind the words. Although we're often making an informed guess, we can directly ask with the intention of connection and caring and in so doing enliven our relationships, or again, we can silently guess. Even this, in my experience, adds value to the energy of connection and to the interchange.

Confirming That What's Said Is What's Heard

When we're expressing something important to us or to group productivity, we have a need to be understood when speaking with others—either one on one or in a group. So I will often say, "Because what I've said is important to me and I don't know if I've been clear, would you be willing to tell me what you heard me say?" This might come across as a "technique" if I weren't comfortable and sincere about wanting clarity. When people can tell I value clarity, I find they are happy to answer in almost all cases. I might also say something like: "My relationship with you is important to me and what I just said could be of value to our relationship. I would appreciate it if you'd tell me what you heard so I know if I'm being clear. Sometimes I'm not as clear as I like. Does that work for you?" Phrase it in a way that's comfortable for you, but I've found that asking, "Do you understand what I just said?" puts the responsibility on the listener and may be less comfortable for the listener to hear. About half the time, I discover the person has *not* heard or understood what I thought I said. I know if I don't ask, I lose the opportunity to build a connection with that person and to create professional clarity.

In our history as youngsters, many of us have experienced being asked if we understand with the intent to shame or punish us instead of connect. While the intention behind the words remains primary, framing our language in a way that's most likely to create connection can be a productive practice in itself. This is particularly important if we hold structural power on our team or in our workplace or provide performance reviews.

Performance Reviews

Using the language of OFNR is especially effective in performance reviews. Not only can we decrease the likelihood of conflicts, discomfort, low morale, and defensiveness when we use observations instead of judgments, but we can determine needs on both sides and make requests to have them met. Managers and employees I've worked with report regularly that the one aspect of their job they dislike the most is giving or receiving performance reviews. The process likely has created more anxiety and distance and lowered morale more than anyone ever intended.

Feedback in the form of objective observations rather than evaluations can enhance communication and help employees understand what is expected of them in a constructive way, as illustrated by the following story.

An administrative assistant who worked in our offices several years ago assisted me with setting up an executive team retreat. When Jayda arrived to begin coordinating logistics, I noticed she was wearing something I enjoyed seeing her in that I hadn't seen before. I commented, almost in passing, that I liked her outfit—the color tones and combination and the style of her skirt—and thought she looked professional in it. Then we got to work. During our debriefing of the day's events, I asked her what she'd gotten value from that day. To my surprise, she said it was the comment I made about liking her outfit. She then related the story to me of how she once had a performance review at another company where she was told that her choice of office attire was "unprofessional." She asked what specifically they didn't like and no one could make an observation. They just said, "Dress more professionally." After this, Jayda spent an hour or more in her closet each day before work, trying to assess what was "professional." Her confusion and frustration brought her to tears many times as she stood there in her closet. I was then shocked to learn that this had been occurring every morning before work for five years. For this reason, the experience of me making the comment about how I liked her attire accompanied by a few specific observations felt like heaven to her. As her employer, I thought she looked professional and could tell her specifically the elements of her outfit that met that criterion.

(Name has been changed.)

As explained previously in Chapter Four and illustrated by Jayda's experience, observations are helpful when they provide specific details that we like and want to see continue or actions we would like to see changed. Instead of saying, "Your reports were excellent this quarter," it would be more helpful to say, "Your reports this quarter had three more sections of information and a format with twice as many illustrations. I look forward to the next batch. Thank you." Or, instead of, "You were late getting those reports to me," it's likely more connecting to say, "I've noticed you've been bringing me the reports on Friday that are due on Wednesday. Are you open to talking about what's going on so we can find a way to support each other with the information and schedule we both want?"

The lists of Feelings Inventory for the Workplace and Needs Inventory for the Workplace in Chapter Three (also in the Appendices) provide reminders to help us connect with our own feelings and needs as well as those of others. The Non-Feelings and Non-Data chart in Chapter Four can help us make distinctions that result in an empathic and thus effective performance review as opposed to one based on either positive or negative evaluations or judgments and blame.

The idea is to use whatever words and actions have the highest probability of showing that you hold the other person's needs equal to yours.

State of Grace Document

In conjunction with NVC, a valuable tool for revealing needs and helping to ensure sustainable collaboration between people both during and following a performance review is the State of Grace Document developed by Maureen K. McCarthy and Zelle Nelson.

Beyond self-awareness, our world now demands collaborative awareness. How can we do this fast-paced dance without stepping on one another's toes? The State of Grace Document is a collaboration process. It's used to build, sustain, and transition internal and external business relationships with trust and respect to increase the health of both people and profits. Each person writes it along with others involved, whether that means two or twenty thousand plus people.

The Document captures what draws each individual to the people involved, the particular job, company, or group, and everyone's work styles, needs when under stress, and expectations. It also provides a path to return to peace, if the need arises. It's often used to replace or enhance traditional legal contracts. By custom designing their relationship container, individuals are the architects of their work, rather than squeezing it into established relationship definitions. The Document is being used in many languages to establish more resilient relationships between individuals, among teams, and throughout entire organizations, global corporations, and other communities. From performance reviews and new business partnerships to boards of directors and client and supplier relationships, State of Grace Documents form the foundation for the needs-based conversations that are often absent from traditional business.

The following explanation of the components of the Document indicates how it can be used in a performance review.

The five components of a State of Grace Document include:

1. **The Story of Us.** Share what draws you to these people and this situation. Continual reengagement and reconnection to your reason for being there is crucial in a performance review.

2. **Interaction Styles and Warning Signs.** Provide the "blueprint of me"—how you work best, what you "look like" on a good day, and what you might need on a bad day that you may not be able to ask for in the moment. These "blueprints" are updated as people evolve and change.

3. **Expectations.** List your core values and nonnegotiable elements—the structure you need to create and sustain this relationship. The standard performance review elements are typically included here.

4. **Questions to Return to Peace.** Each person contributes to a list of questions that will help everyone involved mediate a return to peace if the need arises, making the difficult times shorter and easier. This list might include questions such as: Do we want to say something we haven't been saying? What are we noticing? How is this situation making us feel? Would you be willing to . . .?

5. **Short- and Long-Term Agreements.** *Short-Term:* If something feels even slightly off, you agree that you will wait no longer than twenty-four hours to three days before you reread the entire Document and use the Questions to Return to Peace. *Long-Term:* You agree that you will wait no longer than a specified amount of time, such as five years, to get back together to find peace if the unimaginable

happens and you can't seem to go over your Questions. This commitment helps avoid carrying the pain of an unpleasant ending for a lifetime and never resolving it. It allows an opening through the healing nature of time. To minimize the pain, you also agree that you will not speak of one another among colleagues and in the industry in a way that might do harm.[70]

Traditional performance reviews address goals or targets and how the work measures up against those targets. State of Grace Documents, when used in place of existing performance reviews, in conjunction with the NVC process explained later in this chapter, or both, create the ability to evaluate not only deliverables but how the relationships involved impact the business. In contrast to reviews in which only one side is accountable, these are reciprocally accountable discussions detailing how colleagues can work together effectively. The structure of the State of Grace Document holds the initial performance review, and in each review going forward, all five components are updated as people and projects evolve.

The State of Grace Document generates true 360-degree collaboration. It:

- creates an ongoing conversation based on how all parties can support one another's needs, rather than one-sided, check-box evaluations.
- shifts the process from hierarchical to circular.
- focuses on sustainable collaboration rather than how the subordinate "should" change.
- acts as a third-party mediator, getting people through the difficult conversations with ease.
- provides a deeper level of understanding of self and others, cultivating interdependence.
- exponentially improves the process and the bottom line.

It's easy to switch from traditional performance reviews to State of Grace Documents, as the capacity is already built into its structure. State of Grace Documents increase speed, creativity, and trust within teams and enrich day-to-day interactions. Combining the Document with the

NVC process of Observations, Feelings, Needs, and Requests creates a connecting and sustainable collaborative environment.

(The Center for the State of Grace Document is listed in the Resources, and Maureen K. McCarthy and Zelle Nelson are listed in Contributors to This Book.)

What About Rewards?

It may seem counterintuitive, but within a needs-based context, praise and rewards are seen in the same light as blame and punishment. Why? Because both positive and negative moralistic judgments are considered evaluations. Either may achieve only temporary results in terms of "good" or "bad" behavior if the recipient isn't acting from inherent motivation and a true desire to meet his or her own need to contribute to others. If the person being praised or blamed, for example, isn't acting out of a connection to needs, the praise or blame will be a form of external manipulation. By manipulation, I mean any action we take that's intended to make people do something or continue to do something out of fear, guilt, blame, praise, or reward instead of from their own internal motivation or desire to contribute. Manipulation is attempting to get someone else to do what we want because of our own needs and at the expense of the needs of the other person.

Rewards are often used to entice people into performing better, but do they work? With his groundbreaking book *Punished by Rewards: The Trouble with Gold Stars, Incentive Plans, A's, Praise, and Other Bribes*, Alfie Kohn "has persuaded countless parents, teachers, and managers that attempts to manipulate people with incentives may seem to work in the short run, but they ultimately fail and even do lasting harm. Drawing from hundreds of studies, Kohn demonstrates that people actually do inferior work when they are enticed with money, grades, or other incentives. The more we use artificial inducements to motivate people, the more they lose interest in what we're bribing them to do. . . . Rewards and punishments are two sides of the same coin—and the coin doesn't buy much."[71]

The alternative to external incentives is intrinsic motivation, in which a connection to our own internal needs motivates us, such as the need to contribute, the need for satisfaction of a job well done, or the need for accomplishment.

To be clear, I'm not opposed to praise or reward in general when it's an act of appreciation that grows out of both the giver's and receiver's needs and is observation based. But praise can be as damaging as blame to individual and group productivity if it's not given in this spirit.

Within a needs-based context, praise and rewards can be as damaging as blame and punishment if they're based on judgment or evaluation meant to manipulate instead of on observation meant to enhance intrinsic motivation for the job or tasks.

What If Nothing Works?

What if someone is so connected to external reward that s/he won't perform without it or has not met others' needs according to the job description on multiple occasions? It could be time to consider whether s/he is well matched to the shared values and *Identity* of the organization. Time to determine what needs of the person's are not being met so a better match can be found—either within the same company or, perhaps, at a different organization.

This is a tricky concept. I was advising the president of a firm I was working with once about the repeated frustrations he and others were experiencing with one particular team member. He remarked to me, "How can firing someone be compassionate?" We discussed the idea that the goal was to find a strategy that meets the employee's need for meaningful work, the president's need for the work to be completed, and the organizational need for *Structure* and clarity of roles between the two parties. Sometimes conflict resolution within organizations is conducted with the idea of changing someone's behavior. But as mentioned in Chapter Two, in *Good to Great*, Collins points out that if you have to manage someone, he or she is likely not matched to the skill or to the values of the group.

For this reason, he says, it's important to get the "right" people in the "right" seats.[72] It's much easier to change and teach skills than it is values, which are established very early in the development of our individual makeup.

Be Sure to Look at Systems Issues

Human Resources professionals have long understood that keeping someone in a job or organization when it's not a reliable fit for either the employee or the employer is neither kind nor productive. However, it's imperative to look at the system around the employee first. This applies the idea we discussed earlier that most interpersonal conflicts in the workplace are systems issues and not people issues. If we mediate between people and ignore the system within which both work, we are putting time and resources into fixing a symptom and not the cause. The situations we don't want will likely recur with this employee or the person's replacement.

If we mediate between people and ignore the system within which both work, we are putting time and resources into fixing a symptom and not the cause.

Following are some of the first questions to ask from a needs-based perspective when interpersonal conflict arises in our workplace settings. I use the term "team member" instead of "employee" here because many organizations are already moving away from the hierarchical idea of a "supervisor" or "manager" and "employee" and refer to people as team members instead.

1. Has the team member received observation-based training where all are clear what performance achievement will look like and sound like?
2. Is a system in place to ensure that the training met its objectives and the team member can incorporate the training objectives into his or her work flow?
3. Does the team member have the necessary systems to receive critical information and support on a regular, reliable basis to perform well?
4. Does the team member have the necessary resources to perform well?

5. Is an accountability system built around the team
    member and the tasks or job performance that: a) is
    observation based, b) provides immediate feedback, and
    c) is transparent to the larger team? In other words, does
    the team member have a system for self-management
    supported by transparency of performance? Here's an
    example: Suppose I'm the team leader for ten salespeople.
    Instead of "managing" them, I first discuss with them our
    markets and goals so they know our benchmarks. Then my
    job becomes to make sure they have transparent feedback,
    such as posting progress toward our goals on our shared
    team information space. That way, team members can
    see if they're meeting their goals and if their fellow team
    members are tracking toward their goals, as well. When
    critical information is transparent, people can self-manage
    around agreed-upon goals and parameters.
6. Does the team member have the authority and autonomy
    to make choices to produce the desired results within the
    parameters of how this position fits into the larger work
    system?

If the team leader or those creating the system within which the
team operates haven't addressed these types of systems issues, then
providing conflict resolution between this team member and other
team members or the team leader is a short-term fix to a long-term
problem. It's also inherently unfair to the team member and costly to
the organization if resources are being deployed to fix the symptom and
not the root causes.

Similar to the way being triggered at the interpersonal level
can be perceived as a gift because it points to our unmet individual
needs, team members who aren't performing the way we would
like can be gifts because they often point to flaws in our workplace
systems. By remaining objective and focusing on individual and
organizational needs, a performance review can be an opportunity for
both individual performance improvement and systems review and
improvement.

Needs Performance Observations

One way to encourage direct communication that's likely to be more connecting than separating in the workplace is a process I call Needs Performance Observations (NPO), which is conducted between two people—a manager or team leader and a team member—or between peers or team members. In a group or 360-degree review where everyone is reviewed by several people they choose from the team, for example, it's still conducted between two people, but in multiple pairs. Each person fills it out for him- or herself first and then for the other person. First and foremost, it's a self-review.

Our clients combine the NPO with other components, such as a matrix of accountabilities or goals. I use the NPO in conjunction with the job's "Position Description and Impact Statement," which lists the needs to be met by the person in that position.

The key to combining the Position Description and Impact Statement and the NPO is the section on needs impacts in the job impact statement. As an abbreviated example of needs impacts, when the administrative assistant to the president of a company is fulfilling the position description, the following needs will be met.

Impacts:

    A.   Ease, productivity, and enjoyment for the president in her leadership, management, team, client, and vendor relations

    B.   Order in the office

    C.   Coordination and collaboration among team members

In my consulting with managers and employees alike, one of the frustrations they voice most often is this: An employee or co-worker is technically doing the work specified in his or her traditional job description, but in doing so, s/he is contributing to many other unmet needs. For example, a project team design engineer produces technically accurate plans. However, she contributes to more confusion and tension than other team members would like because of her unwillingness to share key project information with others. In the needs impact section of her job impact statement, one of the critical needs to be met in this position is "collaboration." Thus contextual relationships in the work are valued as much as the work product and content.

The main sections of the NPO are described below, which you can adapt to your own uses. Because all organizations are comprised of smaller teams, the NPO is scalable for use within teams in large organizations.

OVERVIEW OF THE NEEDS PERFORMANCE OBSERVATIONS FORM

As a preface to the dialogue that takes place using this form, it's important that both parties have shared clarity about the organizational needs, particularly the Source Needs of *Identity*, *Life-Affirming Purpose* and *Direction*. Absent this shared reality, performance discussions can become circular and painful because everyone is speaking from the context of the organizational needs without clearly knowing what they are. In other words, if there's conflict or not as much ease as people would like, it may well be because not everyone is clear about the organizational needs and priorities rather than because of the people.

Once this shared clarity has been ensured, participants fill out the NPO form working in pairs.

SECTION 1: What's Working

Share three SPECIFIC OBSERVATIONS of what you see or hear from each other that support your work productivity and enjoyment. These observations are what you would like to see continue that you appreciate in each other or each other's performance. Also express *why* these behaviors are of value to you—specifically what needs are being met. Growing research shows that when we focus on what's working, these conditions are likely to continue and increase.[73] Specific reference to organizational and team goals is critical in this section.

SECTION 2: Getting Clear On What We'd Like to See and Hear More of

Share three SPECIFIC OBSERVATIONS of what you'd like more of in your work with each other. No strategies or solutions yet, just what you'd like more of.

SECTION 3: Insights

After sharing Sections 1 and 2 with each other, discuss any insights, surprises, or new understandings you have about what the other person said in Sections 1 and 2. What did you learn about each other and the way you'd like to work together? (If you aren't certain you've had any insights or new understandings, check to see if you made specific observations in the previous sections. When we make judgments, evaluations, and comparisons instead of specific observations—what we can all agree we see and/or hear—we tend to have more difficulty gaining understanding into our own or another's requests and needs.)

SECTION 4: Specific, Doable Requests—The Strategies for Progress

Based on what you've learned about SPECIFIC OBSERVATIONS and what you'd like to see continue and what you'd like to see more of, what are you willing and able to do?

Choose three *specific, doable* action items that you can accomplish with confidence and that represent a move toward progress.

SECTION 5: Next Steps

Set a time and place to briefly meet again for fifteen minutes within the next seven working days to see how you're doing with the strategies you discussed, using SPECIFIC OBSERVATIONS to measure your progress.

Share the value of the NPO, and if the value was high, plan another NPO review in six months. If the value was low, schedule another NPO review for the next month. Repeat as necessary. Each NPO will take less and less time as you become more versed in making specific observations.

Power in the Workplace

One of the many interpersonal issues we face in the workplace involves structural power and authority. Miki Kashtan is co-founder and lead trainer of Bay Area Nonviolent Communication (BayNVC) and a Center for Nonviolent Communication certified trainer. She tells the story of how power struggles in the workplace can be transformed into collaboration using a needs-based consciousness and observations instead of judgments.

Carol was adamant: "Ben can't tell me how to run *my* department. It's too bad he doesn't like the new production schedule. It's my prerogative to make these decisions, and I don't intend to negotiate everything with him."

I asked Carol if she wanted the freedom to act, respect for her authority, and a sense of flow and trust in her relationship with Ben. Carol concurred and added that she also wanted more ease in their communication.

Later I talked with Ben, and he expressed significant pain about his experience of Carol making decisions that limited his ability to carry out his job responsibilities. He related several such incidents to me. When I suggested that we could find a way for him to be fully open with Carol about his concerns, he laughed in disbelief. "There's no way I can tell her the truth. She doesn't want to hear it. In this economy I can't risk losing my job." I could sense Ben's passion and commitment to the success of the department and the organization, and that he wanted the authority and support to carry out his various initiatives. I also imagined, and he agreed, that he wanted clear and prompt communication. Without it, he was often left in the middle of a project without either freedom or guidance.

Despite his disbelief, Ben was willing to work on how he might present his concerns to Carol. We talked about how he could filter out his many judgments of her and instead focus on the clearest description of her actions that were challenging for him and what was important for him in those incidents. After some weeks, he agreed to risk presenting his concerns to Carol. To his utter amazement, Carol was entirely receptive and graciously took responsibility for acting without considering the effect of her decisions on Ben.

I wasn't as surprised as Ben was. To meet with Carol, Ben had to learn a few powerful lessons that dramatically altered his way of approaching her. The most obvious one was the experience of empowerment from becoming willing to face consequences and trust he can survive them. Coming to the meeting with less fear meant he was more relaxed and calm, which made it easier for Carol to hear him.

Another significant milestone for Ben was developing curiosity about Carol's experience. As he stretched to understand her, he was reminded that she's a human being just like him. In addition, when he could see things from her perspective, he could more easily understand their shared purpose and speak to that when he brought up his concerns. Because Carol didn't experience Ben's view as an attack, she had nothing to oppose and could open to hearing his concerns.

When I met with Carol afterward, it became apparent that while she felt more receptive to Ben, she was still concerned about what she saw as his inability to accept her authority. The dilemma she was facing is common: when would she involve Ben in decisions, and when would it make more sense for her to make executive decisions and expect Ben to follow and support her authority?

In exploring this dilemma, Carol learned that getting Ben, or anyone else, to do something just because she has the power is expensive. The price she pays is not only losing Ben's goodwill and productivity; she could also foresee information being withheld from her when it's contrary to her viewpoint, with potentially negative consequences for the department. At the same time, she knew that plenty of situations would require her to make decisions quickly, with ease, and without *having* to involve Ben or anyone else. That freedom was essential to her in order to fulfill her responsibilities.

At this point we brought Ben into the conversation. Together we identified three things Carol could do to address this dilemma with Ben. One was to distinguish between the *convenience* and the *necessity* of making decisions without consulting with Ben. The second was to share with him more transparently about decisions she made on her own. And the third was to invite feedback about the effect of her decisions on his ability to perform his job. Over time, this combined strategy would increase trust and result in exactly what they each wanted. Ben would have more willingness to accept decisions Carol made without consulting him, and Carol would have more willingness to include him in decisions.

Is collaboration across power differences possible or an oxymoron? When people in authority assert their power as a matter of principle rather than based on need, and when people with less authority operate out of fear, there won't be enough trust for collaboration. When communication and agreements are explicit, roles are clear, and learning is an integral part of the work, power differences are much less likely to interfere with the flow of collaboration and mutual support toward a common goal.

(Miki Kashtan is listed in Contributors to This Book. The situation described here combines elements of real situations with which she's been involved. The names have been changed.)

An Enlightening Exercise

In a Needs-Based Leadership and Communication Training, I asked participants to pair up and do an exercise based on the process of NVC. They had all learned the basics but were still new to using this language in their conversations. For this exercise, they were to take turns speaking and listening and ask each other, "In the sessions so far, what is one thing that has been of value?" I gave them the following guidelines.

Person speaking:

- Make an **observation** about what's been of value.
- What do you **feel** about this one thing?
- What **need** is met or unmet in connection to this?
- What's one **request** you have of yourself or someone else to meet or continue to meet this need?

Person listening:

- **Listen** silently if you are clear about the other person's observation, feeling, need, and request.
- If you are not clear, ask **clarifying questions** such as the following.
- **Observation** – "What did you see or hear that was of value?"
- **Feeling and Need** – "Are you feeling excited because this gives you hope?"
- **Request** –"What's one request that would meet or keep meeting this need?"

Remember to WAIT

I gave them only a few minutes for these conversations, but the results were enlightening for them and gratifying for me. They found that the process required them to think about what they were going to say and become clear—the WAIT concept of Why Am I Talking?—and "organize and distill" their thoughts so they could "cut to the chase." I reminded them that people can take in about forty words in one segment, so I encouraged them to be brief.

We talk throughout the day and we don't often do it consciously, but it's a practice to have clarity about what we want to say as well as to listen to the deepest levels of what others are expressing. In fact, every time we open our mouth, we put an obligation on whoever hears what's coming out to listen. This can be burdensome if we aren't clear why we're talking or what we want the other person to do about it. The NVC process gets to the heart of the conversation more quickly than our usual speaking patterns. Then we can request what we want from our listeners and ask if that works for them. Remember that

We talk throughout the day and we don't often do it consciously, but it's a practice to have clarity about what we want to say as well as to listen to the deepest levels of what others are expressing.

sometimes people just want us to listen and we don't need to respond. But if we're silently listening for their feelings and needs, we can gain a far deeper understanding of what they are saying—and we can ask clarifying questions that zero in on their underlying feelings and needs. Often we can help a speaker understand his or her own message better by asking these types of questions.

Beyond Ego

Participants seemed genuinely surprised at the honesty that was "beyond ego" resulting from pure observation rather than judgment. It relieved them of worrying about how the other person would react to their statements. One person commented he was (pleasantly) surprised at the response when he stated his needs without hedging. Another found that this type of genuine expression quickly "led to resolution" and someone else "felt relief" and "less fear." Others mentioned a higher "level of trust" and "comfort." By observing without judgment, one of the women said she was able to understand and accept the other person better and could see that it would encourage forgiveness because you realize "there are factors you don't know about so you can't judge."

Fear of Others' Judgments

These management team members had typical adult responses to NVC. It seems that as we grow up, we develop a fear of others' judgments that is refreshingly dissipated in this process. Haskvitz tells of an eighth-grade boy in a Montessori school where she was facilitating. After a game of "empathy poker," in which students guessed one another's feelings and needs based on situations the children brought up, this eighth-grader came up to Haskvitz and said "Thank you." Curious, she asked what he was responding to with gratitude. The boy said it was the first time in school that he had ever wanted to participate because it was about sharing feelings and needs, and he didn't have to worry about whether his answer was "correct" or "incorrect." In fact, either response made him not want to participate in class discussions.

He simply wanted the freedom to share his truth in a way that was accepted. . . . And so do we.

Transparency

As one of the group participants admitted, "Transparency can be uncomfortable," and yes, that's true at first. But you'll find that when you're transparent with honesty and sincerity and within the guidelines of what's considered professional in your work setting, people find it refreshing. It can powerfully transform an uncomfortable situation. Remember that this process of empathic connection is one of revolution because we've been conditioned for years and years. Think of yourself as committing a revolutionary act of productivity.

A story that illustrates this occurred during a meeting of about fifty residents of an RV park within a construction project area for a client. The project team manager was presenting information about the construction impacts. One of the residents grew increasingly agitated and began speaking in a tone that was louder than my colleagues and I wanted and using words that were uncomfortable for the project team manager to hear. Tension filled the room.

At this point, I recognized an opportunity to defuse the situation. I chose two actions. First, I empathized silently to myself about the resident who was speaking, guessing what he might be feeling and his unmet needs. This took only a few seconds. Then, since tensions were high, I stepped in between him and the project manager and out of my need for transparency said to the whole group: "I'm uncomfortable with the language I'm hearing right now. Is anyone else uncomfortable?" I was curious because perhaps only the project team was uncomfortable because of our role in the meeting. After asking, about two-thirds of the people in the room raised their hands. The resident who had been speaking could see his effect on others and self-regulated his voice volume and word choices. I didn't have to say anything more about his behavior. I transparently shared my discomfort and expressed sincere curiosity in my inquiry to the group about their discomfort.

Imagine a workplace where people are transparent about their feelings and needs; where people check with others if they are unclear or want to know if others are clear. People wouldn't have to guess what others need or understand (and now they would want to know), and mind games, undercurrents, and power

When you're transparent with honesty and sincerity and within the guidelines of what's considered professional in your work setting, people often find it inspiring.

struggles would become obsolete. The resulting cooperation would boost productivity, morale, and thus the organization's success.

Intention and Desire to Connect

If you're uncomfortable with the words "feelings" and "needs" stated explicitly in your workplace, don't use them. Just say, "Are you frustrated because you'd like more ease in communication?" Find words that match your culture. What matters is your intention with this process and your desire to connect out of curiosity for what the other person is experiencing.

In 2006, I helped design a training in India using the NVC/IC model for a group of "ambassadors" of a nonprofit organization. They acted as liaisons between the organization and other volunteers as well as community residents. A young local woman on our planning team commented that she thought many people would be uncomfortable with the idea of discussing or naming feelings. Thus we focused primarily on helping them identify the needs that might be met or unmet for those with whom they were working. We coupled that with how to express their individual and organizational needs so that both listening empathically and expressing empathically were skills learned in the training. Workshop leaders reported that, based on feedback, the workshops were a success. Participants reported a sense of empowerment and clarity in how to help others while still maintaining connection to their own needs and those critical to the organization.

As this example illustrates, you can adapt the process to your workplace environment and norms.

Charisma

When people are connected to their own feelings and needs and we're in their presence, we often experience a powerful attraction to them. It's very natural. I believe that people with the kind of true, often quiet charisma that Collins describes in *Good to Great* as professional will coupled with personal humility are people connected with their own needs, whether or not they have structural power. When they do have structural power, it creates a way to connect with others—a natural human resonance—irrespective of "rank." One of the ways I like to define humility is the willingness to be open to points contrary to our own. When we're truly connected to our feelings and needs, we become naturally curious about "what's alive in us" and what's happening in others, as well, without the threat that one or the other of us has to be right or wrong.

When people are connected to their own feelings and needs and we're in their presence, we experience a powerful attraction to them.

Go Slow to Go Fast

We've been indoctrinated by a society that values what we do versus who we are. One of the participants in the Needs-Based Leadership and Communication Training said he tends to leap too quickly to try to "fix" a situation without focusing on needs. He's busier than he would like to be and finds that if he doesn't take the time in the moment to focus on needs, later the inquiry loses its immediacy. While I could certainly understand that, I pointed out (and have observed) that checking out needs saves an exponential amount of time down the road—and not that far down the road. While sometimes it may be beneficial and logical to leap to requests, especially if you know someone well, it's been my experience that in the workplace, the idea is to "go slow to go fast."

Spending time connecting may seem like a luxury, but it's worth taking the time to build context and connection. Clarity and efficiency are greatly enhanced.

I told the group about my business experiences with Japanese companies. There, the emphasis is on relationships. Japanese business people don't want to move into the main work subject until they look for an alignment of needs, values, and background. *Then* they talk about content. They enjoy hearing where you grew up, what your hobbies are— anything that helps them understand who you are as a whole person, not just a professional. In Japan, when two companies merge, one of the first things they do is hold a tree planting ceremony at which both companies are represented and the tree symbolizes what they will grow together.

Reap the Benefits

Based on their feedback, the bottom line for these participants was that having a needs-based consciousness and using the simple steps of NVC in communication as both leaders and employees:

- gave them more "empathy" for and "resonance and ease" with the other person, enhancing "understanding, acceptance, and forgiveness."
- made the communication "more efficient" and "got to the heart of the matter quicker."
- imparted "value in learning to listen in this way where the focus is completely on the other person" and they're "not planning what to say next."
- provided "comfort" in knowing that they could "take care of" their "own needs first" and also "help others meet their needs."
- created a "human connectedness that was beyond intellectual."

I've found these benefits to be true for anyone who learns this process. Clearly, they make it worth the effort it takes to develop the skills of NVC and begin to spread empathy throughout the organization.

※ ※ ※ ※

This chapter has focused on how connecting with our own needs and those of others enhances productivity in the workplace. This interpersonal connection is the foundation of an effective team and an effective organization, which we will address in Chapter Seven.

SEVEN

How to Increase Team or Organizational Productivity

"What is the role of a team leader [versus a traditional supervisor]? Three consistent attributes . . . are associated with the most successful leaders in both traditional and empowered organizations.

1. The ability to create strong mutual respect between the workers and the leader. 2. Assuring that the job gets done. 3. Providing leadership in getting problems solved. . . . Thus the primary target of the team leader's work expands from tasks (the work) to relationships (things that affect how the work gets done), and from individuals (a smaller part of the work unit) to teams (a larger part of the work unit)."[74]

—Kimball Fisher, *Leading Self-Directed Work Teams*

As pointed out in Chapter Four, an organization is a collective. The people within the organization perceive whether its six universal organizational needs are met or not. All organizations, teams, or groups have these needs, whether people are aware of them or not. The organizational needs for *Identity, Life-Affirming Purpose, Direction, Structure, Energy,* and *Expression* arise from the people's own needs and the needs of the customers and markets they serve. Productivity is enhanced when the six (collective) organizational needs are well defined and people in the organization understand what they are and are motivated by them.

During the Planning and Implementation stages, people within the whole system interact with one another individually, within teams, and with those served by the organization. When these communications are conducted with organized and widespread empathy—with the intention of connecting to each individual's feelings and needs, using observations rather than evaluations and requests rather than demands—conflict is minimized and productivity optimized.

We've seen how effective leaders support productivity by helping people meet their individual needs for autonomy and contribution. They practice "non-management" from an objective, needs-based consciousness rather than one of controlling and manipulating with fear, guilt, shame, blame, or even praise and reward.

Here's an example of what can happen when a company adheres to this kind of approach.

W. L. Gore & Associates, creators of the renowned Gore-Tex® waterproof material as well as many other technology-driven innovations, has a nonhierarchical system of interconnected relationships between associates—and no traditional bosses. The company places an emphasis on relationships and direct communication. One look at the company's website (www. gore.com) gives a picture of connection and collaboration. The homepage presents a series of questions, such as: "What happens when a global company . . truly believes . . . knows . . . shows that people are its greatest asset?" And then . . . "What happens when people . . . own their own destiny?"[75]

The site goes on to address these questions, but the short answer is—a lot.

In 2010, Gore marked its thirteenth consecutive year of being named to *Fortune* magazine's list of the "100 Best Companies to Work For" in the United States. It has also been named one of the best places to work in France, Germany, Italy, and the United Kingdom for several years in a row. Company founder Bill Gore once said, "The objective of the Enterprise is to make money and have fun doing so." [76]

The company is clear about its organizational *Identity, Life-Affirming Purpose,* and *Direction* and has developed a unique culture that provides the organizational *Structure* and *Energy* to support its inherent core values and beliefs. The *Expression* of its organizational needs stands out as clear and compelling not only to its associates, who are all part owners through its associate stock plan, but also to its customers, vendors, and suppliers.

"How does all this happen?" asks another question on the website. "Associates (not employees) are hired for general work areas. With the guidance of their sponsors (not bosses) and a growing understanding of opportunities and team objectives, associates commit to projects that match their skills. All of this takes place in an environment that combines freedom with cooperation and autonomy with synergy." . . . Gore is "a team-based, flat lattice organization that fosters personal initiative. . . . This unique kind of corporate structure has proven to be a significant contributor to associate satisfaction and retention." [77]

More and more, organizations are realizing the importance of teams as well as a key phrase mentioned above: "Freedom with cooperation." Collins and Porras point out a similar dynamic relationship between two seemingly opposite paradigms in *Built to Last.* In their terms, the "core ideology provides continuity and *stability,*" while the "drive for progress urges continual *change* (new directions, new methods, new strategies, and so on)." Core ideology "is by its very nature, a *conservative* act," while "the drive for progress can lead to dramatic, radical, and *revolutionary* change." [78] In Integrated Clarity language, the core ideology consists of the inherent, unchanging needs and values, and the drive for progress involves the changing strategies.

Following is another kind of example, in which I worked with a newly formed business association to address their identity and purpose before they implemented strategies.

A 2005 article in the *Arizona Daily Star* business section began, "The Palo Verde Alvernon Business District was having an identity crisis." This merchants association had formed in response to the closure of a major street overpass for construction because local merchants were concerned about the effect of the closure on their businesses. However, the newly formed group was having trouble defining its purpose. It wanted to remain as a support for the more than seven hundred diverse local businesses after the construction was completed.

I was brought in as a consultant and could see that the group members had commitment and a lot of strategies and ideas, but they didn't have a starting point. Trying to duplicate other group models that didn't fit, they were frustrated.

I reminded them that deciding what they wanted to do before defining who they wanted to be as a group was like starting a career without knowing what it is you're passionate about doing. I helped them work through the organizational needs of *Identity, Life-Affirming Purpose, and Direction* so they would know how the group would express itself in terms of communicating to the other businesses in the area. The members identified that the sense of community was important to them and that the purpose of the association was to serve as the voice of that community. Then the group was able to develop a more formal structure and ways to reach out to the businesses.

The association's team found value in defining the group's needs, beginning with *Identity* and *Life-Affirming Purpose*. From that clarity, the other needs could be more effectively addressed, eventually helping to fulfill the needs of the local business community.[79]

In larger organizations, the productivity of its teams determines the success and productivity of the organization as a whole. Therefore, this chapter provides ideas for facilitating team meetings for productive outcomes. It also explains the Organizational Needs Dashboard, a measuring and monitoring tool. The dashboard is a means of sharing data, the organizational equivalent of feelings, and informing all teams of needs met and unmet. Chapter Eight then provides a decision-making tool that can be used for clarity and cooperation in groups or teams across the spectrum of job responsibilities.

Revisiting the IC Framework for Whole Systems

Let's reconsider the whole system orientation of the Integrated Clarity Framework. The Four Steps of the framework are presented in Chapter Four and are also in the Appendices. The four steps with regard to the organization are parallel to NVC's OFNR (Observations, Feelings, Needs, Requests) for individuals. These are:

1. **Identify Data**
   - Observations that can be analyzed, compared, measured
   - Dashboards, metrics, and measurements; data that mark where the organization is versus where we would like it to be and allow for the creation of metrics for best practices

2. **Identify Feelings About Observations and Business Data**
   - Feelings such as: worried, excited, irritated, confident, disappointed, comfortable versus non-feeling judgments or evaluations, such as: incompetent, underperforming, profitable. (Rather, use numbers to describe numeric or financial situations.)

3. **Connect Data to Organizational Needs**

Source Needs	Leveraging Needs
Identity	Structure
Life-Affirming Purpose	Energy
Direction	Expression

4. **Develop Strategic Intentions**

In organizations, requests are strategies. Strategic planning and implementation on a whole system level are intended to meet organizational needs that people in the system perceive and monitor.

The difference between a strategy and a plan is that a strategy is a request to meet a need or continue meeting a need that's already been met. A plan is a composite of a number of strategies, or requests, put together for a group or organization in a coordinated and orchestrated implementation schedule. Like a strategy for an individual, the plan is stated:

- in terms of concrete observations (e.g., #1 in regional market share),
- in the affirmative (what we will do, not what we won't do),
- with a present moment request ("Are we willing to make this initiative our first priority?"), and
- from the basis of need ("What human needs will we serve by our actions?").

The strategy is a request, and the outcome is the destination. A "positive" outcome is defined in specific, observable terms because "positive" is an evaluation or judgment and otherwise can have different interpretations. *Outcome goals* are defined as what we'd like to have happen but don't have control over, whereas *process goals* are actions we're going to take that we have 100 percent control over. The Integrated Clarity model places a premium on process goals. We don't want to be attached to outcomes—just to keep what works and not keep what doesn't. Many factors outside our control can influence outcome.

The following is an example of how to carry out the Four Steps on the organizational level in meetings, or strategic conversations, which involves an interplay of organizational needs and individual needs.

In 2010, I facilitated a strategic planning retreat for a group of executives. While driving me to the meeting, the CEO briefed me on key principals who would be in the sessions. When she started talking about a particular department head, she became visibly more agitated and sighed several times, expressing her frustration with the communication patterns she had with this member of her team. I empathized with her about her hopelessness that this pattern would never change and about her need for connection and progress. She thought their conversations were circular and that when she asked this executive for solutions, her team member came back with more questions instead of answers—and around and around they went, with not as much progress as either of them wanted. When I guessed that she was ready, I asked her if she would like suggestions about how to connect with this person. She said, "Yes, please. I'm desperate for change around this and have run out of ideas."

During the facilitation, the department head she had been referring to spoke longer than anyone wanted. His continual focus was on his department's budget and what he perceived would be a significant decrease in his budget due to organization-wide cost trimming. He even said, "I don't know why I'm talking so long about the budget, but I feel these things have to be said and put on the table."

As facilitator, I could see how he was losing connection with the group the longer he spoke and the more frequently he spoke about the same issues. Because it was early in the retreat and they were all establishing their voices, I didn't intercede into the group dialogue, but from what I heard, I guessed at how frustrated he was and how he was experiencing an unmet need to be understood.

At lunch, I overheard one of his team members comment to another about how pleased he was that they were all being so positive despite their serious issues regarding finances—"except for one person."

After lunch, the department head spoke again, and the same pattern occurred. This time, I interrupted him, not to take attention away from him but to find ways to keep him more connected to the group while he expressed something important to him. I said I had noticed his comment that he wasn't sure why he was talking longer than he wanted (observation about individual need for clarity), and I repeated some specific financial information back to him (observation about organizational need for *Energy*). I then told him I was equally puzzled about the main reason he was speaking and began guessing that he felt worried (feeling) about his department and had a need for transparency (need).

Then came the turning point that led to immediate productivity for individuals in the meeting as well as organizational productivity in the future. Out of my own need for clarity, I asked him if he had a request of himself and others. He paused and said, "Oh. A request? Yes. I want a meeting to clarify not just my budget but the budgets of other departments." I then asked him a few more questions about which people he wanted in the meeting and when he would like to hold it. I supported him in making the request instead of continuing to speak without knowing why he was speaking. The pattern of circular dialogue and speaking longer than he wanted ended because all along he wanted to make a request but didn't have clarity about making it. Thus time was saved and productivity gained for the whole team.

Further, all the people he wanted to attend his requested meeting said they would come, and they included another department head, who had an idea for a collaborative project between their departments for new customer markets. In addition, the second department head offered to share his ideas about how he works with the corporate budget guidelines. So the meeting born out of one person's frustrations grew into possibilities for growth and collaboration for all.

You can see how conducting meetings in this way helps to meet both individual and organizational needs. The following are guidelines for facilitating meetings using NVC and framing the conversations in terms of IC's universal organizational needs, which can help you gather information and opinions and make decisions expeditiously. Plus it will meet everyone's needs, which can boost morale, create cohesion, and give everyone the satisfaction of making progress.

Facilitating a Meeting

In Chapters Four and Six, we discussed the acronym WAIT, which stands for Why Am I Talking? Although it's an effective question that enhances productivity in meetings, it's preceded by a more critical question: Why Am I Meeting? So before you facilitate (or attend) a meeting, gain clarity about the needs you want the session to meet, and when you call the meeting (or accept an invitation to one), be clear, at least with yourself and if possible with every team member, about the purpose of it and your role in it.

Your meeting takes on an entirely different flavor when you ask questions that are intended to connect and track feelings and needs. Facilitate the process, not the people. All people have inherent wisdom. I suggest never asking a question to which you know the answer. For example, instead of asking, "What are the three main points we discussed last week?" ask, "What are you remembering as the three main points we discussed last week?" The first question has correct or incorrect answers. With the second question, the person answering can only be correct.

When facilitating, never ask questions to which you already know the answers.

Track needs. As a facilitator, you're acting as a needs "traffic cop," tracking people's needs and letting one person or need at a time through and holding back others until it's their turn so various needs don't become intertwined. Distinguish separate issues. Slow down to speed up. Allow people to connect with feelings and needs. You want to ensure that everyone has the opportunity to be heard.

You might say, "Before we move to that, I want to understand what Joe said." The others then tend to respond to what that person said. In this way, the conversation is responsive to what's alive in the moment. Never assume that things stay the same. People are always changing, and if you are facilitating, they will see you as a leader if you keep responding to what's alive in the moment. If you are not the facilitator, you can still be a leader of the moment, helping track needs and supporting the facilitator in this way.

Remember that you don't have a relationship with the group per se—only with individuals within the group. It's still an interpersonal relationship, but on a more complex level. Throughout a conversation, ask questions such as, "Is this helping your need for clarity, comfort, or specificity?" or "Does that help?" or "Did I answer your question?" This process gives your conversation structure throughout the meeting and keeps it from ballooning into multiple directions at once.

Track requests or strategies. You might ask, "Would you like to make a request for help to meet your need for more specificity?" Keep requests in the present moment (e.g., "Would you be willing to write up that report?". . . instead of "Would you write up that report?") Then check to make sure that the requests or strategies for the meeting have been met.

Track agreements. For example, say to everyone, "So we're in agreement, then, that we're going to _____."

Interrupt when necessary. Yes, sometimes it's expeditious to interrupt if someone is going on longer than most want or talking about a topic no one is interested in or that's repetitious. Interruption is powerful if you do it with care and with connection to needs. You may want to explain in advance by saying, "Sometimes I will interrupt if I see that people aren't connecting with what one of you is saying because I want people to stay connected as much as possible." You can also be direct and in the moment: "I'm going to stop you now because I can see that others aren't following you and I want to maintain understanding on this issue."

Along those lines, continue to ask people to reflect back what you or others have said so you can be sure what is said is clear. It's the speaker's responsibility to make sure he or she is expressing clearly, not everyone else's to understand. In a group, if one person hasn't heard what you or someone else has said, others generally haven't either. As a formal facilitator (or as a participant who takes the role of facilitator informally for a moment from time to time), it's your job to maintain connections.

Use OFNR. When you're facilitating (formally or informally), remember to connect with yourself as well as encourage others to use Observations, Feelings, Needs, and Requests to keep the contextual connections alive and not just focus on the content. That's the basic premise of this process. If you focus only on content, people become tired. If the need for connection is met, they are energized.

We have some work to do in our meetings. When I asked participants in one of my groups to explain why they thought that 30 to 50 percent of what is said is not heard, they gave the following reasons:

- Our inner dialogue gets in the way.
- Our own needs become a filter.
- We're preoccupied with defending ourselves or planning our response.
- We're focused on hearing what would most support our own agenda—what we want to hear.
- We've already judged the person's response because of preconceived notions about that person.
- The delivery isn't clear, so we can't hear it. (The speaker didn't apply the WAIT principle.)
- The ego gets in the way. The person speaking is more interested in making sure everyone thinks s/he is important than getting across what s/he has to say.
- Either or both the speaker and listener are too nervous because they're afraid of the other person's judgments.

As a facilitator, you can help people avoid these ways of thinking and develop a genuine interest in what others have to contribute. When you stay present to "what's alive in the room" and encourage the expression of feelings and needs, it brings an openness that tends to dissipate these kinds of concerns. It humanizes the process by connecting people empathically. Thus concrete discussions about specific issues take on a completely different flavor of productivity and authentic agreement, which saves cost and time in the future. One of the situations most damaging to productivity arises when people don't truly agree during the discussion and planning phases of an initiative. They may say they agree out of fear, guilt, or shame and then choose to not fully support the initiative during the implementation phase.

> *When you stay present to "what's alive in the room" and encourage the expression of feelings and needs, it brings an openness that leads to more authentic agreement, which supports strategic implementation.*

Sometimes something big happens in a meeting, and if people aren't aligned, they might ignore it. Some are aware of it, some aren't.

The meeting then turns into several small groups with different levels of understanding. As a facilitator, you can say, "I want to stay connected to what the group is doing, but at the same time, I just heard ____. I wonder if everyone else heard that."

Even if you are not the designated facilitator, you can facilitate at certain times by asking for clarification to meet your own needs. It's highly likely that others share your unmet needs.

Be transparent. You can adjust your level of transparency to meet your comfort level. It simply means to be honest. It isn't always being "nice," but to me, it's being kind. Being transparent can get to the heart of the matter quickly, which boosts productivity. Think back to my story about starting a strategic conversation with an executive team in which a number of the department heads kept doing paperwork or other tasks. I didn't want to waste their time or mine if what I had to say wasn't of interest to them, so I just told them I had something I thought was of value that I wanted to share with them but didn't want to continue if they weren't interested. I then had their attention—not because they were suddenly interested in what I had to say (because they didn't know exactly what it was), but because they were refreshingly surprised by my transparency. From then on, we made progress, and the connection turned out to be quite productive for all of us.

Staying connected to your own needs and being transparent means taking a risk, but I've found that much more often than not, people respond in a powerful way that I like. They aren't accustomed to authenticity, to realness, but at some level, we all crave it.

Appreciate appreciation. Focusing on and appreciating what's working while also being aware of what's not working can stimulate organizational change and energize the workforce. When appreciation, recognition, and acknowledgment are connected directly to needs through OFNR, they perpetuate the behavior we want to continue.

Use the power of the "finish line." Groups thrive when they have a shared reality of what needs they're meeting with a focused use of resources on a particular timetable that members either agree to or develop together. This vision of the finish line is part of the organizational need for *Direction*. Shared clarity and agreement on what team members would like to accomplish, what needs these actions would meet, and when they would like to achieve certain milestones can invigorate a team. When teams have connection as well as thinking, planning, and doing, these projects can be highly energizing for team members—and the markets they serve, as well. Collins echoes this in his concept of the Big Hairy Audacious Goal (BHAG) in *Built to Last*. "A BHAG engages people—it reaches out and grabs them in the gut. It is tangible, energizing, highly focused. People 'get it' right away; it takes little or no explanation."[80]

Check in and check out.

Sometimes you can have participants check in. If this level of sharing is not comfortable in your work culture, open with a more practical question. The one I like to begin with, especially in groups of different types of participants

Groups thrive when they have a shared reality of what needs they're meeting with a focused use of resources on a specific, observable timetable.

meeting for the first time is, "What would make this meeting of value for you by the time you leave?" If the topic falls into the meeting agenda, we list it as a discussion item. If it doesn't, we place it on a list of items for another meeting. Every idea and request is captured and addressed. Everyone learns a great deal about the other participants by hearing what would be of value for him or her. This is a subtle way to connect that adds value to the concrete discussion.

Always offer participants the opportunity to "check out" at the end of the meeting by asking them each to briefly state what they are feeling, what they have learned from the session, and what needs were met or unmet. I like to ask people to give one or two words— literally—to summarize how they are thinking or what they are thinking as they leave the meeting. Fifteen participants can do this in one minute or less. Every group I've worked with has enjoyed this check-out process immensely. I always give people the option to pass, and while very rarely do people say "pass," when they do, it's still connecting to hear their choice.

Organizational Needs Dashboard

In order to meet needs, we have to know what they are. Many teams and organizations track their key performance indicators on a dashboard of some kind, which documents the information they consider most important to keep an eye on collectively. Dashboards might be in the form of regular reports, spreadsheets, or internal websites. Financial and sales information are often the first to populate dashboards because of the ease with which numerical and market information can be translated into reports on an ongoing basis.

The purpose of a dashboard is to present information so that all can see it, track it on a regular basis, see if they are getting closer to or further away from agreed-upon goals, and make operational and strategic decisions based on current information.

In an organizational needs dashboard, all of these indicators fit under one of the six universal organizational needs as outlined in IC. In this way, the individual needs-based consciousness has an organizational counterpart. The needs of both the organization and individuals—from employees and shareholders to customers and communities—can be met at the same time with strategies that meet as many needs as possible. Consider these examples:

Core values. These fit with *Identity*. In needs-based consciousness, these values are not something we aspire to, but something that is part of our natural makeup, genetically encoded in our organizations and teams from their inception. Needs and values can be used interchangeably in this context. We know what needs are core because of the level of stimulation triggered when this need is met or goes unmet. Many groups I've worked with aren't connected to their intrinsic values. Instead, they think of what they'd like to be only to find that it's more difficult than they thought to become something they're not. In other words, if they have values that aren't part of their current core needs, they'll be frustrated and less likely to be successful because they aren't aligned to their authentic *Identity*.

Collins provides an example in *Good to Great*: "When Gillette executives made the choice to build sophisticated, relatively expensive shaving systems rather than fight a low-margin battle with disposables, they did so in large part because they just couldn't get excited about cheap disposable razors."[81] It's not easy to shift from developing inexpensive to expensive products. It requires more R&D, retooling of manufacturing, new marketing efforts, and so on. This is a huge change; but the change is likely worth the effort and expense if the result aligns with core values.

While organizational needs or values change more slowly than individual needs because they reflect a collective change in the perception of a group of people, they are mutable nonetheless. For organizations that have the kind of widespread empathic connection to the customer that Patnaik

If organizations have values that aren't part of their current core needs, they'll be less likely to be successful because they aren't aligned to their authentic Identity.

documents in *Wired to Care*, responding to the needs of their customers stimulates internal changes faster than traditional organizations that are more introspective. The first is customer driven while the second is management driven.

An organization is in no danger of losing touch with the organizational needs of *Identity* or *Life-Affirming Purpose* if it's customer driven. This tension between maintaining a stable core (*Identity*) and being responsive to the organization's market (*Life-Affirming Purpose*) is the "both/and" dynamic that Collins and Porras describe in *Built to Last* as "preserve the core and stimulate progress." [82]

Over time, we see patterns that reveal more stable core needs and needs that aren't as important to us as individuals or the organization as a whole. But at any given time, any of these needs might be more or less active, which invites us to be present to each moment as new.

Thus both individual needs and organizational needs change in terms of being met or unmet in any given moment. Being aware of this allows us to fully receive the most current information about people and the markets around us.

Sales. The information about the customer and what needs your product or service meets for them is part of *Life-Affirming Purpose*. Sales targets and numbers fit with the financial part of the need for *Energy*.

Marketing, product development, and innovation. How we connect and communicate with the customer and the feedback we receive from them about how we are or aren't meeting their needs fits with the need for *Expression*. The more empathically connected we are to people either in or representing our current and future markets, the more likely we are to be able to create products and services that will add value to them and our organizations.

There are no "right" or "wrong" categories in which to track key indicators within the organizational needs framework. What's important is to make the dashboard needs based and ensure it works for those who use it. People find that following critical indicators and making key distinctions about what needs they meet, similar to the economic driver concept in the *Good to Great* Hedgehog Concept discussed earlier, makes the organizational needs dashboard manageable and effective.

＊ ＊ ＊ ＊

This chapter has shown how to increase team and organizational productivity through a needs-based consciousness and tools to track progress in meeting organizational and individual needs. Chapter Eight explains how to shorten the time for this task and maintain group connection and cohesion using needs-based decision-making tools.

EIGHT

Needs-Based Decision-Making Tools

*[When you make a decision] "... the one thing
you should always be doing is considering your emotions,
thinking about why you're feeling what you're feeling."* [83]

—Jonah Lehrer, *How We Decide*

Needs-based consciousness in decision making in our workplaces and teams runs contrary to what most of us are accustomed to, which is the idea that the majority rules. We haven't been trained and educated in the concept that all needs matter and that strategies exist to meet all needs at the same time. Our workplaces are filled with processes born out of the thinking and models of domination hierarchy. These antiquated approaches developed around the idea of preserving the *status quo* of power systems or meeting the needs for stability and order so that structural power remained with certain predetermined groups of people.

Today, many in our world and our workplaces recognize that a rise in consciousness in which more needs are met for more people—from customers to employees to shareholders—creates more value for all stakeholders, including those who have structural power. In the early history of humankind when chaos and unpredictability were common in most parts of the world, resources were scarce and essential to life.

According to Buckminster Fuller, as early as two to three decades ago, the world began producing enough life resources such as food to feed the entire global population. Hunger, therefore, is no longer an agricultural or resource problem, but a system problem of distribution and consciousness. This situation translates to our workplaces. In our work settings, most of us likely have our basic needs met, such as shelter, water, light, and the like. Our primary concerns can now focus on meeting the need for raising our consciousness in how we Connect-Think-Do.

Chances are you've been in groups that have made decisions using the traditional model for decision making. How do you feel when the majority rules and you are in the minority—when you don't agree with the decision proposed and no one seems to care why?

In the traditional model of majority rule, the question is black or white: Are you for or against this proposal? The objective: get at least 51 percent to agree with the proposal. The problem with this approach is you have limited choices in meeting both the *need for progress* for the group and the *need for group cohesion* at the same time. Any single proposal holds the risk that almost half the group, 49 percent, might disagree with it and would then have to live with the proposal that the other 51 percent approved. The need for progress is met in that a decision is made, but the need for group cohesion goes unmet.

This can be a problem for three reasons. First, those who vote against the proposal might see something no one else sees and have an alternate viewpoint to contribute. Diversity of opinions can increase productivity. Second, having been left out or left behind, those who vote no aren't invested in the success of the decision and are likely to work against it or at minimum not work for it. Third, they might feel their needs haven't been heard. In the absence of needs awareness, their needs don't matter as much as the need for a decision and progress. The group as a whole is de-energized, having lost connection with those who voted no.

Majority-rule models value efficiency and progress above connection and group cohesion. On the flip side but still equally unable to hold both the need for progress and group cohesion, we have models that value group process over getting to a decision. I experience these processes as taking longer than most group members are willing to tolerate, and often participants are left with a sense of disappointment when decisions aren't made and progress isn't achieved. You've been to these kinds of meetings. It seems like everyone has an opinion, everyone wants to be heard, and yet the group has no system to progress the variety of thoughts and ideas. Instead, it appears to be a circular conversation where many people repeat what's already been said without adding anything new to the dialogue.

The Consent Model

Enter the needs-based Consent Model. I call it a consent rather than consensus model because by applying NVC-inspired needs awareness, this model goes beyond a desire for consensus, or agreement; it strives to achieve mutual understanding of one another as well as the issues at hand. I find that for many people, consensus implies we all have to agree. When I facilitate groups, the idea of "consent" creates more space for dialogue and a discussion of needs behind positions and opinions than "consensus."

What's the difference? In the Consent Model, the question becomes: Can you live with this agreement? Not only that, but on what level can you live with this agreement, and what changes would meet your needs? It's important for the group to hear from the people who say no and find out what needs of theirs are unmet that keep them from saying yes. It's equally important for the people who say no to hear from the people who say yes regarding what cost their no might hold for these people. The decision-making process becomes a structured opportunity to highlight connecting to one another's feelings and needs—and building the relationship *context*—instead of just focusing on the topic or proposal—the *content* of the discussion. With a needs-based consent model, the context of group

> *By applying NVC-inspired needs awareness, the Consent Model goes beyond a desire for consensus, or agreement; it strives to achieve mutual understanding of one another as well as the issues at hand.*

connection and the content of the proposal or issue addressed hold equal weight. Thus you progress the group as well as the issue. Meeting both types of needs delivers a higher return on the group's investments of time and resources in discussion and decision making.

The Gradients of Agreement and Decision-Making Spectrum tools help create a needs-based connection among members of a group or team that is both efficient and collaborative.

The Gradients of Agreement Tool

In 1996, Sam Kaner with Lenny Lind, Catherine Toldi, Sarah Fisk, and Duane Berger developed a seven-step scale that expresses a range of choices for team members voting on a proposal or idea.[84] Applying an NVC-inspired needs-based consciousness to each gradient of agreement adds another level of connection for team members and builds on the Kaner model. In this way, while members of a group may disagree about the proposal (content), they are continuously working to strengthen and energize their understanding of one another's feelings and needs behind their opinions. In so doing, they are building their relationship (context) at the same time.

The Consent Model uses the Gradients of Agreement tool (Fig. 8-1, p. 191), with which decision makers can choose one of seven degrees of what I call levels of "comfort" with a proposed decision. On this gradient, 7 means Full Agreement, or very comfortable, and 1 means Block, or very uncomfortable. Any choice lower than 7, or complete agreement, creates an opportunity for needs to be heard, and six out of seven meet both needs for progress and group cohesion. Those who vote 1 are often willing to move up on the scale once their needs have been heard.

In groups I've facilitated, when a small percentage of people want to block a proposal because key needs are completely unmet by supporting it, I've found two dynamics in every instance so far that support the group members' need for both progress and cohesion: the Consent Model that uses the Gradients of Agreement tool, and the process of articulating and connecting to feelings and needs. The following story is an example.

Fig. 8-1. Gradients of Agreement

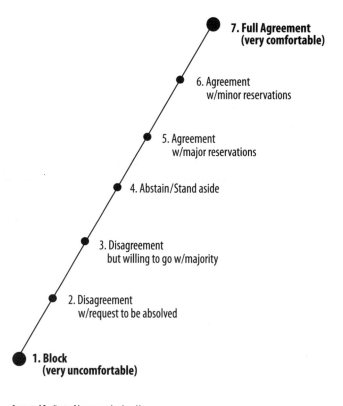

7. Full Agreement
(very comfortable)

6. Agreement
w/minor reservations

5. Agreement
w/major reservations

4. Abstain/Stand aside

3. Disagreement
but willing to go w/majority

2. Disagreement
w/request to be absolved

1. Block
(very uncomfortable)

Concept of Gradients of Agreement developed by
Sam Kaner with Jenny Lind, Catherine Toldi, Sarah Fisk, and Duane Berger
(www.communityatwork.com)

© 2011 Elucity Network, Inc. as developed by Marie R. Miyashiro

I facilitated a decision-making strategic planning process in a work team of sixteen people representing four different business units. Economic pressures were limiting the group's choices in terms of what services they could offer in the future. Resources were scarce and every team member realized that investing in one initiative meant there would be fewer resources for other initiatives. Two team members disagreed with a proposal to add a new service, one abstained, and thirteen passionately supported it. Having heard what the others felt, those who disagreed were willing to move up on the gradient scale. They could hear the others' needs. It was also critical that those who agreed hear the needs behind the disagreements and be able to connect to those feelings and needs. The needs behind both the agreement and disagreement are important, and all participants have the opportunity to voice not only their thoughts but their feelings and needs.

For example, one team member voiced concern that if the proposal passed, he didn't think he was qualified to contribute to the new service program because of the type of training he had received. Having heard his concerns, all other team members voiced their confidence in his professional qualifications.

This particular issue had been stalemated for more than four years. The group director attributes both the group's progress and group cohesion to the Consent Model as well as the process of articulating and connecting to feelings and needs. He later emailed me that he thought the decision-making and strategic planning sessions represented "a pivotal point in their history" as a department.

Using the Consent Model with the Gradients of Agreement, a group still moves forward even if all don't fully agree with the proposal. They give consent to some degree and everyone's needs are heard. If anyone remains at 1 as a block, a new proposal is crafted based on the needs of that person (or people) saying no until a level of consent can be reached. Polling or voting in this model is intended to add clarity and understanding of needs instead of resulting in polarization. This is accomplished by assuring that the needs and feelings behind each vote that is less than agreement are heard and received by all. I find it interesting that when people see that others are not at a 7 in full agreement, they become naturally curious about why and intuitively want to understand the others' points of view.

I often ask people to go up to the Gradients of Agreement scale on a flipchart and write their name at the place that best represents their agreement and comfort level with the proposal. For many groups, this becomes a ritual of deeper understanding when there isn't consent to proceed—or celebration when there is consent. Visually, this is a powerful exercise for collaboration in that it makes transparent where all members stand regarding a proposal in a way that is pure observation. In this model, there are no "naysayers," "whiners," "winners," or "losers." No proposal or opinion is "good" or "bad." All that remains are the needs behind each proposal and the people in the room.

The Consent Model and Gradients of Agreement tool allow everyone's feelings and needs to be heard and a decision to be made that everyone can live with, facilitating both progress and group cohesion.

When facilitating a group decision, I use this process:

1. Summarize the background or history of an issue.
2. Discuss the specifics of the issue.
3. Develop a proposal.
4. Vote or poll transparently using the Gradients of Agreement.
5. Go back to those who were below a 4 and bring out their unmet needs—especially if at 1. I ask people if they feel their needs have been sufficiently heard and understood. If they say no, I go back to asking about needs and, if necessary, guess as to what their needs might be. If they say yes, I ask if they are willing to move up the Gradient.
6. Celebrate the decision or craft a new proposal starting with those who said no to the earlier proposals.
7. Continue until I find a proposal all can live with.

During the process, I look to see if people are saying more than the others can absorb. In other words, when someone is expressing the needs behind their disagreement, I watch to see if other people become triggered. If this happens, I ask them each to reflect what they think they heard that was hard for them to hear and their feelings and needs connected to it. When the first party feels heard, I then ask the people who were listening to express their feelings and needs given what they heard. Then, the first person who is now listening, empathizes (does the same) with them, and so forth. We do this until the connection of understanding is established between the parties who disagreed originally and those who agreed originally.

Using the Consent Model and the Gradients of Agreement, participants can usually reach a decision about a specific proposal in thirty minutes rather than hours. Miki Kashtan (www.baynvc.com) has a detailed process flow that she uses for proposals, polling, and consent that involves specific proposal-making and decision trees.[85] While her process has variations from the one I've developed and explained above, both are examples for moving very divergent groups from chaos to consent in a matter of minutes, while maintaining connection.

Kashtan makes a powerful and common sense suggestion in service of efficiency: people speak only to add something new to the dialogue, not to concur with or repeat what's already been said. It's surprising how fast the discussion advances when participants share only new information or viewpoints.

Using the Consent Model and the Gradients of Agreement, participants can usually reach a decision about a specific proposal in thirty minutes rather than hours.

The Decision-Making Spectrum Tool

The chart in Fig. 8-2 is self-explanatory. It's been adapted from a spectrum developed by the International Association for Public Participation and, in turn, adapted by a variety of clients for use with their particular processes.[86]

In my experience mediating conflicts between team members or working with groups, I find that many conflicts stem from a lack of clarity about who has decision-making authority for different issues. Ultimately, everyone on a team or in a department is responsible for some work process or product. Clarifying levels of authority supports ownership of the work. If someone thinks he's empowered to design a new sales program or office protocol and his suggestions are vetoed at every turn by his supervisor, then he's in a conflict of procedure, not personality. I find that when people can make the key distinctions in the chart below, their tendency to personalize the issue dissolves.

Fig. 8-2. Decision-Making Spectrum in Organizations

INCREASING LEVEL OF AUTHORITY IN DECISION

Each level is progressive and includes the elements of the previous level.

INFORM-1	CONSULT-2	INVOLVE-3	COLLABORATE-4	EMPOWER-5
GOAL To provide you with accurate information on the situation, needs, strategies, and requests.	GOAL To obtain feedback from you on the situation, needs, strategies, and decisions.	GOAL To work directly with you to ensure that your concerns and hopes are consistently understood and considered.	GOAL To partner with you in the decision, including needs identification, developing strategies, and prioritizing preferred solutions.	GOAL To partner with you and transfer authority to you for strategy development, decisions, and solutions implementation.
PROMISE We keep you informed.	PROMISE We keep you informed, understand your concerns and hopes, and tell you how we used your feedback.	PROMISE We work with you to ensure that your concerns and hopes are directly reflected in the strategies and decisions developed.	PROMISE We look to you for direct advice in formulating strategies and decisions, incorporating them to the maximum extent possible.	PROMISE We implement what you decide.
SAMPLE TOOLS Newsletter, briefing memos, email updates, procedure manual, bulletins, employee handbook	SAMPLE TOOLS Surveys, focus groups, informational meetings, two-way dialogues, one-on-one conversations	SAMPLE TOOLS Planning meetings, project workshops, polling, project update meetings, interactive website	SAMPLE TOOLS Decision-making committees, advisory boards, budget teams, partnering sessions	SAMPLE TOOLS Delegated decisions, self-directed work teams, autonomous projects within agreed-upon parameters

© 2011 Elucity Network, Inc. as developed by Marie R. Miyashiro
Adapted from the International Association for Public Participation (www.iap2.org)

Ideally, you sit down with your team members or your manager or employee and review the chart together at the beginning of a new task or as part of a regular feedback session. Combining the NVC process of

OFNR (Observations, Feelings, Needs, Requests) with this chart both builds relationship, or context, and defines the content of the task or assignment. For ease, some groups combine the categories of Consult, Involve, and Collaborate. At either end of the spectrum, Inform and Empower stand apart.

A converse relationship between parties exists in regard to authority on the Decision-Making Spectrum. For example, if my team leader Empowers me (one side of chart) with responsibility to develop a new sales program, I can Inform him (other side of chart) of my progress.

Conflicts often stem from a lack of clarity about who has decision-making authority for different issues, work processes, or products. Clarifying levels of authority frames these conflicts as symptoms of procedure, not of personalities.

In summary, the Consent Model uses the language and process of Observations, Feelings, Needs, and Requests along with the Gradients of Agreement and the Decision-Making Spectrum. Decisions made in this way produce whole team support for agreed-upon initiatives, increased understanding, cohesion, and connection among team or group members, as well as progress on issues and initiatives that meet organizational needs.

* * * *

This chapter has explained a way of making decisions that considers everyone's needs as well as the needs of the organization. Chapters Nine and Ten provide ways to deal empathically with two issues we may experience in the workplace more frequently than we'd like—expressing anger and connecting with people when we find it especially difficult to do so.

PART III

Transforming Our Workplaces

NINE

Healing Workplace Anger, Guilt, Fear, and Shame

"We are never angry because of what others say or do. . . . The cause of anger lies in our thinking—in thoughts of blame and judgment." [87]

—Marshall Rosenberg, *Nonviolent Communication: A Language of Life*

In Part III, I discuss topics that I've had questions or heard concerns about from many employees and managers, and comment on topics I consider important to creating the empathic workplaces of the future. These chapters also serve to further deepen our understanding and application of needs-based consciousness as presented through the lenses of NVC and IC in previous chapters.

This chapter addresses anger, guilt, fear, and shame in the workplace—some of the least productive but most common feelings people report to me that create discomfort for them and others. Chapter Ten examines work relationships in which we're not as comfortable or skilled as we would like to be in our interactions. Finally, in Chapter Eleven, we look at how to begin the process of creating an empathic workplace and the implications of this endeavor in conscious capitalism, a sustainable society, and our own lives.

Why Do We Feel Angry?

When was the last time you felt angry at work—or some variation of angry, such as irritated, frustrated, impatient, agitated, or annoyed?

Within many workplace settings, people experience discomfort talking about or acknowledging most feelings, but I find anger is one feeling people are more comfortable with than I would like. Many consider anger to be a legitimate emotion that motivates work production, assures quality for the consumer, or somehow protects the company or organization. However, it's often expressed in a way that creates separation rather than connection. The separation comes from thinking that someone or something else is responsible for how we feel. Someone else has done something wrong or is deserving of punishment.

When we tell ourselves, "You made me angry," "I feel hurt because of what you said," or "You're not showing me the respect I deserve," we trick ourselves into believing that the cause of our anger lies outside ourselves. At first, we may not be aware that the cause of our anger is related to our own thinking.

Rosenberg identifies three parts to our thinking and behavior when we're angry:

1. We're wanting something we're not getting.
2. We're telling ourselves that someone "should" be giving it to us.
3. We're preparing to speak or behave in a way that will virtually assure we won't get what we want—or at least assure that even if we get it, it won't be given in the way we'd want it most. [88]

Look for these elements in the following story shared by attorney and NVC mediation trainer, Ike Lasater, who was introduced in Chapter Three. In this vignette, Ike shares how powerful anger can be even when we know better—*and* how powerful NVC can be in defusing it.

About seven years after I first met Marshall Rosenberg and learned of NVC, I was attending a board meeting for an organization in which I was heavily involved. In many previous board meetings, the group had been working on two related proposals that I saw as inextricably linked. The board chair was one of the advocates of the first, and I was one of the advocates for the other.

We finally voted on the first proposal, and as soon as that was complete, the chairperson proposed to table consideration of the second proposal—the one I was interested in—until the next board meeting.

I immediately concluded this was a Machiavellian plot to permanently table the second proposal. I suspected this had been planned all along, and I'd been duped into voting on the first item without knowing what procedure would be used to deal with the policy in which I had an interest. I didn't trust the chairperson's motives, and I immediately flashed to anger; I could feel my face flush with heat and the hair on the back of my neck stand on end.

I stood up to speak.

Now, I had been doing my best for seven years prior to this meeting to integrate NVC into my day-to-day life. In my anger at what I interpreted was happening, I was able to maintain just enough awareness to communicate in a variation of the classic NVC "training wheel" format: "When I hear . . . , I feel . . . because I need . . . . Would you be willing to . . .?"

After I stood up, I explained that I saw the suggestion to delay consideration of the second proposal to the next meeting as part of a plan to have it delayed indefinitely. I said I was angry about this (which was obvious because spittle was literally spewing from my mouth and my face was red) and went on to say that I needed to trust what was going on and I did not. My request was, "Is there anybody who is seeing it the way I'm seeing it?"

Then I sat down. I quickly realized I'd just accomplished a form of self-empathy out loud by expressing in this NVC format, and it had helped me reconnect with myself. I had met my need for empathy by expressing, as opposed to being empathized with by someone else or empathizing silently with myself.

When I sat down, my anger was gone. It left as quickly as it had come; of course, I was still feeling the aftereffects of the neurotransmitter and hormone releases in my body, but I was no longer angry.

Someone I trusted implicitly in the room turned to me, looked me straight in the eye, and said, "I'm not seeing it the way you're seeing it, and if at the next board meeting this doesn't get taken up and dealt with, I assure you I will stand shoulder to shoulder with you to make sure it gets considered." With that, I replied, "Okay, that's all I need," and I was able to be back in the board meeting connected to myself and the rest of the group.

What amazed me was how different this experience was from previous times when I had experienced anger in meetings. I'd been in many meetings as a trial lawyer and had served on various nonprofit boards. Whenever someone had been angry in those contexts, we conducted a lot of "billiard shot" communication about it afterward. In my experience, the expression of anger had generally been disruptive and had created harmful collateral aftereffects. That was not the case this time.

I didn't receive any feedback later that people were distressed by my expression, nor did I experience any lingering effects of it myself. It was like a spring shower; the thunderstorm came and then went, leaving the air fresh. This experience showed me the power of NVC and self-empathy in being able to communicate my anger in a way that was clean and clear, leaving no dark clouds behind.

(Ike Lasater with Julie Stiles, both of whom are listed in Contributors to This Book.)

Anger is a valuable feeling because it signals us that something is not working within us, for us, or around us, and it's calling for our immediate attention. People tend to judge anger as "bad." How we express it is another issue, but feeling anger can be productive if we know how to engage with it and express it in healthy ways. If we could become aware of our own judgments about anger and recognize it's neither good nor bad but just calling our attention to something that isn't working, or perhaps even dangerous, anger can be of enormous value for us. With this realization, we can take steps to meet the underlying need(s) this emotion is signaling.

I've had challenges myself with the way I've expressed anger with others, likely stemming from cultural norms with which I was raised. NVC has helped me evolve by giving me more understanding of this feeling and options for working with it productively.

Anger's Toll in the Workplace

Anger can derail us and is a powerful de-motivator for workplace productivity. The implication of blame and the energy of punishment can be damaging to team motivation and interpersonal work relationships with co-workers or customers. Many customer service units are desperate to find ways to help their employees connect with the customer even when the customer is expressing anger in a way that's difficult or painful for the service representative to hear.

My professional and personal experiences with anger also point to an interrelationship between anger and other feelings that can be damaging in the workplace, such as guilt, fear, and shame. When we hear or see something that's difficult for us to accept, we have four options for how to respond based on what we've learned in previous chapters. We can: blame ourselves (feel guilty); blame others (feel angry); connect to our own feelings and needs (self-empathy); or connect to another's feelings and needs (empathy). When someone (particularly with structural power) expresses anger intending to blame, punish, or humiliate another in the presence of a group, it can stimulate shame not only for the person receiving it but also for those witnessing it. Anger can also easily stimulate fear.

How we interpret someone's expression of anger with blame or intention to punish depends on many factors. These include our past experiences in general, our past experiences with this particular person, and other conditions in our life that range from personal health issues to stress levels. I've learned that it's not as black and white as we might first think. When someone is expressing anger in a way we don't like, we tend to say they're "wrong" or behaving in "inappropriate ways." As part of my job, I'm often interacting with people who are highly triggered, raising their voices or using language some might find uncomfortable. My intrapersonal dialogue guessing their feelings and needs is part of what allows me to stay connected with them and feel more comfortable than some others might feel. I tell myself that their behavior is not about me but about their own feelings and needs. They often are meeting me for the first time, so we have no history between us.

Being stressed and overscheduled so we have no time for self-care and connecting with ourselves, much less with others, also contributes to our agitation and possible overreaction to another's anger—and it can also contribute to our own feeling and expression of anger.

As explained in Chapter Five, certain dietary choices can also sabotage our best efforts to remain calm and express empathy in the workplace. I've worked with executives who pumped themselves up daily with six to eight cups of coffee and a consultant who drank up to six double espressos a day! Several of them explored the relationship between their coffee consumption and their feelings of impatience or worry, which are forms of agitation. To a person, they felt calmer and more at ease with workplace stress and relationships upon lowering their caffeine consumption. This natural stimulant can also contribute to lack of sleep, which can cause people to become more easily irritated during the day. While it may not contribute to anger for all people, it elevates the nervous system and primes it to respond to stimuli. It can magnify any anger that arises and add a nervous energy to people's responses that's likely to be interpreted as anger by others.

Judith Orloff Faulk, the course developer of a program called Choices, shared her perspective that anger is a cover feeling, not an authentic one. It covers other feelings, such as hurt, sadness, or fear. We may habitually feel angry as a way to avoid experiencing or integrating the pain of these emotions. For some, this could be true of shame and guilt, as well.

Fear is another form of thinking that can sabotage efforts of both self-empathy and empathy with others. Note the inner dialogue mentioned by group participants in Chapter Seven in relation to why we hear only 30 to 50 percent of what is said. Scary stuff! Fear can trigger the fight or flight response in us, making it unlikely that we'll connect with others in an authentic way.

Dr. Tania Singer talks about the two competing capacities we all have as humans—the capacity for love and the capacity for fear. "The ability to be compassionate toward others has to be cultivated in the sense that [we] have to learn how to deal with [our] fear," says Singer. She points out that as our fear grows, our capacity for compassion diminishes and that these two elements are "always in a dialectic balance with each other." To cultivate compassion, she suggests we learn about our fears, recognize them, and learn how to "down-regulate" them so our hearts can open to the outside world because we're no longer afraid for ourselves or of losing something.[89]

We've likely all had experiences where one or more of the feelings of fear, guilt, or shame were triggered, and instead of acknowledging these feelings and relating them to our unmet needs, we became angry, thus diminishing our capacity to empathically connect with our team members or customers.

Fully "Expressing" and Receiving Anger in the Workplace

Rosenberg says, "To fully express anger requires full consciousness of our need. In addition, energy is required to get the need met. Anger, however, co-opts our energy by directing it toward punishing people rather than meeting our needs."[90]

Instead of participating in what he calls, "righteous indignation," we can practice self-connection and empathy with our own unmet needs. I can personally attest to the effectiveness of this approach. Here's an example.

Part of my work involves large construction team projects with up to forty people in a diversity of roles and backgrounds, from private engineering firms to community relations professionals, all working on projects involving more than $100 million. One of the team leaders, who has authority but with whom I've had little contact, commented about one of my recommendations through an email that was sent to the whole team. He was unaware of how successful the empathic approach has been with community relations on similar projects. Some people might feel anger or "righteous indignation" in that situation. After all, I had been brought in to advise the team on my particular area. But I was aware that I was feeling ashamed, even though there was no reason for me to feel this way given this situation (the ideas I presented were received as sound by other team members) and even though I knew logically that his intent was not to shame me. I connected those feelings to my needs for respect and support. These feelings arise more often when I lose sight of my own connection to the needs I'd like to serve by being part of this team.

For example, when I reconnected with my need to support business owners and employees and managers impacted by the construction, I hear this team member differently. What I heard as criticism translated into guessing that he's feeling worried and having a need for predictability about how the neighborhoods will respond. Or, perhaps he's stressed because he has a need for competence and has a history of someone else questioning his competence. Or, he could be nervous because his interactions with people in my role have not been enjoyable for him in the past and he'd like to feel more comfortable on this project.

To be clear, he's not responsible for my feelings of shame or guilt and my need for respect. While he contributes to these feelings and the need, he's not responsible for them.

In this circumstance, I first engaged in self-empathy. When I noticed a shift from the sense of feeling blamed to a feeling of appreciation for this work and my part in it, I was then able to empathize with the other party. As I connected empathically both to myself and my team member, I no longer had a need to be understood or express my side of the story, nor did I feel guilty or ashamed. That was all transformed simply through my internal process. Nothing had changed in the real world situation, but everything had changed in my inner dialogue.

I find this process helpful, and I suggest to my clients that they practice a healthy dose of self-empathy or ask for empathy from others when they're triggered by someone else's anger or blame at work *before* they strategize about ways to communicate with this person. The reason? Many times, when our needs are met in other ways, we don't need to make requests of others, just ourselves. Because I don't report to this person and I've been reassured by the people I do report to that they want me to implement my recommendations, I developed connection with this person through silent empathy.

If, after these processes of self-empathy and empathy for the other person, I'm still experiencing anger and have a need to express it, I can again follow the OFNR process flow with myself. Then if the further requests I make of myself (such as going for a walk) still don't meet my needs, I can then (with as much gentleness as I can muster) make a request to the person who stimulated these feelings in me to allow me to express them. While others are not responsible for the feelings we have, they can have an effect on these feelings.

I would then:

1. contextualize my request to meet or talk with this person by emphasizing how much I value our relationship or whatever appreciation of that person I experience.
2. make as clean an observation as I could about what I saw or heard that was triggering for me.
3. share what I felt and what needs weren't met by what was triggered—in terms of both my individual needs and the organizational or team needs.
4. make a request of the other party to: first, confirm that what I said was what was heard along with my intention for connection and not blame; second, see what the other person thought; third, explore requests we might both have to see what would be of most value to each of us going forward.

Feelings of anger, guilt, fear, or shame come from the way we interpret what we see or hear. Even though they are triggered by outside stimuli, they originate within us, so we have the power through self-empathy and empathically connecting to others to transform and heal the pain we have around these feelings and their connected needs.

Having heard the explanation above for the true causes of anger, managers or employees sometimes express disbelief. "What if someone's done something awful? Isn't that a reason to be angry?" they ask. Yes, many situations in work and life can trigger huge fundamental needs for us. But if we think back to the lunch date exercise in Chapter Three, we can logically apply that same reasoning to any situation that triggers our anger. Circumstances aren't as black and white as we may tend to believe. People always act in service of their own needs, and how we interpret their actions is based on our own needs.

That said, we may encounter situations in which we may choose to use "protective use of force," as Rosenberg calls it. This means we have to act unilaterally without considering the other person's needs. In *Words That Work In Business,* Lasater explains this situation from his own point of view: "If I have sought to care about and include the needs of the other person, attempted to get clear about my needs, communicated my needs and made requests, and formulated and revisited agreements, then at some point I become unwilling to continue trying to engage with the other person in a communication process. The question becomes, With what attitude do I take action? If I want to exercise the protective use of force, then to the best of my ability, I take action without anger, and without any attempt to punish the other person or induce feelings of shame, guilt, blame, or depression. I do whatever inner work is necessary for me to act with some sense of compassion for myself and for the other person. Without compassion, I have only the typical method of resolving issues in the workplace: using force over another person." [91]

Words That Work In Business expands on using NVC for various workplace challenges, including anger, prejudice, humor that can be uncomfortable for some, power issues, complaints, broken agreements, sharing work areas, answering emails, and more.

Healing in the Workplace

I've been exploring for myself and with clients what I call "antidotes," or remedies, for anger, guilt, fear, and shame, and I've found the following antidotes to be of value. You may know your own strategies or identify them through trial and error.

Fig. 9-1. Antidotes for Feelings That De-Motivate

FEELINGS IN THE WORKPLACE	ANTIDOTE PRACTICE
Anger (irritation, annoyance, impatience)	Appreciating what's working/what we have
Guilt	Self-acceptance
Fear, Fatigue	Self-care
Shame	Self-appreciation

© 2011 Elucity Network, Inc. as developed by Marie R. Miyashiro

Self-appreciation might involve more awareness with the words we use to describe ourselves, even if only to ourselves. Self-care might mean addressing our health issues, resting when we're tired, and eating healthy food. Self-appreciation could also mean standing up for ourselves, holding true to our values, and knowing that we are just as worthy of respectful treatment as any other human being.

I find that one of the most challenging aspects of living this process and applying it to my own work settings and personal relationships is forgiving myself for the times when I've made choices that aren't in alignment with my values as expressed in this book. When I'm not as connected to whatever is going on for me or not as resourceful with others as I'd like to be, I feel regret, but instead of feeling guilt or shame about it, I work to empathize with the needs I was trying to meet and grieve the needs I didn't meet. This is the process Rosenberg calls mourning and self-forgiveness.

Many of my clients experience the same challenge of first being authentic with this process personally. As mentioned earlier in the book, our language and our habitual behaviors are deeply entrenched. This is an important point because I will be the first to admit that this process takes practice. It takes a "race of rebels" to instigate this new dimension of connection within our workplaces and become role models for others. The return on investment of time and effort to practice this new skill will increase as more and more people begin to realize its effectiveness and become "on fire," as one of my group participants expressed. As the fire spreads, it can blaze a path of transformation within the organization that leads to harmony, increased productivity, and true prosperity. The idea is not to do the process perfectly. It's to do it. Period.

✳ ✳ ✳ ✳

This chapter has focused on how to transform specific feelings that are demoralizing and disconnecting in the workplace into understanding based on needs. In Chapter Ten, we'll look at how to connect with that one person or those few people who seem to be beyond the reach of our current connecting skill level and resourcefulness.

TEN

Connecting With People Who Stretch Our Skills

"A difficult person is someone who presents issues or acts in ways that are beyond our current skill level to meet openheartedly: the difficulty is in us, and not about the other person." [92]

—Inbal Kashtan, Miki Kashtan, BayNVC

For many years, I've been seeing titles of other books, chapters, or articles about conflict resolution that are phrased something like, "Communicating With Difficult People," or "How to Handle Difficult Conversations." I'm not in agreement with these titles as they either evaluate or prejudge a person as "difficult" and in so doing imply that the problem is with the other party, or they evaluate or prejudge an interaction as "difficult." As you've read previously, the IC/NVC process avoids evaluations—even positive ones—in favor of observations that are objective.

I came up with this chapter title to emphasize that people are never difficult; instead, they are acting in ways that are beyond our current skill levels of connecting, understanding, and communicating. In fact, our interactions with people who challenge our resourcefulness are gifts because they point us in the direction of our important unmet needs. To review, if the needs being triggered were met, we wouldn't experience discomfort or uneasiness in our interactions with this person. The cause of our unpleasant feelings, then, is not the "difficult person" or "difficult conversation," but our skill level in connecting to our own and the other person's feelings and unmet needs. We know this is true from two facts. First, the lunch date exercise in Chapter Three demonstrated that people have different responses to the same situations. Second, somebody, somewhere is likely to think of the person we might judge as "difficult" as "kind," "fun," "loveable," and so forth. So much of our interpretation of others depends on our own history.

Why Do We Experience Some People in This Way?

I propose four main reasons that contribute to experiencing others in our workplace in a way that requires us to stretch our skills and resourcefulness to have the kind of connection we would like.

1. Similar Unmet Needs

First, I find that when two people sense tension or conflict in their interactions, they often but not always have similar unmet needs. For example, if both you and I have an unmet need for being understood, it's likely these unmet needs will bump up against each other when we interact. Because we both have a need to be understood, we each might be listening with the intent to respond instead of with the intent to empathize with the other's feelings and needs.

Customer service and human resources personnel encounter this frequently. Customers who are satisfied are less likely to call for customer service than those who are dissatisfied or have questions. In trainings I've conducted for people who respond to complaints, I emphasize establishing a level of connection and empathy with people expressing unmet needs before answering their questions or providing information, even if their request is for information. Connecting before explaining, defending, or educating and informing sets the contextual foundation for the answers to their questions or the information they're requesting.

Someone might call and say, "Your company owes me a new product. It was damaged during shipping. When can I get a new one?" This could be addressed by empathically connecting to this person's feeling and need first. "Are you disappointed because you wanted to use the product right away?"

I recommend establishing a level of connection and empathy with people expressing unmet needs before answering their questions or providing information.

We know when people feel heard because we notice a pause in their speaking or a slight shift in the energy level of their expression. Most people tend to relax a bit into the dialogue or interaction when they feel sufficiently heard. It may be subtle, but the signs are usually there. Then, after we've made the connection, we can answer the question directly.

Or, we might ask the customer if she would like understanding about her disappointment and frustration. "Would it be helpful to you if I understood what it was like for you to receive your product that way in more detail?" She might say yes or she might say, "No, I've already spent enough time on this. It was supposed to come and be ready for use, but it doesn't work at all." Her dialogue points us to many of her possible unmet needs. Need for efficiency, ease, or integrity might be several guesses.

If she says yes, we might ask, "Please tell me what happened." As she shares, we can be silently empathizing, guessing her feelings and needs. When it sounds as if she's complete and we can be fairly confident that she feels heard, we can ask, "Would you like information about our product replacement options?"

If we interpret the customer's tone, intent, or message as blame, judgment, or anger, we'll likely have a higher chance of being

Most people tend to relax a bit into the dialogue or interaction when they feel sufficiently heard.

frustrated ourselves and want to be understood, as well. Haskvitz refers to this as an "empathy collision," where both people want empathy and understanding at the same time and neither has any of it to give in that moment. An emotional collision is imminent.

So when I'm stumped about why I'm not able to connect as easefully as I'd like with someone, I begin by silently guessing a possible shared unmet need. Because I have ready access to my own feelings and needs, this gives me a possible reference for the other person's needs. I'm guessing at this point, but it gives me much more structure when I'm engaging with this person, and that's crucial. Even if I guess wrong and the person's need is completely different than the one I imagined, I can engage in a process of elimination about likely needs. This very act can add a level of comfort for me that enhances our connection and may even result in the dissipation of my judgments of them.

Over and over, I have seen the power of NVC and IC at work within a small core of people at first, and then watched it spread to entire teams and organizations. It takes only a few people who really want it, understand it, and practice it.

2. "Culture" or Values Clash

A second reason we might have interactions with certain people that are beyond our skill level has to do with organizational or team cultures. This is particularly important given the emphasis on diversity and cross- or multi-cultural teams. The priority of different needs may be apparent not only between two organizational cultures, such as in a merger, but also within organizations. Working from the framework of the six universal organizational needs helps us to recognize and connect with the needs of the larger organization, as well as its embedded departments and teams that may have additional value needs specific to their professional roles. Accountants, for example, likely have a different emphasis on needs for detail and accuracy than sales representatives, who might value connection time and a broader

Be alert to values and needs a person may have that are related to his or her role in the workplace.

vision of the future. The key here is to be alert and sensitive to any needs and values that this person is likely to hold given his or her role within the organization.

3. Constant Changes

Third, our own history of interactions with this person or with people who remind us of this person can filter our current interactions. For this reason, I've heard Rosenberg remind us that every interaction with every person is new because we can never know what someone is experiencing moment to moment. One minute s/he might be feeling calm and have a need for communication. Literally, the next minute s/he might be feeling concerned and have a need for resolution. Every feeling is also new in each moment because our experience of whether our needs are met or unmet changes based on what we are telling ourselves and what we think others are telling us.

Knowing this helps free us from the myth that we can ever "know what someone is like" based on past experiences or have expectations of how people in organizations might choose collective behavior. There are no "good" or "bad" people or organizations—only choices and behaviors with which we may or may not agree. All people and organizations are acting in service of their own needs, even when they make choices we abhor because they don't meet needs that are important to us or others.

In a needs-based consciousness, we strive to find strategies that meet all needs. This is possible because the need to contribute to others is genetically encoded in each of us as part of our evolutionary history. We are a social species. As such, understanding others on the deepest levels of empathic connection is a natural act. We're not learning something new but remembering something we've forgotten. For this reason, when we meet people who invite us to stretch our skills of connection, they are giving us the gift of remembrance.

The need to contribute to others is genetically encoded in each of us as part of our evolutionary history. We're not learning something new but remembering something we've forgotten.

4. Our Own Energy Levels

A final reason we might encounter situations in which people stretch our capacity to easefully connect with them relates to our own physical, mental, and emotional energy levels. It takes energy to connect with—or even want to connect with—another person. While the need for connection is natural because we're social beings by nature, our energy capacity at any given moment may be less than what we'd like it to be. As discussed in Chapter Five with regard to health, if we're rested and feeling content, connecting with a person can be an entirely different experience than if we're tired and stressed.

The organizational need for *Energy* works the same way. At any given time, an organization's *Energy* (the combination of its financial, people, and technological resources according to the Integrated Clarity framework) may be less than what people in the organization want it to be. If people in an organization or on a team share an experience of being overwhelmed by their workloads and have a need for focus, they will collectively respond differently than if they share the experience of feeling energized and have their need for meaning through work met.

Our personal fluctuating energy levels and organizational **Energy** *needs can influence the level of ease with which we connect to others in the workplace or with our customer groups.*

Every one of the reasons listed above relates to us and to our organizations and teams and not to the other person or people. That person is not difficult. This customer is not challenging. That company is not bad. Instead, we find ourselves in situations where we don't possess the level of skill or energy we'd like in creating connections and interactions that are easeful and enjoyable for us.

Stretching Our Capacity and Skills to Connect

It takes a personal and sometimes organizational investment of energy to connect with people who say or do things we experience as triggering our unmet needs. This process requires us to self-empathize for the discomfort we're feeling so we can be present for the other party. It's a balancing act of engaging with the other person while doing our own inner empathy process about what we find challenging. We are stretching ourselves in both ways now by self-connecting as well as empathizing with the other party. These two processes might be happening in the same interaction or we might have the advantage of some time between interactions to do this work.

When we add a group dynamic on top of this, like a meeting setting, we now have organizational information to process, and all three levels of communication (intrapersonal, interpersonal, organizational) are active at the same time. Interactions can become quite complex when we're triggered in these settings.

Helpful Strategies

Strategies we can use to address situations when we're stretched include the following:

1. Whenever possible, we can avoid interacting with others when we're highly triggered and feeling angry, impatient, fatigued, overwhelmed, and the like. In my experience, it's worth rescheduling a meeting if at all possible to provide time for deeper self-connection with the intention of creating more productivity for all. We're not productive when we're triggered because our focus tends to move toward defending, explaining, or justifying rather than hearing what's happening in the moment.

2. If it's not feasible to schedule time for ourselves, which is often the case, I've learned to empathize silently with myself during a meeting. The process isn't outwardly detectable, and I might do it for a few seconds here and there when my focus on it doesn't take away from contributing to the meeting. For example, when we're seated and getting ready to begin, I might avoid small talk and take out a pad of paper and lean away from the table for privacy and draw a three-column

table with "F" for feelings at the top of one column and "N" for needs and "R" for requests at the top of the others. In a few seconds, I make some guesses. People to whom I've taught this technique find, as I do, that even thirty seconds of this can lead to a substantial level of self-connection, which then influences their choices in the meeting in a way that's more productive for them and the group.

3. If I don't have the time, energy, or motivation to do self-empathy, I simply say to myself, "Okay. Let's put my feelings and needs aside for a moment and see if I can guess this person's feeling and needs and what requests s/he might have." WATT Why Are *They* Talking? becomes my focus instead of WAIT, Why Am *I* Talking? as discussed in Chapter Six.

4. Requesting a short period of "speed empathy" or listening time from a trusted colleague or someone outside our work setting is also a strategy I like. I've called and have been called by work colleagues who simply say, "Do you have three minutes? I could use some empathy around this." Literally a few minutes later, we're complete. It's quite empowering to be heard for no other reason than you want it and it works for the other party, as well.

5. Then there's always what I call surrendering. Sometimes, I forget all the words and processes and just say to myself: "I'm at a complete loss here. What do I do next?"

    This is a form of empathy in that I've acknowledged I'm at the end of my resourcefulness rope. I find that this provides the additional benefit of creating space for unknown possibilities. Converse to what we might think is required of us at work, we don't know all the answers and never will. I find a sense of relief and a planting of a seed of potential when I approach some situations in this way.

The idea that the challenges we encounter in interacting with people originate within us is empowering. If challenges begin within us, they can end within us.

✳ ✳ ✳ ✳

This chapter has focused on the idea that there are no "difficult people" or "difficult conversations," only people and situations that invite us to stretch our capacity and skill for connection. Chapter Eleven ties in the implications of everything we've covered so far with the trends of conscious capitalism and organizational social responsibility. It also delineates the next steps to help you and your organization launch your own exploration of this expanded dimension of needs consciousness and human connection.

ELEVEN

Implications for the Future of Workplaces

"The search for morals and meaning at work, as well as the desire to experience the peace and purpose of the Sacred in the stressful world of business, are 'inner' truths, alive in the hearts of millions of people. These internal realities profoundly influence people's behavior—like the choice to invest in a corporation that embraces higher social, environmental and ethical standards than its peers; the decision to work only for a company that honors your soulful, creative instincts; or the pledge to shop only at retailers who refuse to traffic in 'sweatshop' labor." [93]

—Patricia Aburdene, *Megatrends 2010: The Rise of Conscious Capitalism*

Looking to the Future

While other books and consultants work specifically on the issues of corporate social responsibility and conscious capitalism, a needs-based consciousness can serve as the foundation for these trends. At their core, both direct us back to our universal needs and thus engender a way of doing business for the twenty-first century and beyond.

Regarding connection and communication within organizations, in *The Change Handbook,* Rosenberg and I expressed a wish for every organization to experience clarity about its universal organizational needs and for its employees, shareholders, customers, and other stakeholders to gain clarity about their individual needs and values.

"We believe when this happens, every worker will experience more ease in finding their seat in an organization that meets their needs. Each organization will draw to it people who are most in alignment with it."[94] This reduces the likelihood of conflicts due to misaligned values.

In *Megatrends 2010: The Rise of Conscious Capitalism,* Patricia Aburdene, who co-authored the *New York Times* bestseller *Megatrends 2000,* highlights several points in her introduction that resonate with the needs-based consciousness championed in this book:

- No invention in business or technology can be accomplished *without* human consciousness.
- Technology is consciousness externalized.
- The inner world of ideals and beliefs shapes our actions.
- These inner truths are our values, and they play a crucial role in change.
- The synergy of changing values and economic necessity is transforming capitalism.[95]

I believe that in the next five to fifteen years, the skill of empathy will be one of the most sought-after qualities by large corporations, universities, nonprofits, government agencies, and small businesses. The call to return to what is natural for us—empathic connection— is powerful. It's now being fueled by rampant accounting scandals, financial market disruptions, and growing deficits, as well as desires for more personal meaning in our work and to make a contribution that matters in the course of our workday.

So what is involved in transitioning an organization from the old paradigm to this new empathic dimension? This chapter addresses what to expect and possible next steps.

How to Integrate NVC and IC Into Your Organization's Culture

First, realize that transformation begins internally and personally before it spreads within the organization. Over time it becomes the normal way of communicating and operating. For this reason, the process begins

with a core group of leaders and employees learning and practicing
NVC together as a communication tool and structural framework for
teams or the organization. A facilitator or small group of practitioners
explain and model the key concepts and distinctions. As leaders become
familiar with the process and how it relates to the organizational needs
(IC), they become role models of the process and facilitators themselves.
NVC and IC are not taught in the traditional way as much as they are
shared and lived.

It's helpful to establish a supportive infrastructure that includes:

- assessment of the current organizational status (see
  Appendices for an abbreviated assessment tool);
- regular, ongoing training in NVC and IC;
- practice, inquiry, and relating the concepts to the
  organization;
- strategic conversations to determine organizational needs
  using NVC and IC tools;
- a process to monitor success, such as an organizational
  needs dashboard;
- follow-up, with periodic assessments to determine which
  needs are most and least met.

With Regard to the Language of NVC

It's important to integrate the language and process of empathy into
our own consciousness so it comes naturally and isn't perceived
as a "technique" to manipulate others. The idea is to empower and
help others meet their needs and the organizational needs as we've
defined needs in this book. The more people create sincere empathic
connections with one another and with customers, the more they will
enliven the organization because they're responding to "what's alive" in
others. As people become empowered and feel their need for respect
being met, productivity improves.

With Regard to Organizational Needs

Everything flows from determining, clarifying, and articulating the Source Needs of *Identity, Life-Affirming Purpose,* and *Direction.* It's crucial to conduct strategic conversations about these organizational needs before jumping into investments in operations and infrastructure—the Leveraging Needs of *Structure, Energy,* and *Expression.* Once these six universal needs are determined, it's important to support their fulfillment by investing in whatever non-IC training (such as technical) and equipment is necessary to empower employees. In the IC process, these training investment decisions rely heavily on employees at the work level.

How Much Time Will This Integration Take?

Although this question is often asked, it's difficult to answer because of the variables involved, such as size of the organization, commitment level and involvement, and starting point given the initial assessment. In addition, the process is continually being refined by each person using it, and the organizational needs are revisited over time for ongoing transformation.

That said, Kimball Fisher in *Leading Self-Directed Work Teams* suggests that about 10 to 20 percent of a person's work time be devoted to learning.[96] Although Fisher is referring to self-directed and empowerment work models and isn't speaking about learning NVC and IC per se, the principle is applicable. When integrating the NVC and IC processes into an organization, you'll want to incorporate time for formal classroom training, practice groups, coaching, mentoring, and team meetings. However—and this is an important distinction—all this training and practicing focuses on work-related tasks so people are accomplishing their work as they learn, with better results as they improve. Coupling organizational needs with individual needs into the same framework allows for learning this needs-based approach within the context of daily work and business goals.

Once the organization or team: determines and meets the six organizational needs (at least initially); communicates these to the entire organization (or at least the parts relevant to each business unit); and establishes a standard of training in NVC and IC, it will eventually reach a critical mass of employees using the process. At this point, the transformation in terms of harmony, productivity, and profit will become more readily apparent. Plus, the organization will attract new employees and customers who are in alignment with its clear *Identity, Life-Affirming Purpose,* and *Direction.*

Coupling organizational needs with individual needs into the same framework allows for learning this needs-based approach within the context of daily work and business goals so people are accomplishing their work as they learn.

Customer Focus

I remind clients and colleagues that the ideas in this book are not new. These principles have been around for many decades now. But these kinds of organizations, as David Lei and Charles R. Greer define them in their research paper, "The Empathetic Organization," are different. Lei and Greer studied The Container Store, Apple Computer, Harley-Davidson, and Mary Kay. They note the following: "While every organization and business seeks to work closely with its customers, the empathetic organization attempts to build competitive advantage by harnessing the knowledge it learns from each customer to conceive entirely new products and solutions that ultimately set a key performance standard for the industry. . . . From the company's perspective, customers are a rich source of knowledge and insights that help [The] Container Store develop new storage ideas. A key premise behind [The] Container Store is that managers and employees realize that the customer is not solely interested in buying a product. Instead, customers are looking for knowledge, ideas, and a feeling of personal understanding in getting the help they need to create and shape their own personalized experiences and emotional attachments. . . . As a result, customers leave [The] Container Store feeling as if they were the creative forces behind the work." [97]

Interest in the value of empathy is expanding into other areas and professions. The traditional field of health care and medicine has begun to research empathy as part of its evolving clinical training models. Johanna Shapiro's study "How Do Physicians Teach Empathy in the Primary Care Setting?" is just one of many examining this subject.[98]

Meeting customer needs is key. Some organizations can be so inwardly focused with empathic connection among their own team members that the empathic connection with customers can become lost or subsumed. I find that these types of organizations emphasize their own healing as a part of their *Identity* values and place less emphasis on the customer. I believe that if an organization exists to meet the needs of the customers it serves, then it's logical to make customers the primary focus. The healing and value that employees or internal team members experience are by-products of the organization's *Life-Affirming Purpose* and *Direction* in service of meeting customer needs.

Researchers are now looking at ways to teach empathy to professionals in the traditional fields of health care and medicine.

Again, NVC presents itself as a plausible training framework for empathy, whereas none of the research results outline a methodology to teach it.

Supportive Workplace Environments

Successful companies combine the elements of a needs-based consciousness and empathic connection. Emerging markets such as Brazil boast some of the most unusual approaches to successful workplaces. Take Semco, S.A., for example, a manufacturing firm with no standard hierarchies, office or work hours, or salary schedule. Employees are empowered to set these to meet their needs as well as the needs of the customer and the company.[99]

What about situations in which "members of an organization or society expect and agree that power should be stratified and concentrated at higher levels of an organization or government"?[100] The Center for Creative Leadership study "Empathy in the Workplace"[101] notes that managers working in highly paternalistic organizational cultures such as those in China, Hong Kong, Poland, Singapore, Malaysia, and Taiwan find that empathic skills play a critical role in creating an environment of support and protection.[102] Even in hierarchical systems, empathy was positively correlated with performance: the more empathic the people were, the higher the level of leadership and manager performance.

Even in hierarchical systems, empathy was positively correlated with performance: the more empathic the people were, the higher the level of leadership and manager performance.

The Social Sector and Beyond

When an organization and the people in it raise their consciousness to the level of needs awareness and empathic connection, the best of business practices can be applied in social sector organizations such as schools, universities, social programs, and so forth without fear that a profit motive will corrupt or distort their social missions. When a company and its people operate from individual as well as organizational needs awareness, the most beneficial outcome unfolds for both as well as for the company's customers and community and the greater environment.

Whether people are practicing these skills in a for-profit or nonprofit organization, learning them at work can encourage the transference of these skills to our home lives. This is just one reason many of us who teach and share NVC and IC hope that a critical mass of practitioners can shift the workplace paradigm in favor of needs awareness and empathic connections.

Successful, Happy People

I've interviewed, met with, coached, and facilitated thousands of employees and managers. One characteristic of successful, happy people stands out: they think in ways that don't involve blaming others. They highly value personal responsibility as well as encouragement, empathy, and compassion.

These people demonstrate that if we want to be successful and happy, we can choose empathy as it's defined in this book over being "right," which necessitates that someone else be "wrong." As it turns out, Gerald Jampolsky's statement that "You can be right or you can be happy" makes a salient point.

If we doubt that a business philosophy based on the principles discussed here can achieve both enterprise success and happiness for its people, we can look at *Joy at Work*. In this book, Dennis Bakke writes about his experiences as CEO of AES, an $8.6 billion energy firm with forty thousand employees in 2002. Its uncommon workplace culture, which Bakke championed, also yielded robust financial results. However, he says, "Winning, especially financially, is a second-order goal at best. Working according to certain timeless, true, and transcendent values and principles should be our ambition." Bakke proposes ". . . a broader definition of organizational performance and success, one that gives high priority to a workplace that is filled with joy for ordinary working people. Such a place gives all workers an opportunity to make important decisions and take significant actions using their gifts and skills to the utmost."[103]

As final words, I'd like to emphasize that increased success, productivity, profitability, and richness of empathy, compassion, and meaning are possible if we each endeavor to develop empathic connection as a professional skill. We can cultivate this skill at higher levels as we learn and grow; and when we fail, we can try again, relying on our personal resilience, humility, and courage. The workplaces we dream of are not only possible but probable using the framework presented in these pages. Let's celebrate all victories, large and small, that mark our steady but inevitable progress toward the expanded world of deep empathic connection, both with ourselves and with one another.

✳ ✳ ✳ ✳

Please see the Resources section of this book for help in bringing about this transformation for you and your organization. I'm grateful for your interest and I'm confident that if you hold the intention to travel this road, you will receive value and meaning from your experience.

APPENDICES

Feelings Inventory for the Workplace

SAD
Ashamed
Blue
Brokenhearted
Depressed
Disappointment
Discouraged
Disheartened
Fragile
Helpless
Hurt
Lonely
Miserable
Numb
Vulnerable

GLAD
Delighted
Eager
Encouraged
Excited
Happy
Hopeful
Inspired
Optimistic
Proud
Relieved
Satisfied
Thrilled

MAD
Agitated
Angry
Annoyed
Bitter
Disgusted
Enraged
Frustrated
Furious
Impatient
Irate
Jealous
Pessimistic
Resentful

TIRED
Burned Out
Distracted
Exhausted
Fatigued
Flat
Frazzled
Hopeless
Indifferent
Lethargic
Off Center
Restless
Weary

WORRIED
Alarmed
Anxious
Concerned
Disturbed
Guarded
Nervous
Overwhelmed
Panicky
Scared
Shocked
Suspicious
Tense
Terrified
Wary

CONFUSED
Cautious
Conflicted
Doubtful
Hesitant
Puzzled
Reluctant
Skeptical
Torn
Troubled
Uncomfortable
Uneasy
Unsettled
Unsure

CALM
Absorbed
Awed
Blissful
Comfortable
Confident
Content
Fulfilled
Loving
Peaceful
Relaxed
Secure
Serene

FRIENDLY
Appreciative
Cordial
Fondly
Grateful
Open
Receptive
Sensitive
Social
Tender
Trusting
Warm
Welcoming

EXCITED
Adventurous
Amazed
Creative
Curious
Energetic
Engaged
Exhilarated
Fascinated
Free
Inspired
Interested
Intrigued
Invigorated
Passionate

Needs Inventory for the Workplace

RESOURCES
PHYSICAL NEEDS
Air/Food/Water
Comfort, Ease
Consistency
Equipment, Tools
Health
Movement, Exercise
Privacy
Respectful physical contact
Rest/Relaxation
Safety, Security
Supplies
Time, Efficiency

COMMUNICATION
MENTAL NEEDS
Awareness
Clarity, Direction
Data, Research
Decision Making
Discernment
Education, Training
Information
Reflection
Stimulation, Challenge

AUTHORITY
EMPOWERMENT
Autonomy
Choice
Co-creation of strategies
Collaboration
Discipline
Freedom
  (emotional, spiritual, and physical)
Individuality
Solitude

ACCOUNTABILITY
INTEGRITY
Authenticity
Contribution
Effectiveness, Progress
Feedback, Tracking
Honesty
Humility, Self-reflection
Morality
Punctuality
Quality
Self-worth
Sincerity

INTEGRATION
INTERDEPENDENCE
Acceptance
Appreciation
Clarity
Closeness
Community
Compassion
Connection
Consideration
Cooperation
Emotional Safety
Empathy
Harmony
Inclusion
Intimacy
Love
Reassurance
Respect
Support
Trust
Understanding
Validation
Warmth

SELF-EXPRESSION
CREATIVITY
Creating, Generating
Growth, Progress
Learning, Mastery
Meaning
Play, Fun, Laughter
Teaching

SELF-ALIGNMENT
NATURAL ENERGY
Beauty
Equality, Mutuality
Harmony, Peace
Inspiration
Order
Purpose, Meaning
Respect

MARKING OF TRANSITIONS
CELEBRATING BEGINNINGS
Ceremony/Ritual
Delight
Enjoyment
Excitement
Healing
Humor
Passion

ACKNOWLEDGING ENDINGS
Accept learning
Accept limitations
Acknowledge regrets
Grieve dreams unfulfilled
Mourn lost relationships

THE FOUR STEPS OF THE
INTEGRATED CLARITY® FRAMEWORK

A needs-based approach to workplace productivity

Individual People Orientation Nonviolent Communication (NVC)	Whole System Orientation Integrated Clarity (IC)
1. Make Observations. • What am I seeing or hearing? • Objective, concrete, factual	**1. Identify Data.** • Observations that can be analyzed, compared, measured: metrics, dashboards
2. Identify Feelings. • Feelings vs. non-feeling judgments or evaluations about observations and business data	
3. Connect Feelings to Human Needs. Universal needs that all people share, such as respect, learning, purpose, and autonomy	**3. Connect Data to Organizational Needs.** **Source Needs** **Leveraging Needs** 1) Identity 4) Structure 2) Life-Affirming Purpose 5) Energy 3) Direction 6) Expression
4. Make Requests to Meet Our Needs. *Examples of a request:* "Would you be willing . . . 1) to tell me what you heard me say?" 2) to complete this report and have it on my desk by five o'clock?"	**4. Develop Strategic Intentions.** In organizations, requests are strategies. Strategic planning and implementation on a whole system level are intended to meet organizational needs that people in the system perceive and monitor.

Integrated Clarity®
SIX UNIVERSAL ORGANIZATIONAL NEEDS

Identity
Who we are. Our unique, authentic collective self — our values and what we are passionate about.

Expression
How we express and appreciate our unique place in the market. Growth as a natural by-product of reaching and serving customers.

Life-Affirming Purpose
Why we exist. Our connection to how our operations serve the universal human needs of our customers.

Energy
How we fuel our operations. Financial (profit), Human Operational Capital (morale), Technology Accelerators.

Direction
Where we are going and by when. Our intentions and strategies to live our Identity into the future.

Structure
How we leverage our Identity, Purpose, and Direction. Our use of communication, authority, accountability, resources, and information.

© 2011 Elucity Network, Inc. as developed by Marie R. Miyashiro

10 Minutes to Clarity®
Organizational Needs Assessment

Elucity Network, Inc's 10 Minutes to Clarity Organizational Needs Assessment is an online instrument that measures sixteen key aspects for team, business unit, or whole system effectiveness. The assessment creates a valuable baseline to determine what individual and organizational needs are being met. Based on the results, recommendations for training, strategic planning, and management decisions can be determined.

Perceptions about eight key team, business unit, or organizational needs or aspects are measured:
- IDENTITY – who we are collectively
- LIFE-AFFIRMING PURPOSE – why we exist
- DIRECTION – where we are going together
- STRUCTURE – our accountability and authority balance
- ENERGY – the power of our resources, people, and technology
- EXPRESSION – how we show up in our markets
- COMMUNICATION – the effectiveness of our communication
- CHANGE MANAGEMENT – how well we cope with change

Perceptions about eight individual needs are also measured:
- RESPECT
- TRUST
- ACKNOWLEDGMENT
- LEARNING
- MORALE
- INDIVIDUAL PRODUCTIVITY
- HUMILITY
- PERSONAL MEANING FROM THE JOB

This assessment builds on key organizational research and integrates this with the needs-based consciousness of the Nonviolent Communication and Integrated Clarity models. Finally, people needs and organizational needs can blend seamlessly for conscious growth and profit and sustainability.

* * * *

The following questions are examples of what Elucity Network, Inc.'s **10 Minutes to Clarity Organizational Needs Assessment** measures. Ask yourself how you, your team, or your organization would rank the following statements. If you'd like more information about the complete assessment, please contact: survey@empathyfactoratwork.com.

Pick a number from 1 to 7 for each statement below.

1 = very strongly disagree   5 = agree
2 = strongly disagree   6 = strongly agree
3 = disagree   7 = very strongly agree
4 = neutral; neither disagree nor agree

- People know what our organization stands for—its core values, culture, mission, etc.

- Roles are filled with the people who have the skills and potential for performing at the highest level.

- Understanding the needs, expectations, and experiences of first-time and potential customers or clients is an important part of the regular work routine.

- People know what the big-picture goal is for our organization three years from now.

- When organizational changes happen, the organization supports its people through their personal process in coping with the changes.

- The people who do the work make their own decisions and have the authority to shape how the work is done without supervisors' approval.

- People understand how our organization makes money, including their role in it.

- Through a consistent way of receiving feedback and measuring satisfaction, people see and hear how their work impacts customers and their co-workers.

- Our organization provides materials and training to its people about ways to communicate the organization's unique strengths and qualities.

- Communication works smoothly throughout our organization.

- It's common to hear recent success stories with our clients or customers.

- People have access to all the necessary information to do their jobs well.

- People share the credit with others on successful efforts.

- People are excited and passionate about their roles in our organization.

- People seek feedback, give feedback, and work to improve themselves.

- People see their work as having a higher purpose— something greater than delivering a service, maintaining financial sustainability, or even being the best in our field.

- When decisions are made, people give consideration to how that decision might affect customers or others in our organization.

- People trust one another to do what they say they will do and to get the job done.

- People have access to all the needed resources and equipment to fulfill their roles well.

- It's common throughout our organization for people to express appreciation and acknowledgment.

- People are willing to learn both personal (communication, teamwork, etc.) and technical skills to improve their organizational performance.

For more information about Elucity Network, Inc.'s 10 Minutes to Clarity online needs assessment, contact:
survey@empathyfactoratwork.com
www.empathyfactoratwork.com

NOTES

Chapter One—*Introducing the Third Dimension and Integrated Clarity*®

1. Abbott, *Flatland.*
2. Schwab and DeGioia, Faith and the Global Agenda, Values for the Post-Crisis Economy, World Economic Forum 2010, p. 5.
3. Fuller, *Critical Path.*
4. Russell, *Waking Up in Time: Finding Inner Peace in Times of Accelerating Change.*
5. Wiseman, *The Luck Factor: The Four Essential Principles,* p. 89.
6. Marshall Rosenberg's NVC Workshop, Phoenix, AZ., April 2005.
7. 2006 Annual Report for The Center for Nonviolent Communication.
8. Rosenberg, *Nonviolent Communication: A Language of Life.*
9. Holman, Devane, Cady, eds., *The Change Handbook: The Definitive Resource on Today's Best Methods for Engaging Whole Systems.*

Chapter Two—*Capitalizing on the Human Element*

10. Sisodia, Wolfe, and Sheth, *Firms of Endearment: How World-Class Companies Profit from Passion and Purpose.*
11. Gabel and Walker, "Leadership By Design: How One Individual Can Change The World–Leadership Principles of Buckminster Fuller," 2006.
12. Association for Federal Information Resources Management Conference, Washington D.C., C-Span, October 19, 2010.
13. Fisher, *Leading Self-Directed Work Teams: A Guide to Developing New Team Leadership Skills,* p. 122. Fisher cites the work of Harvard Business School researchers Pamela Posey and Janice Klein.
14. Salovey and Mayer, "Emotional Intelligence," *Imagination, Cognition and Personality,* Vol. 9, No. 3, 1989–90, pp. 185–211.
15. Goleman, "What Makes a Leader?" *Harvard Business Review,* 1998.
16. Martinuzzi, "What's Empathy Got to Do With It?"
17. Gallup Polls, "Why People Follow," 2008.
18. Stawiski, Deal, and Ruderman, "Building Trust in the Workplace," Center for Creative Leadership, April 2010.
19. PR Newswire, "Survey by Center For Creative Leadership Shows 'Soft Skills' Make a Difference in Tough Times," January 14, 2002.
20. Patnaik, *Wired to Care: How Companies Prosper When They Create Widespread Empathy.*
21. Collins, *Good to Great: Why Some Companies Make the Leap . . . and Others Don't,* p. 22.
22. Collins, *Good to Great: Why Some Companies Make the Leap . . . and Others Don't,* p. 37.

23. Wikipedia on Pixar. http://en.wikipedia.org/wiki/Pixar. Accessed February 14, 2011.

24. Fisher, *Leading Self-Directed Work Teams*, p. 31.

25. Fisher, *Leading Self-Directed Work Teams*, p. 31.

26. Fisher, *Leading Self-Directed Work Teams*, p. 32.

27. Fisher, *Leading Self-Directed Work Teams*, p. 31.

28. Collins, *Good to Great: Why Some Companies Make the Leap . . . and Others Don't*, p. 7.

29. Deming, www.deming.org

30. Collins, *Good to Great: Why Some Companies Make the Leap . . . and Others Don't*, pp. 95–96.

31. Covey, *The 7 Habits of Highly Effective People: Powerful Lessons in Personal Change*, pp. 150–69.

32. Davenport, "Five Ways Pixar Makes Better Decisions," July 15, 2010, blog for the *Harvard Business Review*.

33. www.kellogg.northwestern.edu/execed/Programs/SOUL.aspx

34. Sisodia, Wolfe, and Sheth, *Firms of Endearment*, p. 4.

35. Bridges, *Managing Transitions: Making the Most of Change*, p. 143.

Chapter Three—Basic Principles of Nonviolent Communication

36. Boroditsky, "Lost in Translation," *The Wall Street Journal*, July 24, 2010, pp. 4 and 5.

37. Patnaik, "Innovation Starts with Empathy," 2009.

38. Martinuzzi, "What's Empathy Got to Do With It?" 2006.

39. Robison, "What Leaders Must Do Next," *Gallup Management Journal*, June 11, 2009.

40. Interview with Singer, 2010. http://ccare.stanford.edu/node/89

41. Covey, *The 7 Habits of Highly Effective People: Powerful Lessons in Personal Change*, pp. 240–41.

42. Interview with Michelle Peluso on Morning Edition of National Public Radio, April 14, 2005.

43. Berry, "Empathy as a Key to Business Success," January 13, 2009.

44. Patnaik, "Innovation Starts with Empathy."

45. Boroditsky, "Lost in Translation," p. 5.

46. Boroditsky, "Lost in Translation," p. 3.

47. Patnaik, *Wired to Care: How Companies Prosper When They Create Widespread Empathy*.

48. Patnaik, "Innovation Starts with Empathy."

49. de Waal, *The Age of Empathy: Nature's Lessons for a Kinder Society*, p. 43.

50. PR Newswire, "Survey by Center for Creative Leadership Shows 'Soft Skills' Make a Difference in Tough Times," January 14, 2002.

51. Lasater with Stiles, *Words That Work In Business: A Practical Guide to Effective Communication in the Workplace*, p. 111.

Chapter Four—Applying Needs-Based Awareness to the Workplace

52. Collins, *Good to Great: Why Some Companies Make the Leap . . . and Others Don't*, p. 210.
53. Aburdene, *Megatrends 2010: The Rise of Conscious Capitalism*, pp. 1–2.
54. Lehrer, *How We Decide*, p. 26.
55. Lehrer, *How We Decide*, p. 15.
56. Miyashiro and Rosenberg, *The Change Handbook*, pp. 126–27.
57. Collins, *Good to Great: Why Some Companies Make the Leap . . . and Others Don't*, pp. 90–119.
58. Collins, *Good to Great: Why Some Companies Make the Leap . . . and Others Don't*, p. 96.
59. Collins and Porras, *Built to Last: Successful Habits of Visionary Companies*, pp. 91–114.
60. Fisher, *Leading Self-Directed Work Teams: A Guide to Developing New Team Leadership Skills*, pp. 15–16.
61. Collins, *Good to Great: Why Some Companies Make the Leap . . . and Others Don't*, p. 9.
62. Collins, *Good to Great and the Social Sectors: A Monograph to Accompany Good to Great*, p. 19.

Chapter Five—How to Increase Self-Productivity

63. Lehrer, *How We Decide*, pp. 142–43.
64. Lehrer, *How We Decide*, p. 249.
65. Greenspan, *Healing through the Dark Emotions: The Wisdom of Grief, Fear, and Despair*, pp. 80–81.
66. *Healing through the Dark Emotions*, p. 81.
67. Haskvitz, *Eat by Choice, Not by Habit: Practical Skills for Creating a Healthy Relationship with Your Body and Food*.

Chapter Six—How to Increase Interpersonal Productivity

68. Suttie, "Compassion across Cubicles," *Greater Good*, Spring/Summer 2006, p. 31.
69. Brown, TEDxTalks: www.youtube.com/watch?v=X4Qm9cGRub0&feature=player_embedded
70. www.stateofgracedocument.com/WkspDlds/SoGDComponents2007.pdf
71. Kohn, *Punished by Rewards: The Trouble with Gold Stars, Incentive Plans, A's, Praise, and Other Bribes*, back cover.
72. Collins, *Good to Great: Why Some Companies Make the Leap . . . and Others Don't*, p. 41.
73. "What is Appreciative Inquiry?" http://appreciativeinquiry.case.edu/intro/whatisai.cfm

Chapter Seven—How to Increase Team or Organizational Productivity

74. Fisher, *Leading Self-Directed Work Teams: A Guide to Developing New Team Leadership Skills*, pp. 122–23.
75. http://www.gore.com/en_xx/index.html
76. "Working in Our Unique Culture." http://www.gore.com/en_xx/careers/whoweare/ourculture/gore-company-culture.html
77. "About Gore." http://www.gore.com/en_xx/aboutus/index.html
78. Collins and Porras, *Built to Last: Successful Habits of Visionary Companies*, p. 85.
79. Velez, "Diverse Business Group Needs to Shape Its Identity," *Arizona Daily Star*, January 17, 2005.
80. Collins and Porras, *Built to Last*, p. 94.
81. Collins, *Good to Great: Why Some Companies Make the Leap . . . and Others Don't*, p. 109.
82. Collins and Porras, *Built to Last*, p. 82.

Chapter Eight—Needs-Based Decision-Making Tools

83. Lehrer, *How We Decide*, p. 249.
84. Kaner with Lind, Toldi, Fisk, and Berger, *Facilitator's Guide to Participatory Decision Making*.
85. Kashtan. www.baynvc.com
86. International Association for Public Participation. www.iap2.org

Chapter Nine—Healing Workplace Anger, Guilt, Fear, and Shame

87. Rosenberg, *Nonviolent Communication: A Language of Life*, pp. 142–43.
88. Handout from the Center for Nonviolent Communication. Direct inquiries to: www.cnvc.org
89. Interview with Singer, 2010. http://ccare.stanford.edu/node/89
90. Rosenberg, *Nonviolent Communication*, p. 144.
91. Lasater With Stiles, *Words That Work In Business: A Practical Guide to Effective Communication in the Workplace*, p. 109.

Chapter Ten—Connecting With People Who Stretch Our Skills

92. Kashtan and Kashtan, Handout, "Responding to Challenges from Participants: Preparation Notes," p. 1.

Chapter Eleven—Implications for the Future of Workplaces

93. Aburdene, *Megatrends 2010: The Rise of Conscious Capitalism*, p. xvii.
94. Miyashiro and Rosenberg, *The Change Handbook*, p. 132.
95. Aburdene, *Megatrends 2010: The Rise of Conscious Capitalism*, pp. xvi–xvii.
96. Fisher, *Leading Self-Directed Work Teams: A Guide to Developing New Team Leadership Skills*, p. 148.
97. Lei and Greer, "The Empathetic Organization," *Organizational Dynamics*, Vol. 32, No. 2, Elsevier Science, Inc., 2003, pp. 142–43.
98. Shapiro, "How Do Physicians Teach Empathy in the Primary Care Setting?" *Academic Medicine*, Vol. 77, No. 4, April, 2002.
99. Semler, *Maverick: The Success Story Behind the World's Most Unusual Workplace*, pp. 2–3.
100. House, Hanges, Javidan, Dorfman, and Gupta, *Culture, Leadership and Organizations: The GLOBE Study of 62 Societies*, p. 12.
101. Gentry, Weber, and Sadri, "Empathy in the Workplace" white paper, Center for Creative Leadership, New York, 2007, pp. 5–6.
102. Gentry, Weber, and Sadri, "Empathy in the Workplace" white paper, p. 11.
103. Bakke, *Joy at Work: A Revolutionary Approach to Fun on the Job*, p. 18.

BIBLIOGRAPHY

Books

Abbott, Edwin A. *Flatland.* Illustrated Edition. Middlesex, United Kingdom: The Echo Library, 2007.

Aburdene, Patricia. *Megatrends 2010: The Rise of Conscious Capitalism.* Charlottesville, VA: Hampton Roads Publishing Company, 2007.

Bakke, Dennis. *Joy at Work: A Revolutionary Approach to Fun on the Job.* Seattle: PVG, 2005.

Bridges, William. *Managing Transitions: Making the Most of Change.* Cambridge, MA: Da Capo Lifelong Books, 2009.

Collins, Jim. *Good to Great: Why Some Companies Make the Leap . . . and Others Don't.* New York: HarperCollins, 2001. Copyright © 2001 by Jim Collins.

Collins, Jim. *Good to Great and the Social Sectors: A Monograph to Accompany Good to Great.* Boulder, CO: Jim Collins, 2005. Copyright © 2005 by Jim Collins.

Collins, Jim and Jerry I. Porras. *Built to Last: Successful Habits of Visionary Companies.* New York: HarperCollins, 2002. Copyright © 1994, 2002 by Jim Collins and Jerry I. Porras.

Covey, Stephen R. *The 7 Habits of Highly Effective People: Powerful Lessons in Personal Change.* New York: First Fireside edition, 1990. (Also Free Press, a Division of Simon & Schuster, Inc., 2004.)

De Waal, Franz. *The Age of Empathy: Nature's Lessons for a Kinder Society.* New York: Three Rivers Press, 2009.

Fisher, Kimball. *Leading Self-Directed Work Teams: A Guide to Developing New Team Leadership Skills.* New York: McGraw-Hill, 2000.

Fuller, R. Buckminster. *Critical Path.* New York: St. Martin's Press, 1981.

Greenspan, Miriam. *Healing through the Dark Emotions: The Wisdom of Grief, Fear, and Despair.* Boston: Shambhala Publications, Inc., 2004.

Haskvitz, Sylvia, M.A., R.D. *Eat by Choice, Not by Habit: Practical Skills for Creating a Healthy Relationship with Your Body and Food.* Encinitas, CA: PuddleDancer Press, 2005.

Holman, Peggy, Tom Devane, Steven Cady, eds. *The Change Handbook: The Definitive Resource on Today's Best Methods for Engaging Whole Systems,* second edition. San Francisco: Berrett-Koehler Publishers, Inc., 2007.

243

House, Robert J., Paul J. Hanges, Mansour Javidan, Peter W. Dorfman, and Vipin Gupta. *Culture, Leadership and Organizations: The GLOBE Study of 62 Societies.* Thousand Oaks, CA: Sage Publications, 2004.

Kaner, Sam with Lenny Lind, Caterine Toldi, Sarah Fisk, and Duane Berger. *Facilitator's Guide to Participatory Decision Making.* Philadelphia: New Society Publishers, 1996.

Kohn, Alfie. *Punished by Rewards: The Trouble with Gold Stars, Incentive Plans, A's, Praise, and Other Bribes.* New York: Houghton Mifflin Company, 1993.

Lasater, Ike With Julie Stiles. *Words That Work In Business: A Practical Guide to Effective Communication in the Workplace.* Encinitas, CA: PuddleDancer Press, 2010.

Lehrer, Jonah. *How We Decide.* New York: Houghton Mifflin Harcourt Publishing Company, 2009.

Patnaik, Dev. *Wired to Care: How Companies Prosper When They Create Widespread Empathy.* Upper Saddle River, NJ: FT Press, 2009.

Rosenberg, Marshall. *Nonviolent Communication: A Language of Life.* Encinitas, CA: PuddleDancer Press, 2005.

Russell, Peter. *Waking Up in Time: Finding Inner Peace in Times of Accelerating Change.* First Edition, 1992. Novato, CA: Origin Press updated ed., 2008.

Semler, Richard. *Maverick: The Success Story Behind the World's Most Unusual Workplace.* New York: Warner Books, Inc., 1993.

Sisodia, Rajendra S., David B. Wolfe, and Jagdish N. Sheth. *Firms of Endearment: How World-Class Companies Profit from Passion and Purpose.* Upper Saddle River, NJ: Wharton School Publishing, 2007.

Wiseman, Richard. *The Luck Factor: The Four Essential Principles.* New York: Hyperion, 2004.

Articles and Other Sources

Association for Federal Information Resources Management Conference, Washington D.C., C-Span, October 19, 2010.

Berry, Tim. "Empathy as a Key to Business Success." January 13, 2009. http://timberry.bplans.com/2009/01/empathy-as-a-key-to-business-success.html

Boroditsky, Lera, professor of psychology, Stanford University and editor in chief of *Frontiers in Cultural Psychology.* "Lost in Translation." *The Wall Street Journal,* July 24, 2010.

Brown, Brené, Ph.D., researcher and professor, University of Houston Graduate College of Social Work. TEDxTalks: www.youtube.com/watch?v=X4Qm9c GRub0&feature=player_embedded

[The] Center for Nonviolent Communication. 2006 Annual Report.

[The] Center for Nonviolent Communication. www.cnvc.org. Handout.

Davenport, Tom. "Five Ways Pixar Makes Better Decisions." July 5, 2010, blog for the *Harvard Business Review.* http://blogs.hbr.org/davenport/2010/07/ how_to_make_good_decisions_les.html

Deming, W. Edwards. www.deming.org

Gabel, Medard, and Jim Walker, "Leadership By Design: How One Individual Can Change The World—Leadership Principles of Buckminster Fuller," 2006. http://www.readyaiminspire.com/Buckminster_Fuller_Leadership_ By_Design.html

Gallup Polls, "Why People Follow," 2008. http://strengths.gallup.com/private/ Resources/Followers_Study.pdf

Gentry, William A., Todd J. Weber, and Golnaz Sadri, "Empathy in the Workplace" white paper. Center for Creative Leadership, New York, 2007.

Goleman, Daniel. "What Makes a Leader?" *Harvard Business Review,* 1998. https://www.mercy.edu/faculty/Georgas/inbs640/files/ WhatMakesaLeader.pdf

International Association of Public Participation. www.iap2.org

Lei, David, and Charles R. Greer, "The Empathetic Organization." *Organizational Dynamics,* Vol. 32, No. 2, Elsevier Science, Inc., 2003.

Martinuzzi, Bruna, founder of Clarion Enterprises, Ltd. "What's Empathy Got to Do With It?" www.mindtools.com/pages/article/newLDR_75.htm

Miyashiro, Marie, and Marshall Rosenberg, "Energizing How We Talk and What We Talk about in Organizations." Peggy Holman, Tom Devane, Steven Cady, eds. *The Change Handbook: The Definitive Resource on Today's Best Methods for Engaging Whole Systems.* Second Edition. San Francisco: Berrett-Koehler Publishers, Inc., 2007.

Patnaik, Dev, business strategist and adjunct faculty member at Stanford University, founder and principal of Jump Associates. "Innovation Starts with Empathy," 2009. http://designmind.frogdesign.com/articles/the- substance-of-things-not-seen/innovation-starts-with-empathy.html

Peluso, Michelle. Interviewed by National Public Radio, Morning Edition, April 14, 2005.

PR Newswire, "Survey by Center For Creative Leadership Shows 'Soft Skills' Make a Difference in Tough Times." January 14, 2002.

Robison, Jennifer. "What Leaders Must Do Next." *Gallup Management Journal*, June 11, 2009. http://gmj.gallup.com/content/120791/leaders-next.aspx

Rosenberg, Marshall. NVC Workshop, Phoenix, AZ, April 2005.

Salovey, Peter, and John D. Mayer, "Emotional Intelligence." *Imagination, Cognition and Personality,* Vol. 9, No. 3, 1989–90.

Schwab, Klaus, and John J. DeGioia. Faith and the Global Agenda: Values for the Post-Crisis Economy, World Economic Forum 2010. www.weforum. org/pdf/faith/valuesreport.pdf

Shapiro, Johanna. "How Do Physicians Teach Empathy in the Primary Care Setting?" *Academic Medicine,* Vol. 77, No. 4, April, 2002.

Singer, Tania, Ph.D., Director of the Max Planck Institute for Human Cognitive and Brain Sciences, 2010. Interviewed by The Center for Compassion and Altruism Research and Education at Stanford University, 2010. http:// ccare.stanford.edu/node/89

Stawiski, Ph.D., Sarah, Jennifer J. Deal, Ph.D., and Marian Ruderman, Ph.D. "Building Trust in the Workplace." Center for Creative Leadership, April 2010. http://www.ccl.org/leadership/pdf/news/ BuildingTrustIntheWorkplace.pdf

Suttie, Jill. "Compassion across Cubicles." *Greater Good,* Spring/Summer 2006. http://greatergood.berkeley.edu/greatergood/archive/2006springsummer/ SpringSummer2006_Suttie.pdf

Velez, Tiana. "Diverse Business Group Needs to Shape Its Identity." *Arizona Daily Star,* January 17, 2005.

"What is Appreciative Inquiry?" http://appreciativeinquiry.case.edu/intro/ whatisai.cfm

Wikipedia on Pixar. http://en.wikipedia.org/wiki/Pixar. Accessed February 14, 2011.

www.baynvc.com

www.gore.com

www.kellogg.northwestern.edu/execed/Programs/SOUL.aspx

www.stateofgracedocument.com/WkspDlds/SoGDComponents2007.pdf

RESOURCES

Elucity Network, Inc.
Elucity Network, Inc. offers strategic planning, executive team and work group training and development, employee communications training, customer relations communications and training, change management workshops, and personal or team productivity trainings. Elucity's founder, Marie R. Miyashiro, presents workshops and keynote speeches that cover a wide range of business and nonprofit topics for conferences and consulting engagements with clients.
 Website: www.empathyfactoratwork.com
 Email: info@empathyfactoratwork.com
 Tel: 520.777.7271
 Address: P.O. Box 64338, Tucson, AZ 85728 USA

Center for Nonviolent Communication (CNVC)
The Center for Nonviolent Communication is a global organization that supports the learning and sharing of NVC and helps people peacefully and effectively resolve conflicts in personal, organizational, and political settings. Its website lists certified trainers, NVC training organizations, and other NVC practice and educational resources.
 Website: www.cnvc.org
 Tel: 505.244.4041
 USA Toll free: 1.800.255.7696
 Address: 5600 San Francisco Rd. NE, Suite A
 Albuquerque, NM 87109 USA

PuddleDancer Press
PuddleDancer Press publishes books and materials on Nonviolent Communication for beginning, intermediate, and advanced NVC practitioners.
 Websites: www.puddledancer.com; www.nonviolentcommunication.com

NVC Academy
NVC Academy is an online learning center for NVC. Programs include telecourses, audio and video recordings, mentoring, and other practice and educational resources.
 Website: nvcacademy.com
 Tel: 928.774.5210
 Address: 212 Quincy Avenue, #204, Long Beach, CA 90803 USA

NVC Toolkit for Facilitators

This 506-page resource is a comprehensive collection of resources for people who share and teach NVC. It can be ordered through:

www.nvc.toolkit.org
www.cnvc.org
www.amazon.com

Bay Area Nonviolent Communication, or BayNVC

Website: www.baynvc.org
Email: nvc@baynvc.org
Tel: 510.433.0700
Toll Free (outside Bay Area): 866-4-BayNVC (866.422.9682)
Address: 55 Santa Clara Ave, Suite 203, Oakland, CA 94610 USA

Center for the State of Grace Document

The Center for the State of Grace Document promotes sustainable collaboration around the globe by creating new models for interdependent and resilient business and personal relationships.

Website: www.stateofgracedocument.com
Maureen K. McCarthy and Zelle Nelson
Email: maureen@stateofgracedocument.com
Email: zelle@stateofgracedocument.com
Tel: 847.859.9046
Address: 2021 Greenville Highway, Flat Rock, NC 28731 USA

The Center for Collaborative Communication
(formerly known as Brooklyn Nonviolent Communication)

Website: www.collaborative-communication.org
Email: info@collaborative-communication.org
Tel: 718.797.9525
Address: 340 Decatur Street, Brooklyn, NY 11233 USA

Eat by Choice Movement

Website: www.eatbychoice.net
Email: silgiraffe@aol.com
Tel: 520.572.9295
Address: 6301 N. Panorama Drive, Tucson, AZ 85743 USA

Oregon Network for Compassionate Communication

Website: www.orncc.net
Email: info@orncc.net
Tel: 503.450.9909
Address: 1430 Willamette St. #4, Eugene, OR 97401 USA

CONTRIBUTORS TO THIS BOOK

Raj Gill B.Sc., ART., CPCC
Center for Nonviolent Communication Certified Trainer
Communication with Compassion, Certified Professional Coach/Speaker
Prosperity Circles Coaching Intl
Email: raj.gill@telus.net
Tel: 604.531.2564

Raj's NVC Toolkit for Facilitators is available at www.nvctoolkit.org.

Sylvia E. Haskvitz
Center for Nonviolent Communication Certified Trainer
Website: www.eatbychoice.net
Email: silgiraffe@aol.com
Tel: 520.572.9295

Certified in 1989, Sylvia was among the first CNVC certified trainers. She is Dean of Educational Services with Elucity Network, Inc. and works with families and coaches individuals and couples in person or by phone. Also the author of the book *Eat by Choice, Not by Habit* with accompanying guidebooks for adults and children, Sylvia offers Eat by Choice workshops around the country, helping people create a healthy relationship with their body and food.

Miki Kashtan, Ph.D.
Center for Nonviolent Communication Certified Trainer, Strategic Vision, Lead Trainer, Bay Area Nonviolent Communication (BayNVC)
Website: www.baynvc.org
Address: 55 Santa Clara Ave. #203, Oakland, CA 94602

Blog – The Fearless Heart: http://baynvc.blogspot.com
TV show – The Conflict Hotline: http://bit.ly/conflict-hotline
Consciousness Transformation Community: http://ctc.learnnvc.org
Certified Trainer for the Center for Nonviolent Communications: www.cnvc.org

Miki co-founded Bay Area Nonviolent Communication (BayNVC). She enjoys working with organizations interested in developing more collaboration in their culture.

Dian Killian, Ph.D.
Center for Nonviolent Communication Certified Trainer
Director, Center for Collaborative Communication
Website: www.collaborative-communication.org
Tel: 719.797.9525

Dian Killian provides customized Collaborative Communication training, Leadership Communication Coaching, Communication Audits, and Leadership and Team-Building Retreats. Her clients include Fortune 500 companies, the UN Development Program, and nonprofit and educational organizations.

Ike Lasater
Author of *Words That Work In Business: A Practical Guide to Effective Communication in the Workplace*
Websites: www.wordsthatwork.us; www.nvcmediation.com

Ike is co-facilitator of NVC mediation immersion programs in Australia, Poland, and the United States. He practiced law for twenty years as counsel in high stakes business and environmental cases in California and co-founded a twenty-person law firm before beginning to offer mediation trainings using NVC. For six years, he was on the board of directors of the Center for Nonviolent Communication.

Kathleen Macferran
Center for Nonviolent Communication Certified Trainer
Strength of Connection
Website: www.strengthofconnection.com
Email: kathleen@strengthofconnection.com
Tel: 206.780.1021
Address: PO Box 10009, Bainbridge Is, WA 98110-0009

Kathleen has been a Certified Trainer with the Center for Nonviolent Communication (CNVC) since 2003, working with businesses, schools, medical staff, community organizations, families, and prison inmates. She has been a trainer for CNVC International Intensive Trainings and a Trainer Candidate Assessor for CNVC.

Maureen K. McCarthy and Zelle Nelson
Center for the State of Grace Document
Website: www.stateofgracedocument.com
Email: maureen@stateofgracedocument.com
Email: zelle@stateofgracedocument.com
Tel: 847.859.9046
Address: 2021 Greenville Highway, Flat Rock, NC 28731 USA

The Center for the State of Grace Document promotes sustainable collaboration around the globe by creating new models for interdependent and resilient business and personal relationships.

Julie Stiles, M.A.
Website: www.juliestiles.com
Email: jlstiles24@gmail.com
Blog: http://oceanrosetale.wordpress.com/

Julie is a writer and executive assistant at Words That Work (www.WordsThatWork.us). She's the author of *Dying for Now: Living Your Transformative Journey* about the transformation of consciousness and helps professionals shape their ideas for publication. Julie also hosts a blog on the loss and reclaiming of feminine power and is a holistic health coach.

INDEX

About Nonviolent Communication

Nonviolent Communication has flourished for more than four decades across sixty countries selling more than 1,000,000 books in over thirty languages for one simple reason: it works.

From the bedroom to the boardroom, from the classroom to the war zone, Nonviolent Communication (NVC) is changing lives every day. NVC provides an easy-to-grasp, effective method to get to the root of violence and pain peacefully. By examining the unmet needs behind what we do and say, NVC helps reduce hostility, heal pain, and strengthen professional and personal relationships. NVC is now being taught in corporations, classrooms, prisons, and mediation centers worldwide. And it is affecting cultural shifts as institutions, corporations, and governments integrate NVC consciousness into their organizational structures and their approach to leadership.

Most of us are hungry for skills that can improve the quality of our relationships, to deepen our sense of personal empowerment or simply help us communicate more effectively. Unfortunately, most of us have been educated from birth to compete, judge, demand, and diagnose; to think and communicate in terms of what is "right" and "wrong" with people. At best, the habitual ways we think and speak hinder communication and create misunderstanding or frustration. And still worse, they can cause anger and pain, and may lead to violence. Without wanting to, even people with the best of intentions generate needless conflict.

NVC helps us reach beneath the surface and discover what is alive and vital within us, and how all of our actions are based on human needs that we are seeking to meet. We learn to develop a vocabulary of feelings and needs that helps us more clearly express what is going on in us at any given moment. When we understand and acknowledge our needs, we develop a shared foundation for much more satisfying relationships. Join the thousands of people worldwide who have improved their relationships and their lives with this simple yet revolutionary process.

About PuddleDancer Press

PuddleDancer Press (PDP) is the premier publisher of Nonviolent Communication™ related works. Its mission is to provide high-quality materials to help people create a world in which all needs are met compassionately. By working in partnership with the Center for Nonviolent Communication and NVC trainers, teams, and local supporters, PDP has created a comprehensive promotion effort that has helped bring NVC to thousands of new people each year.

Since 1998 PDP has donated more than 60,000 NVC books to organizations, decision-makers, and individuals in need around the world.

Visit the PDP website at www.NonviolentCommunication.com to find the following resources:

- **Shop NVC**—Continue your learning. Purchase our NVC titles online safely, affordably, and conveniently. Find everyday discounts on individual titles, multiple-copies, and book packages. Learn more about our authors and read endorsements of NVC from world-renowned communication experts and peacemakers. www.NonviolentCommunication.com/store/

- **NVC Quick Connect e-Newsletter**—Sign up today to receive our monthly e-Newsletter, filled with expert articles, upcoming training opportunities with our authors, and exclusive specials on NVC learning materials. Archived e-Newsletters are also available

- **About NVC**—Learn more about these life-changing communication and conflict resolution skills including an overview of the NVC process, key facts about NVC, and more.

- **About Marshall Rosenberg**—Access press materials, biography, and more about this world-renowned peacemaker, educator, bestselling author, and founder of the Center for Nonviolent Communication.

- **Free Resources for Learning NVC**—Find free weekly tips series, NVC article archive, and other great resources to make learning these vital communication skills just a little easier.

PuddleDancer PRESS

For more information, please contact PuddleDancer Press at:

2240 Encinitas Blvd., Ste. D-911 • Encinitas, CA 92024
Phone: 760-652-5754 • Fax: 760-274-6400
Email: email@puddledancer.com • www.NonviolentCommunication.com

About the Center for Nonviolent Communication

The Center for Nonviolent Communication (CNVC) is an international nonprofit peacemaking organization whose vision is a world where everyone's needs are met peacefully. CNVC is devoted to supporting the spread of Nonviolent Communication (NVC) around the world.

Founded in 1984 by Dr. Marshall B. Rosenberg, CNVC has been contributing to a vast social transformation in thinking, speaking and acting—showing people how to connect in ways that inspire compassionate results. NVC is now being taught around the globe in communities, schools, prisons, mediation centers, churches, businesses, professional conferences, and more. Hundreds of certified trainers and hundreds more supporters teach NVC to tens of thousands of people each year in more than 60 countries.

CNVC believes that NVC training is a crucial step to continue building a compassionate, peaceful society. Your tax-deductible donation will help CNVC continue to provide training in some of the most impoverished, violent corners of the world. It will also support the development and continuation of organized projects aimed at bringing NVC training to high-need geographic regions and populations.

To make a tax-deductible donation or to learn more about the valuable resources described below, visit the CNVC website at www.CNVC.org:

- **Training and Certification**—Find local, national, and international training opportunities, access trainer certification information, connect to local NVC communities, trainers, and more.

- **CNVC Bookstore**—Find mail or phone order information for a complete selection of NVC books, booklets, audio, and video materials at the CNVC website.

- **CNVC Projects**—Participate in one of the several regional and theme-based projects that provide focus and leadership for teaching NVC in a particular application or geographic region.

- **E-Groups and List Servs**—Join one of several moderated, topic-based NVC e-groups and list servs developed to support individual learning and the continued growth of NVC worldwide.

For more information, please contact CNVC at:

9301 Indian School Rd., NE, Suite 204, Albuquerque, NM 87112-2861
Ph: 505-244-4041 • US Only: 800-255-7696 • Fax: 505-247-0414
Email: cnvc@CNVC.org • Website: www.CNVC.org

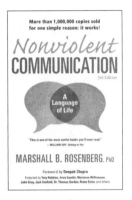

Nonviolent Communication:
A Language of Life, 3rd Edition
Life-Changing Tools for Healthy Relationships

Marshall B. Rosenberg, PhD

$19.95 — Trade Paper 6x9, 264pp

ISBN: 978-1-892005-28-1

In this internationally acclaimed text, Marshall Rosenberg offers insightful stories, anecdotes, practical exercises, and role-plays that will literally change your approach to communication for the better. Nonviolent Communication partners practical skills with a powerful consciousness to help us get what we want peacefully.

Nonviolent Communication has flourished for more than four decades across sixty countries selling more than 1,000,000 books for a simple reason: it works.

"No one deserves our gratitude more than the late Marshall Rosenberg, who lived his life just as the subtitle of one of his books states: What You Say Next Will Change Your World."

— **Deepak Chopra, MD**, founder of the Chopra Center for Wellbeing and author of more than eighty books

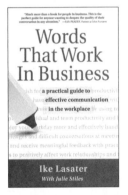

Words That Work In Business
A Practical Guide to Effective Communication in the Workplace

by Ike Lasater
with Julie Stiles

$12.95 — Trade Paper 5-3/8x8-3/8, 144pp

ISBN: 978-1-892005-01-4

Do You Want to Be Happier, More Effective, and Experience Less Stress at Work?

Do you wish for more respectful work relationships? To move beyond gossip and power struggles, to improved trust and productivity? If you've ever wondered if just one person can positively affect work relationships and company culture, regardless of your position, this book offers a resounding "yes." The key is shifting how we think and talk.

Former attorney-turned-mediator, Ike Lasater, offers practical communication skills matched with recognizable work scenarios to help anyone address the most common workplace relationship challenges. Learn proven communication skills to: Enjoy your workday more; effectively handle difficult conversations; reduce workplace conflict and stress; improve individual and team productivity; be more effective at meetings; and give and receive meaningful feedback.

Available from PuddleDancer Press, the Center for Nonviolent Communication, all major bookstores, and Amazon.com. Distributed by Independent Publisher's Group: 800-888-4741.

Trade Booklets From PuddleDancer Press

Being Me, Loving You: *A Practical Guide to Extraordinary Relationships* **by Marshall B. Rosenberg, PhD** • Watch your relationships strengthen as you learn to think of love as something you "do," something you give freely from the heart.
80pp, ISBN: 978-1-892005-16-8 • **$8.95**

Getting Past the Pain Between Us: *Healing and Reconciliation Without Compromise* **by Marshall B. Rosenberg, PhD** • Learn simple steps to create the heartfelt presence necessary for lasting healing to occur—great for mediators, counselors, families, and couples.
48pp, ISBN: 978-1-892005-07-6 • **$8.95**

Graduating From Guilt: *Six Steps to Overcome Guilt and Reclaim Your Life* **by Holly Michelle Eckert** • The burden of guilt leaves us stuck, stressed, and feeling like we can never measure up. Through a proven six-step process, this book helps liberate you from the toxic guilt, blame, and shame you carry.
96pp, ISBN: 978-1-892005-23-6 • **$9.95**

The Heart of Social Change: *How to Make a Difference in Your World* **by Marshall B. Rosenberg, PhD** • Learn how creating an internal consciousness of compassion can impact your social change efforts.
48pp, ISBN: 978-1-892005-10-6 • **$8.95**

Humanizing Health Care: *Creating Cultures of Compassion With Nonviolent Communication* **by Melanie Sears, RN, MBA** • Leveraging more than 25 years nursing experience, Melanie demonstrates the profound effectiveness of NVC to create lasting, positive improvements to patient care and the health care workplace.
112pp, ISBN: 978-1-892005-26-7 • **$9.95**

Parenting From Your Heart: *Sharing the Gifts of Compassion, Connection, and Choice* **by Inbal Kashtan** • Filled with insight and practical skills, this booklet will help you transform your parenting to address every day challenges.
48pp, ISBN: 978-1-892005-08-3 • **$8.95**

Practical Spirituality: *Reflections on the Spiritual Basis of Nonviolent Communication* **by Marshall B. Rosenberg, PhD** • Marshall's views on the spiritual origins and underpinnings of NVC, and how practicing the process helps him connect to the Divine.
48pp, ISBN: 978-1-892005-14-4 • **$8.95**

Raising Children Compassionately: *Parenting the Nonviolent Communication Way* **by Marshall B. Rosenberg, PhD** • Learn to create a mutually respectful, enriching family dynamic filled with heartfelt communication.
32pp, ISBN: 978-1-892005-09-0 • **$7.95**

The Surprising Purpose of Anger: *Beyond Anger Management: Finding the Gift* **by Marshall B. Rosenberg, PhD** • Marshall shows you how to use anger to discover what you need, and then how to meet your needs in more constructive, healthy ways.
48pp, ISBN: 978-1-892005-15-1 • **$8.95**

Teaching Children Compassionately: *How Students and Teachers Can Succeed With Mutual Understanding* **by Marshall B. Rosenberg, PhD** • In this national keynote address to Montessori educators, Marshall describes his progressive, radical approach to teaching that centers on compassionate connection.
48pp, ISBN: 978-1-892005-11-3 • **$8.95**

We Can Work It Out: *Resolving Conflicts Peacefully and Powerfully* **by Marshall B. Rosenberg, PhD** • Practical suggestions for fostering empathic connection, genuine co-operation, and satisfying resolutions in even the most difficult situations.
32pp, ISBN: 978-1-892005-12-0 • **$7.95**

What's Making You Angry? *10 Steps to Transforming Anger So Everyone Wins* **by Shari Klein and Neill Gibson** • A powerful, step-by-step approach to transform anger to find healthy, mutually satisfying outcomes.
32pp, ISBN: 978-1-892005-13-7 • **$7.95**

Available from PuddleDancer Press, the Center for Nonviolent Communication, all major bookstores, and Amazon.com. Distributed by IPG: 800-888-4741. For more information about these booklets or to order online, visit www.NonviolentCommunication.com

ABOUT THE AUTHOR

PHOTO BY LYN SIMS

MARIE R. MIYASHIRO, A.P.R. is the founder and president of Elucity Network, Inc., an empathy-based consulting and training firm based in Tucson, Arizona. A student of compassionate communication, she holds a degree in communication studies from Northwestern University and is accredited by the New York-based Public Relations Society of America. She is also certified in planning by the International Association of Public Participation and has studied with noted organization development consultant Sam Kaner, Ph.D., of the international consulting firm Community At Work.

Since 1985, Miyashiro has consulted with Fortune 500 companies, small businesses, nonprofits, universities, and government agencies in the United States and Asia through Elucity Network, Inc. and Marie Reiko Public Relations and Communications.

In 2004, Miyashiro developed Integrated Clarity® (IC), a process that distills current organizational research about what makes organizations enduring and perform at the highest levels into a framework that is needs based. IC is designed to meet both personal and organizational needs and integrates Nonviolent Communication as a way to bring empathy as a professional skill into the workplace. Other significant influences include Marshall Rosenberg (*Nonviolent Communication: A Language of Life*), Jim Collins (*Good to Great*), Kimball Fisher (*Leading Self-Directed Work Teams*), William Bridges (*Managing Transitions*), Marshall Thurber, Judith Orloff Faulk, and Center for Nonviolent Communication Trainers, Sylvia Haskvitz and Miki Kashtan. Since then, clients have been reporting excitement about the effectiveness of this needs-based process and have experienced increased productivity, significant breakthroughs, and a deepening of personal meaning from their work.

A synopsis of the Integrated Clarity framework appears in the second edition of *The Change Handbook: The Definitive Resource on Today's Best Methods for Engaging Whole Systems* (Berrett-Koehler Publishers, Inc., 2007) in the chapter "Integrated Clarity: Energizing How We Talk and What We Talk About In Organizations" by Marie Miyashiro and Marshall Rosenberg.

Elucity Network, Inc.

Elucity Network, Inc. provides organization development consulting, strategic planning facilitation and consulting, leadership and work team development, and communication training for businesses, nonprofits, government agencies, universities and healthcare organizations.

The firm collaborates with organizations worldwide such as: The Center for Collaborative Communication in New York City, New York; Bay Area Nonviolent Communication in the Oakland/San Francisco Bay area, California; Basileia in Charlottesville, Virginia; Community At Work in San Francisco, California; and trainers and consultants in Canada, Australia, and Western Europe.

To find out more about Elucity Network, Inc. or Integrated Clarity, visit www. EmpathyFactorAtWork.com. You're invited to contact Marie Miyashiro with questions or feedback about the information in this book at info@EmpathyFactorAtWork.com or 520-777-7271.